Breakdown

lor Downing is an award-winning television producer and
orian. He was educated at Latymer Upper School and read History
hrist's College, Cambridge. He went on to become managing
director and head of history at Flashback Television, a leading
dependent production company. His most recent books include the
tselling *Cold War* (with Jeremy Isaacs), *Secret Warriors*, *Night Raid*,
The World at War, *Olympia*, *Spies in the Sky* and *Churchill's War Lab*.

Praise for *Breakdown*:

'An impressive, balanced and often deeply moving book. As the
Somme's anniversary approaches, anyone who wishes to understand
it and its terrible consequences should buy *Breakdown*'   *The Times*

'The tragic fate of the Lonsdales forms one of the most telling
subplots in *Breakdown*, the historian Taylor Downing's superb
account of the military's response to the epidemic of shell shock ...
Downing manages to offer a useful perspective by unpacking the
pivotal role the cataclysm in the Somme played in the birth not just
of military psychiatry, but a new era in our understanding of mental
health ... Downing's book is a necessary reminder that trauma is an
injury, and not a sign of weakness'   *New Statesman*

'This is a thoughtful, intelligent '
highly readable and highly recom

D1147711

'A humane and intensely moving

'What is innovative about Downing
of "the crisis of shell shock" with the military history of the Somme.
He tells h   Downing
is too cle   ver being
the same   *cial Times*

000002095437

ALSO BY TAYLOR DOWNING

Secret Warriors
Night Raid
The World at War
Spies in the Sky
Churchill's War Lab
Cold War (with Jeremy Isaacs)
Battle Stations (with Andrew Johnston)
Olympia
Civil War (with Maggie Millman)
The Troubles (as Editor)

Breakdown

The Crisis of Shell Shock
on the Somme, 1916

Taylor Downing

ABACUS

First published in Great Britain in 2016 by Little, Brown
This paperback edition published in 2017 by Abacus

1 3 5 7 9 10 8 6 4 2

Copyright © Taylor Downing 2016

A CIP catalogue record for this book
is available from the British Library.

Maps drawn by John Gilkes.

ISBN 978-0-349-14101-5

Typeset in Palatino by M Rules.
Printed and bound in Great Britain by
Clays Ltd, St Ives plc

Papers used by Abacus are from well-managed forests
and other responsible sources.

MIX
Paper from
responsible sources
FSC® C104740

Abacus
An imprint of
Little, Brown Book Group
Carmelite House
50 Victoria Embankment
London EC4Y 0DZ

An Hachette UK Company
www.hachette.co.uk

www.littlebrown.co.uk

For those who suffered

And continue to suffer

Contents

List of Maps

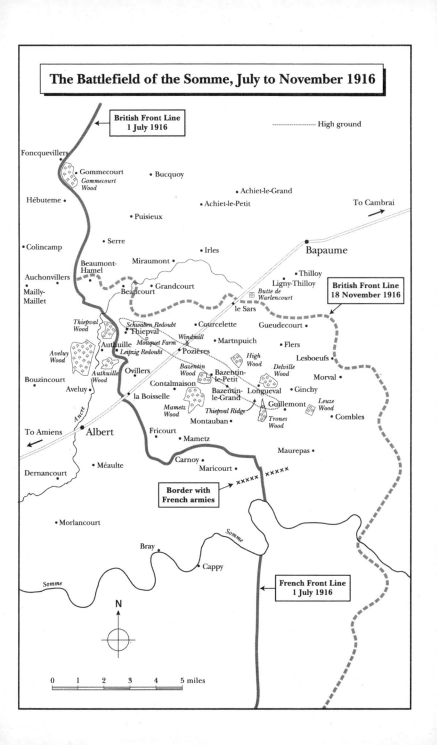

The Battlefield of the Somme, July to November 1916

British Front Line
1 July 1916

------------------- High ground

Foncquevillers •

• Gommecourt
*Gommecourt
Wood*

• Bucquoy

• Achiet-le-Grand

To Cambrai

Hébuterne •

• Achiet-le-Petit

• Colincamp

• Puisieux

• Serre

• Irles

Bapaume •

Auchonvillers •

Beaumont-
Hamel

Miraumont •

• Thilloy

Ligny-Thilloy •

British Front Line
18 November 1916

Mailly-
Maillet •

Beaucourt •

• Grandcourt

*Butte de
Warlencourt*

le Sars •

*Thiepval
Wood*

Schwaben Redoubt
Thiepval •

• Courcelette

Gueudecourt •

Authuille •
*Aveluy
Wood*

Mouquet Farm
Leipzig Redoubt

Windmill
• Pozières

• Martnpuich

• Flers

Bouzincourt •

*Authuille
Wood*
Ovillers •

*Bazentin
Wood*

*High
Wood*

Lesboeufs •

Aveluy •

Contalmaison •

Bazentin-
le-Petit

*Delville
Wood*

Morval •

la Boiselle •

Bazentin-
le-Grand

Longueval

• Ginchy

*Leuze
Wood*

To Amiens

Albert •

*Mametz
Wood*

Thiepval Ridge
Montauban •

Guillemont •

*Trones
Wood*

• Combles

Fricourt •

• Mametz

Maurepas •

Dernancourt •

• Méaulte

Carnoy •

Maricourt •

xxxxx   xxxxx

Border with
French armies

• Morlancourt

Somme

Bray •

Cappy •

French Front Line
1 July 1916

Somme

N

0   1   2   3   4   5 miles

Prologue

It was not the first war he had fought in. Archibald McAllister Burgoyne left his native Lancashire in 1893 to emigrate to southern Africa, where he worked in the rapidly expanding mining industry. When clashes with the Boer population escalated into war in 1899 he signed up to do his bit by volunteering to fight as a trooper in the South Rhodesian Volunteers. After the Boer War was over he went back to mining until again he felt the call to imperial duty in August 1914, when the mother country plunged into the first full European war in one hundred years.

Aged forty-one, Burgoyne volunteered as a private in the South African army and in December 1915, after extensive training, he sailed for the Middle East. In Egypt he joined half a million troops from across the Empire – Australians, New Zealanders and Indians. But he did not spend long there. The greatest need for men was on the Western Front and in mid-April 1916 his unit left Alexandria for Marseilles. By the end of that month he and his fellow soldiers, now organised into what was called the 1st South African Brigade, were training for trench warfare not far behind the Allied lines. On 29 April, the Commander-in-Chief of British forces in France, General Sir Douglas Haig, inspected the brigade, many of whose members, like Burgoyne, were more mature than the average troops to be found in France. Haig described the brigade as 'a fine lot of boys'. Burgoyne confided in his diary, 'Pretty old fashioned "boys" some of us.'[1]

When Haig launched his 'Big Push' on an eighteen-mile front to the north of the river Somme on 1 July 1916, Burgoyne and the South African Brigade were stationed at Bray just behind the front line in the southern sector of the assault. The brigade formed a part of 9th Division under Major-General Furse. On 1 July the offensive on that part of the front was largely successful. British troops captured the village of Mametz and a complete breakthrough looked possible, although the opportunity was missed and the Germans soon sent in reinforcements to shore up their front-line defences. Over the next ten days, Burgoyne was involved in the exhausting task of bringing up supplies of ammunition, barbed wire and rations through reserve trenches that were packed with men going forward to the front and others moving back to rest from the heavy fighting. At one point a shell landed in the very next bay to Burgoyne, about ten yards away. His friend Dan received a direct hit. He was blown to pieces from the waist down and body parts were scattered around the trench. But, astonishingly as it seemed to Burgoyne, Dan's top half appeared to be entirely untouched. His face did not even have a mark on it except for a slight scratch on his balding head.

Over the next few days the German shelling increased in intensity. Burgoyne noted in his diary, 'The din is ear-splitting ... The whizzing and whining of the shells overhead is like the passing of express trains. The different shells have quite distinct sounds. Some whine, others almost shriek, some hiss and some sob distinctly.' The men had names for the different types of shells that every soldier soon came to recognise. The 'whizz bangs' were from field artillery, 'Jack

Johnsons' from heavy howitzers, and 'woolly bears' were the bursts and smoke of a big German high explosive shell. It took about four weeks for a soldier to distinguish the sound of one from another.

By 12 July Burgoyne, like tens of thousands of other men along the Somme front, was living in an inferno of almost continuous bombardment. He wrote of the effect it had on him: 'Being shelled in the trenches is crook [dreadful]. One is so helpless. All one can do is lie as low down as possible, and wait for it to come. You can do nothing. There would be some satisfaction if you could get a bit of your own back. But you just sit still and wait for it to stop – or the other thing. I don't wonder at men getting "Shell Shock". Some go mad – temporarily. We have been shelled since 11.30 this morning. A few minutes ago one struck the kitchen, and the cook, his mate and the S[ergeant] M[ajor]'s batman were hit – the former seriously. Seven men have been hit this afternoon. One chap got hit in 15 places. Pieces of shell and debris have been falling in our bay all afternoon.'

On Saturday 15 July, the South African Brigade directly entered the battle along the Somme. By this point, the principal target was a series of woods scattered across the ridge beyond the British lines. Burgoyne's unit deployed in Delville Wood, a bleak, tangled wreck of vegetation where the trees had been shattered but the undergrowth was still thick with shrub and thistle. That night they settled in on the edge of the wood, crawling into the mass of shell craters to get as low as possible. Part of the brigade began to advance into the southern part of the wood. But it was difficult terrain in which to fight and the German defenders put up ferocious opposition. The South Africans had to fight yard by yard to move forward.

The artillery bombardment around Delville Wood seemed to reach a new intensity. The crashing of the shells was almost deafening. Sometimes a shell ricocheted off the trunk of a tree in an unearthly shriek, bringing down branches and leaves. By the middle of Sunday 16 July the walking wounded were coming back and passing Burgoyne and his two mates, who were taking shelter in a shell hole. A soldier from the Highland Light Infantry crawled by on all fours. Two men were hit in the stomach and their screams echoed across the wood from the nearby dressing station, unnerving those in the vicinity. Burgoyne's own platoon sergeant had his arm smashed in an explosion.

Then something even more alarming took place. Burgoyne described it in vivid detail a few days later: 'The worst of all was a young fellow of the 2nd Regt who crawled to our hole on hands and knees. He was unhurt and was carrying his full kit, and rifle with bayonet fixed dragging behind him, by the sling. He was all in. His eyes were bulging, his mouth open and his throat working as though he were swallowing something. "Oh God! Oh God!" he moaned continuously. He stopped just on the edge of our hole, but did not appear to see us. He stared straight ahead. We asked what was the matter – was he hit? For a time he took no notice – did not appear to hear us, in fact. Then, without looking at us he cried "I want to get out; I want to get out." We directed him to the dressing station. "I don't want the dressing station; I want to get out." I pointed to the wall of a house on the edge of the wood and told him to make for that. He struggled to his feet and moved off – doubled up – stopping dead and dropping to the ground at the sound of every shell. His nerves were absolutely gone. He was better out of it. He came near putting the wind up us three and we were glad when he left.'

Burgoyne and his mate had encountered a man who was suffering badly from shell shock. The long stare, the bulging eyes, the lack of normal interaction, the constant swallowing and difficulty in speaking – all were characteristics of the condition. And the effect the man had on Burgoyne and his colleague was also typical. They could not understand what had happened to him; they did not know what to do. But more than anything his presence spooked them. They had no idea what he would do next. He was unpredictable. He might do something that would suddenly bring down a mass of shells on himself, and them. They were indeed 'glad when he left'.

But the hell of what the soldiers called 'Devil's Wood' continued. On 18 July Burgoyne and his unit were ordered to go 'over the top' and occupy the wood. Under heavy machine-gun fire and yet another artillery bombardment they slowly moved through the remaining tree stumps and shattered shrubs. Men were going down everywhere. The shells shrieked low across them, just above their heads. A sergeant on Burgoyne's left was blown into the air and landed only a few yards away, winded but still alive. Before he could collect himself another shell landed near him and buried him under a mountain of earth, leaves and branches. It took Burgoyne and his mates a little while to reach him and dig him out from under the debris. When they retrieved him 'he was unwounded – but quite mad – temporarily I hope. He was jabbering and mumbling like a maniac.' Yet another case of shell shock.

Later that same day a shell landed even closer to Burgoyne. In an instant, he saw a flash, was aware of a column of smoke and earth, felt the heat of the explosion and experienced a sudden numbing pain that shot up his left arm. He was blown into the air, came down a few yards away and rolled to the bottom of a shell hole. His rifle was splintered and in pieces, the butt completely blown off. His bayonet had been fixed but was nowhere to be seen. Burgoyne was aware that his tunic had been ripped in many places, but apart from his shattered arm the only damage he could find was that he had a wound in his ear and blood was trickling down his neck. He was able to get up during a lull in the bombardment and, still carrying the remains of his now useless rifle, he made his way past piles of dead German and British soldiers to a dressing station. Just outside he was shocked to see a head floating in a water-filled crater. There was no body.

At the dressing station he was bandaged up and given his first cup of tea in five days. He was taken off in a very shaky lorry to a Casualty Clearing Station where he was given a large tetanus injection. Burgoyne was one of the lucky ones, as with a 'Blighty' wound he was shipped back to Britain where he slowly recovered in hospital. It took a couple of months to recover from his wounds but he was back in training with the brigade at the end of September. The 9th Division's official war diary simply noted for 18 July, 'The losses by the South African Brigade holding Delville Wood were said to be heavy.'[2]

During the same days that Private Burgoyne and the South African Brigade were struggling to capture Delville Wood, Captain Frederick St John Steadman was serving as a medical officer a few miles to the north in a field ambulance unit with the 60th Division. His field ambulance was an advanced dressing station consisting of two long, low wooden huts each of which in civilian conditions would be used as a ward to hold twenty-four patients. Steadman was struggling in one of these huts to cope with seventy-eight patients wounded during the first week of the battle when the artillery opened up around him. He described it in a letter to his wife: 'North, east and south, the great guns are thundering, belching and flashing. It is like a huge thunderstorm, only it is absolutely continuous, with huge crashes in between, with vivid sheet lightning (along miles of front) which never goes out. Star shells and rockets go up every moment. We can see the German answering shells bursting continually.

The bombardment is terrific. There has been nothing like it in the world before, not even in this war. The officers with us here say that they have heard nothing like it. The earth is trembling and shaking with it ... We are six miles away. What it must be like in the trenches I don't know. Hell can be nothing to it!'[3]

Steadman, aged thirty-five in 1916, was an experienced and caring doctor who tried to give time to each and every one of the pitifully wounded men who were brought in to his field ambulance. He called the patients his 'boys' and tried to minister to their needs while keeping his medical wards as sanitary as possible. One of the major problems was the lice the wounded men brought with them from the trenches. The beds were packed closely. As Steadman wrote, they 'were actually touching each other and in some cases lice were swarming from one man to another'. As the numbers in his ward grew with the arrival of even more wounded men, Steadman struggled to keep up. He described to his wife one of his strongest memories from that day: 'There are some very pathetic cases. I treat each man as though he were a human being, and try to make his short stay comfortable, after all the hell he has been through. So I smile at each man, when he comes in, and try to make him feel at home.'

Steadman described how a Highland soldier arrived, covered with mud from head to foot, and swarming with lice. 'Such a nice fellow too, quite educated, no doubt came from a good home in Dundee. He was very tired and seemed dazed with want of sleep; his face was twitching constantly from the strain he had been through. I greeted him cheerfully and said "Well, what I can do for you?" He looked at me and said "Well, sir, if – then hesitates as though he were about to ask some tremendous favour, quite out of my power to give, or as though he expected me to be angry with the boldness of his request. So I smiled and said, "Well! What is it?" and his lips quivered and he said: "Well, sir, I have not had my clothes off for nearly six weeks; if I could just have a bath?"' Steadman was struck by the pathos of this simple request, 'almost to break down asking for such a simple thing! Mind you, he was suffering from shell shock, having been blown up and rendered unconscious, but uninjured otherwise. All this was forgotten, it was the bath he wanted. I laughed and said "Of course you shall, and what is more, I can give you a clean shirt".'

Arranging a bath, however, was no easy matter. A horse and cart had to go into the nearest village to fill a large carrier with water. This had to be heated in a series of dixies or large kettles over a stove. The whole process took about five hours but it helped the Highlander quickly recover from his mild shell shock and exhaustion. He was back in the line in a matter of days.

As the injured kept on coming, Steadman was amazed at the number who were suffering from shell shock. He had never imagined that such cases could be so terrible. He characterised them as having 'an exhausted look, with their faces twitching, and hands and arms shaking constantly'. In another letter to his wife he wrote: 'We had another bad case of shell shock in. Poor man, he lost his friend near him, but the shell did not touch him – it knocked him down by the loud concussion. The man looks quite insane; it is fearful to watch him. I think he will eventually recover but it is very sad. Another boy of 17 in my ward, also suffering from shell shock, does nothing but cry and say he can't stand the noise. He is quite unnerved. I shall probably send him down the line in a day or two. He is no good here and ought not to have come out, but he gave his age as 19!'

Of another shell shock victim, Steadman wrote: 'I go up to him in the morning, and I sit down on his bed and hold his hand and pretend to feel his pulse, and I say "Well, better this morning?" He leans forward and whispers "The cloud is very bad this morning, sir." I ask "What cloud?" He looks very cunning and says "The cloud out there, sir. I walked to the door of the ward this morning and saw the black cloud and ran back quick. Both of them were in it."' This went on every morning, although, as Steadman explained to his wife, most of the time the man appeared quite sane and talked perfectly rationally. He discovered that a high explosive shell had burst between the man and two of his chums, killing them both but only knocking him down and throwing a great cloud of black smoke over them. 'This is the cloud he thinks he sees every morning, and he thinks he sees his two friends in it. I sent him to the C[asualty] C[learing] S[tation] and home to Blighty this morning. At least I think my note which I sent with him will get him to Blighty. These shell shock cases are very, very sad to watch.'

By late July 1916, Steadman's small unit, which in normal times could cope with forty-eight patients, was receiving fifty wounded men a day, most of whom would be kept in the wards for at least a week. The overcrowding was dreadful but Steadman still tried to give every one of his 'boys' the care they needed. He noted that many of the shell shock victims suffered from appalling nightmares. Again, in a letter to his wife he described a regular pattern. 'I go from bed to bed, having a cheerful chat and a joke with each one ... before passing on to the next bed I look each man straight in the face and say "Anything else?" Sometimes a man hesitates as he knows the other men may overhear what he says to me, so I just bend over close, and he often whispers "The dreams, sir, I dare not go to sleep because I dream so of – (and I know he means of his chum's death). I have about 12 men in the ward suffering like this; all have had their friends killed by their sides. These men can't sleep; if they get to sleep they wake up with a cry, and shriek out.'

Even an experienced doctor like Steadman was taken aback, writing 'It is very sad to see strong brave men, brought down like this.'

However, Steadman understood what his duty was. As an army medical officer he had to return as many men as possible to their battalions as quickly as possible. This applied in equal measure to the dreadfully sad cases of shell shock he struggled to deal with. He wrote: 'Then the beastly time comes when you have to order them back to all the misery of it again; that is the rotten part. You cannot help them long, just a few days, and then back they must go. If they were kept long the hospital would be absolutely crowded out. *There would be no men to fight*' (author's italics). Steadman, at the front end of the terrible chain of casualties pouring back from the Somme, had realised instinctively that if he was too sympathetic to the large number of shell shock victims that came his way then the army, as he said, would simply have 'no men to fight'.

By the beginning of August, Fourth Army under General Sir Henry Rawlinson calculated it had lost more than 125,000 officers and men killed, wounded or posted missing since the opening of the Battle of the Somme.[4] These losses were on a scale never experienced within the British army before. The numbers lost by the British–Dutch forces at the Battle of Waterloo have been estimated at about 17,000, while the number of British dead during the three years of the Boer War had totalled about 22,000. The worst fighting so far in the Great War, during the Battle of Loos in September 1915, had seen total losses of 59,000, less than half of those incurred in the first month on the Somme.

Rawlinson's most loyal supporter through this terrible month was his chief of staff at Fourth Army, Major-General Sir Archibald Armar Montgomery.[5] Montgomery came from an army family in County Tyrone, in the north of Ireland.

He joined the Royal Artillery at Woolwich aged twenty and served for many years in India and in South Africa during the Boer War. In 1906 he attended the Staff College at Camberley, where officers were trained for senior leadership in the British army. Here Montgomery met General Sir Henry Rawlinson. Montgomery was a typical soldier from the country gentry who set great store by tradition and believed unquestioningly in the British way of doing things. But he was tall, charming and diplomatic in dealing with his superior officers, a skill that helped him progress quickly up through the ranks.

In August 1914, Montgomery was a staff officer in the 4th Division and soon crossed to France, where he took part in one of the earliest engagements between the British Expeditionary Force (BEF) and the German army at the Battle of Le Cateau. When Rawlinson took over the 4th Division, Montgomery became his principal staff officer and a close working relationship developed between the two men. Rawlinson was promoted to command IV Corps later in the year and Montgomery moved across as his chief of staff. When, in early 1916, Rawlinson was appointed commander of the newly created Fourth Army, Montgomery once more went him. He had been promoted from major to major-general in just twenty months, an astonishing rise that in peacetime would have taken at least ten years.

It will be seen that there were substantial disagreements between Haig and Rawlinson as to the strategy and tactics to follow in the offensive on the Somme in July 1916. It is pretty clear from his unpublished memoirs that Montgomery was in close agreement with his own direct superior, Rawlinson, in the dispute and thought that Haig was to blame for his insistence on trying to reach objectives that were beyond the range of the artillery. 'We were in fact short of artillery for the task we were asked to achieve,' he later wrote.[6] But as the heavy losses continued throughout the month, Montgomery like Rawlinson grew concerned. Of particular worry for them was the large number of losses from shell shock cases and the impact this was having on the ability of certain units to sustain their fighting spirit. In early August, Montgomery sent out a set of questionnaires to the most senior commanders within Fourth Army asking what lessons should be learned from the last few weeks of battle. They went to every corps commander and most divisional commanders, as well as to some brigade commanders.

The replies make for fascinating reading. Many of the officers in command of units that had suffered the highest casualty rates ever endured in the British army were very clear about what had gone wrong. There was considerable agreement that attacks resulted in heavy losses if they were carried out too hastily, without giving enough time for local commanders to properly reconnoitre and prepare. There was a consensus that attacks carried out with great determination by fresh, motivated troops after only a short bombardment often enjoyed the advantage of surprise, increasing the likelihood of success. There were many other sensible suggestions about the use of artillery, the best way to cross No Man's Land, and the need to improve communications between front lines and headquarters in the rear.

One or two of the officers consulted went further. Brigadier Reginald John Kentish had been in charge of the 76th Brigade during the bitter struggle for Delville Wood. He had seen some of the worst of the fighting in July and was prepared to stick his neck out more than most. His submission, sent in on 3 August, contained a section titled 'The Limits of Endurance of the Infantry Soldier'. In it, Kentish wrote, 'The present intense fighting calls for the greatest test of pluck and endurance for the British Infantry man. There is no doubt that he will respond to every call made on him. But he will

respond in varying degrees.' Kentish continued his line of
thought in a long and convoluted sentence: 'If he is tried too
highly, he may become a danger to his side, and especially is
this likely to be the case if Divisions which have already been
through a very intense period of fighting, and which have
lost a big proportion of NCOs and men, and which have also
so to speak been living in a very heavily shelled zone where
the fire is both frontal and enfilade, are without sufficient
time for recuperation, filled up with men of every unit except
their own, and sent back to the same ground, and to submit
to the same intense situation they have already experienced.
Further if they have taken part in any of the minor, but very
costly piecemeal attacks, which have been a feature of the
operation since the big offensive on 14 July, their moral [sic]
will undoubtedly ... be very much weaker than when they
first entered the sphere of operations.'[7]

Kentish had recognised two important features of shell
shock. Prolonged exposure to intense fire was a major contributory factor. And although it affected individuals one by
one, it was also contagious and could spread among an entire
unit. If not properly and fairly treated, then shell shock could
undermine the fighting spirit of whole groups of men.

The centenary commemorations of the Great War from 2014
have revealed a widespread fascination with the events of
the years 1914–1918. They have also unleashed a tremendous
outpouring of writing about the war, and of television doc-
umentaries and radio programmes. However, many of the
attitudes expressed in this popular revival of interest in the
war have reinforced traditional and outdated interpretations.
For instance, the generals are nearly always presented as
obstinate and incompetent commanders leading courageous
men, the view made famous more than fifty years ago by
the phrase 'lions led by donkeys';[8] and the war is usually

presented as being entirely unnecessary and futile. These views, however, do not reflect the latest research on the war. Scholarly thinking has moved on a great deal over recent decades. The First World War is often seen not as a futile but as a necessary war and one that was certainly popular for at least the first two years of conflict. The 'lions led by donkeys' thesis has been challenged by a reappraisal of the high command and a recognition that the generals were far more successful than has traditionally been realised in leading a citizen army to final victory in the autumn of 1918. But the popular myths of the war endure in the common view and in many of the television programmes.[9]

Included among the many figures in the cast of stock characters that preoccupy public memory of the war is that of the shell-shocked soldier. He is usually portrayed as one of the key victims of the war, someone who could not cope with the ghastly pressures of the modern battlefield in an industrial war of barbed wire, artillery barrages, high explosives and poison gas; another victim of what is usually presented as a brutal, futile war. The shell-shocked soldier has almost become a symbol of the war and even, it has been argued, a metaphor for the inhumanity of a modern, industrial war.[10] However, a great deal has also been written over recent decades about shell shock in the war. Much of this has been concerned with the psychological factors behind shell shock, based on research into the medical debate about trauma. The research has shown how doctors, neurologists and physiologists struggled (or failed) to understand the process of psychological breakdown. The debate about shell shock is seen as the starting point of a steep learning curve that would culminate, much later in the century, with the classification of war trauma as post-traumatic stress disorder. Moreover, the First World War has been indelibly linked with 'the birth of military psychiatry'.[11]

This book does not attempt to explore in any detail the psychology behind war neuroses and the psychosomatic disorders of war. I am not a doctor or a psychologist. *Breakdown* is rather an exploration of the specific *military* reaction to what was perceived as an epidemic of shell shock that occurred during the Battle of the Somme from July to November 1916. Senior figures in the army regarded shell shock not so much as an individual trauma that needed to be understood, requiring sympathy and treatment, but as a collective threat to the army as a whole. Shell shock was believed to be contagious in that a nervy man showing signs of mental distress could easily make other men around him nervy. And there was the constant fear of malingering. If one man was treated sympathetically and taken out of the line for rest and recuperation, then maybe many others would claim to be suffering from shell shock in an attempt to escape from the horrors of the trenches. The possibility that whole companies or battalions might go down with shell shock was seen as a problem that could ultimately undermine the ability of the army to function as an effective fighting force. *Breakdown* focuses on the story of the attempt by the military authorities, often in the most cruel and uncaring way, to prevent this from happening.

It seemed to contemporaries that there were two apparently new features of war for soldiers of the First World War to grapple with. One was poison gas; the second was shell shock. In the view of many they were parallel in effect. The impact of one was often compared with that of the other. Both amazed the senior command and could cause panic among the ranks that had to face them. Lieutenant-Colonel Rogers had been Medical Officer of the 4th Black Watch battalion for most of the war and he reported, 'The very mention of gas would put the "wind up" the battalion at once, even if they had gas masks which, they were told, were perfectly safe.' Rogers thought that gas 'was a very powerful factor in causing anxiety neurosis'.[12]

Following post-war prohibitions, poison gas was not used in combat in the Second World War, although in more recent conflicts in Vietnam, Iraq and Syria chemical warfare has been resorted to once again. However, shell shock or, in more recent terminology, post-traumatic stress disorder, is something that soldiers have experienced throughout the last one hundred years. It has remained a continuing facet of modern warfare.

The conventional wisdom is that the only people to describe shell shock during the First World War were those who tried to treat it: medical officers in the field, military doctors at Casualty Clearing Stations and base hospitals, and psychologists back home in Britain and in the specialist centres that were finally set up in late 1916.[13] However, research for this book has revealed that there are many very moving descriptions of shell shock, both by those who directly suffered from it and by fellow soldiers who witnessed it in the trenches and were thrown off balance by it. The three sets of extracts quoted in the preceding pages illustrate the range of original sources behind much of *Breakdown*. Archibald McAllister Burgoyne experienced the build-up of stress as his battalion prepared to go into action in Delville Wood in mid-July 1916 and he saw men around him going down with shell shock. Major Frederick St John Steadman was one of the doctors stunned by the scale of the problem as men presented with strange and peculiar mental neuroses, for the treatment of which he had received no training; he was amazed as they turned up in what seemed like ever-increasing numbers. And Brigadier Reginald John Kentish was a military leader who had to command several thousand men in battle but who was left reflecting on how much a soldier could endure before he reached his point of breakdown.

Finding some of these new sources has been one of the great rewards of researching this book.

However, the story of shell shock on the Somme has to be put in context. The preliminary chapters of *Breakdown* therefore look at the mass response to the war in late August and September 1914 when three-quarters of a million men, mostly without any personal or family links with the military, volunteered for the army. The networks they were part of, the Pals battalions they formed and Kitchener's New Army, which they shaped, were all very much of their time. And it was this army that went over the top on 1 July 1916 and saw the lion's share of the fighting on the Somme over the following months. War neurosis had been observed since the early months of the conflict, particularly since the onset of trench warfare with its new battlefield geography of front lines, barbed wire and No Man's Land, and characterised by intense artillery barrages. Men had to hunker down in a trench or a dugout and passively accept being under enemy shellfire, sometimes for hours at a time, with all the risks of sudden death, mutilation or burial under a mountain of earth. Many could not take it and broke down.

The army had not expected this reaction to modern warfare and had made no preparations to cope with it. It naturally turned to medical men for advice on how to respond, but the primitive state of the understanding of how men's minds operated, particularly in Britain by comparison to France and Germany, meant there was no consensus. Doctors argued as to whether shell shock was a physical problem or an emotional one; whether it was a form of what was then called 'lunacy', with all the expectations that went with this, or whether it was a new mental phenomenon that anyone and everyone in a modern army on a contemporary battlefield might suffer from.

Perplexed, the military authorities saw the problem as

a threat that cut to the heart of the army's ability to fight – and responded accordingly. An account of their reaction during the Battle of the Somme forms the central chapters of the book. After the experience of reacting to the epidemic of shell shock on the Somme, the army had to decide how to approach shell shock in the ensuing battles along the Western Front. Should men suffering the various forms of anxiety neurosis be categorised as battle casualties under the term 'shell shock'? Was conventional military discipline appropriate? What treatments were available? And when the war came to an end, others had to decide how the state should look after those who had suffered mental distress and might still be enduring the consequences. It was clear that a man who had lost an arm or a leg in the war should be helped to settle back in to society and receive a pension. Did the same apply to those who had experienced a form of nervous breakdown? If so, what level of compensation was appropriate, how should it be defined, for how long should it be paid? And where should the line be drawn between those deserving of state support and those who should be left to look after themselves? Losing a limb was a form of permanent disablement. Was a psychiatric illness merely a temporary disability, and if so when could it be said that one had recovered?

The history of shell shock in the First World War can be seen, as it were, through many different prisms. It can be understood as an important step in the development of psychology. It can be presented as a disease arising from the horrors of modern industrial warfare. It can be seen as the first step on the long journey of comprehending how men's minds respond to combat and to what is now called post-traumatic stress disorder. It can be seen as an issue of military discipline, as an illustration of the brutality of the high command towards the treatment of its soldiers. But the story of shell shock on the Somme, here, is that of how the military responded to what they perceived as a major manpower crisis.

Never was the problem of shell shock more severe than in the months between July and November 1916. It peaked during the bloody battles of the Somme, when for the first time it became an issue of real concern to the military authorities; as a result they became obsessed with avoiding what they called 'wastage'. It is this story of the military response to shell shock in 1916 that is at the core of *Breakdown*.

1

The Pals Battalions

War came to Britain almost literally out of a bright blue summer sky in early August 1914. On that hot, sunny bank holiday weekend, if Britons feared war at all what they expected was civil war in Ireland between the armed factions of Protestant Unionists in the north and Catholic Nationalists in the south rather than a general European war. But, having been at peace on 28 July, by midnight on 4 August all the major nations of Europe except Italy and Spain were at war.

The governing Liberal Party in Westminster and public opinion across the nation had been deeply divided over whether to rally to France's aid when threatened by invasion from Germany. But when the powerful German army invaded neutral Belgium in a well-prepared operation known as the Schlieffen Plan, both the Liberals and British public opinion quickly swung in favour of war. The sense of outrage in the country at Germany's dastardly invasion of 'gallant little Belgium' (as the contemporary phrase had it) was immense. Germany was sent an ultimatum to withdraw its troops. When the ultimatum expired at 11 p.m. London time, midnight in Berlin, on 4 August, His Majesty's government formally declared war on the Imperial German Reich.

Most people were stunned by the speed of events. They

had gone off on holiday to the seaside, and Europe had been at peace. Now, a few days later, Europe was at war. Most people agreed that war came like a 'bolt from the blue'. And as one twenty-year-old later put it, 'It seemed incredible that in our orderly, civilized world such things could happen.'[1]

Since 1906, the War Office had secretly discussed operational plans with the French army to send an expeditionary force to support France in the event that the country was invaded. But it was unclear whether these talks morally committed Britain to come to France's aid. And, in any case, the discussions had taken place in secret and were not known to either Parliament or public.[2] In retrospect, however, it was the appalling *lack* of planning for a major war that was extraordinary. Not only were there no thoughts as to how, in such an eventuality, the British army should be enlarged, or how the resources to house, equip, feed and arm a substantially larger army would be mobilised, but there had been no thinking about how to expand the small manufacturing base on which Britain's arms and munitions industry was reliant. Even the position of Secretary of War was vacant. Prime Minister Herbert Asquith had carried out its responsibilities for five months since the resignation of the previous secretary. This was clearly not appropriate in a time of war. Asquith wrote to his young confidante, Venetia Stanley, on the first day of war, 'It was quite impossible for me to go on [as Secretary of War], now that war is actually in being: it requires the undivided time and thought of any man to do the job properly.'[3]

The government quickly looked around to find who could fill this essential role. The influential *Times* military correspondent, Colonel Charles à Court Repington, spotted that Lord Kitchener was currently in London, away from his duties as British agent in Egypt, and wrote, 'Lord Kitchener is at home, and his selection for this onerous and important post would meet with warm public approval.'[4] Repington's suggestion would meet with immense public acclaim.

Field Marshal Earl Kitchener of Khartoum was the best-known and most widely respected soldier of his generation. He had joined the Royal Engineers in 1870 and had spent much of his life in the Middle East, carrying out a military survey of Palestine in the 1870s, joining the Egyptian army in the 1880s, acting as Sirdar (commander-in-chief) of that army through much of the 1890s, and leading the successful campaign to crush the Islamic insurgents in the Sudan in 1898 which made him a national figure. During the Boer War he was first chief of staff and then commander-in-chief in South Africa and had gone on to act as military head in India from 1902 to 1909. From India he toured the Far East and Australasia, where he advised the Australian and New Zealand governments on the formation of their own armies. In 1911 he was appointed British agent and consul-general in Egypt, effectively military and political head of that nation, guarding the Suez Canal, which was seen as vital to imperial security. With his links to Egypt, India and South Africa, Kitchener was the personification of Britain's imperial mission. With successful military campaigns behind him he was a popular hero. Despite his long absences from Britain he was widely known and his moustachioed, uniformed image was a symbol of bullish, determined imperialism.

Kitchener's appointment as Secretary for War two days after the declaration of war proved a massive hit with the public and inspired British people that the army was going to be under strong leadership. Asquith's daughter later wrote that 'Lord Kitchener was more than a national hero. He was a national institution ... There was a feeling Kitchener could not fail. The psychological effect of his appointment, the tonic to public confidence, were instantaneous and overwhelming.'[5]

Kitchener's widespread popularity would have an enormous impact on events over the coming months. But several problems would arise from his appointment. Kitchener was by nature autocratic, incapable of delegating responsibility or taking advice and he had an immense suspicion of politicians and even of the War Office itself. He once remarked to a friend, 'May God preserve me from the politicians.'[6] He was not at all keen to take up the post of War Secretary but when it was presented to him as his duty he agreed as long as he was given full Cabinet status. He would prove to be a difficult figure to control. At his first Cabinet meeting he stunned his colleagues around the table by announcing that contrary to public opinion, this war was bound to be a long one, and that Britain must now prepare for a struggle lasting at least three years. He argued that wars took unexpected courses and a European conflict could not be ended by a victory at sea but only by major land battles on the continent. In order to play a part 'on a scale proportionate to its magnitude and power' Britain had to be prepared 'to put armies of millions in the field and maintain them for several years'. Such was the awe and respect that Kitchener commanded that the Cabinet unanimously accepted his view in silence.[7] Lloyd George, then Chancellor of the Exchequer, later described Kitchener as practically a 'military dictator' in the first months of the war and recalled that 'The Members of the Cabinet were frankly intimidated by his presence because of his repute and his enormous influence amongst all classes of the people outside. A word from him was decisive and no one dared to challenge it in a Cabinet meeting.'[8]

Kitchener's views prevailed in that the Cabinet agreed to send an expeditionary force of four divisions supported by cavalry to take its position on the left of the French army. Within fourteen days troops were landing in France and beginning to deploy, in line with the eight years of military planning that had gone into preparing for this specific operation. Moreover, the Cabinet agreed to Kitchener's proposal to increase the size of the army by 500,000 men. On 7 August, the newspapers reported his preliminary appeal for 100,000 men between the ages of nineteen and thirty 'who have the safety of the Empire at heart' to enlist. Kitchener's initial plan was to raise six new divisions.

In 1914, the British army was a tiny, all-volunteer professional force. At home it consisted of six regular infantry divisions supported by a cavalry division. Each infantry division also had its own artillery, engineers, signallers and field ambulance units. The core unit of the army was the regiment and each county had its own famous regiments with their own proud histories. At least one battalion from each regiment served in India or elsewhere abroad for periods of up to five years at a time. There was also the Indian Army, a separate force made up of Indian nationals, many from warrior tribes, commanded by British officers but largely financed from within the sub-continent. In addition, within Britain, there were fourteen Territorial divisions, about 250,000 men, created in the army reforms of 1908. Territorial units were made up of men who were often highly motivated and patriotic. But their training was basic, the requirement being only for a minimum of eight and a maximum of fifteen days a year in camp, supported by a few days (or evenings) of drilling in local halls. Their equipment was often old and outdated, little more than hand-me-downs from the regular army. The key feature of the Territorial Force was that it was directly under local responsibility, with county associations in charge of recruitment, equipment and organisation; they were also responsible for negotiations with employers to ensure volunteers were permitted leave of absence to carry out their duties. Professional military men were still in direct command but most of the major towns and counties of Britain took great pride in their local Territorials. The principal intention behind the recruitment of the Territorial Force (apart from its far lower cost than the regular army) was the home defence of Britain if the regular forces were sent abroad. Territorials were not required to serve overseas, although they could do so if they agreed to volunteer. Before 1914, only about 7 per cent of the Territorial Force had agreed to serve abroad, as this would clearly be far more disruptive to life and employment at home.

Kitchener had a strong and instinctive distrust of the Territorials. He disliked the idea that they were under the county associations and not directly under the command of the War Office, and was suspicious of what he called a 'Town Clerk's Army'.[9] He preferred men who knew nothing and could be trained from scratch to those who had a smattering of what he regarded as the wrong sort of training. It has often been argued that his suspicions were unfounded and betrayed the fact that, having been out of Britain for many years, he was unaware of the good work that the county associations had been doing. Certainly, they were beginning to function efficiently by 1914. But Kitchener did not believe that they were up to the task of managing the enormous expansion that he now foresaw. And Kitchener's view also doubtless represented the suspicion often felt by the full-time professional towards the part-time amateur enthusiast. So Kitchener took a momentous decision in August 1914. He decided not to appeal for recruits to swell the ranks of the Territorial Force but for men to come forward to form a New Army. This would be recruited not locally through the county associations but centrally through the War Office and the normal recruiting mechanisms that existed within the Adjutant-General's Department.

The first few days of the war counter the myth that tens of thousands rushed forward to volunteer as soon as war was declared. A few hundred men turned up in London at New Scotland Yard. But very few were actually processed through the antiquated machinery of recruitment. In other cities like Birmingham, the processing of recruits was equally slow. Every recruit was required to take a bath in the one bathroom available; then to be medically examined by the single doctor present; then to be taken through the complex attestation form by the one clerk assigned to the task. In the first week, the average daily intake was only about 1,600 men across the whole country. Many were left outside queuing, but in no way did this add up to the dynamic recruitment boom that was needed to transform the size of the British army. In contrast, by mid-August 261,000 had come forward to enlist in the German army, which was already twenty-five times bigger than the British.

Over the next couple of weeks the machinery of recruitment expanded and became more fit for purpose. New offices were given over to the handling of recruits. Sometimes town halls opened their doors, and often schools, empty of course in midsummer, were taken over. More clerks were allocated to the task, while doctors were taken on in much bigger numbers and were offered 1s 6d for every recruit they examined. During the second week of the war, the daily number of recruits being attested went up to about 6,000. But this was still very much an urban phenomenon based on the largest cities, London, Birmingham, Bristol and Manchester. The response from rural areas and smaller towns was trivial by comparison.

It was in the last week of August, when news came through of the British Expeditionary Force's first battles at Mons and Le Cateau, that the situation began to change. All reporting from the front was subject to strict military censorship, but soon the papers were full of hints of a retreat from Mons. This aroused great concern for the fate of the nation's army and inspired far more interest in the war than the declaration of war itself. In the last week of August, 63,000 men came forward to attest. Then, in a special edition of *The Times* on 30 August, its reporter, Arthur Moore, wrote openly for the first time of the 'terrible defeat of British troops' and of 'broken British regiments'. In addition to describing panic and chaos at the front, Moore ended his piece with an unashamed call for volunteers to come forward: 'Is an army of exhaustless valour to be borne down by the sheer weight of [German] numbers, while young Englishmen at home play golf and cricket? We want men and we want them now ... We have to face the fact that the British Expeditionary Force ... has suffered terrible losses and requires immediate and immense reinforcement. The BEF has won imperishable glory, but it needs men, men and yet more men.'[10] The situation was transformed almost overnight and recruiting fever swept parts of the nation.

Kitchener announced a new recruiting drive for a second group of 100,000 volunteers. The upper age limit was increased to thirty-five (forty-five for ex-soldiers), married men or widowers with children were accepted and new separation allowances were announced. In a single week from 30 August to 5 September the massive total of 174,901 men attested – nearly three times as many as in the previous week. In fact this proved to be the largest number recruited in any week during the war. The highest total in a single day was recorded on Thursday 3 September when 33,204 men joined up – including 3,521 in London, 2,151 in Manchester, 1,653 in Birmingham and 1,014 in Glasgow.

The War Office could not begin to cope with such huge numbers. Kitchener had no alternative but to accept assistance from local authorities, MPs and prominent citizens who came forward to help, despite his original hostility to the county committees. At the same time, the Prime

Minister created a Parliamentary Recruiting Committee, a cross-party group responsible for the organisation of recruiting meetings to mobilise young men across the nation and 'at which the justice of our cause should be made plain and the duty of every man to do his part should be enforced.'[11] Consequently a fundamental shift in the process of recruitment took place. It was taken out of the sole hands of the understaffed War Office and delegated to local communities, who could organise rallies and employ local speakers as they saw fit. The mayors and corporations of the biggest cities, along with self-appointed committees of local dignitaries, industrialists, factory owners and large landowners, all had a stake in raising local units. Recruitment became a matter of local and civic pride as well as of national need. As a consequence Kitchener's New Army began to take on a unique character.

Britain had become a predominantly urban country in the latter half of the nineteenth and the beginning of the twentieth century. The 1911 census recorded that four out of every five people lived in a town or city and it counted five principal conurbations in England with well over one million inhabitants – south-east Lancashire, the West Midlands, West Yorkshire, Merseyside and Greater London (far and away the largest of all with a population of 7.256 million). For most city dwellers the principal form of government they came across was local or municipal. The Victorian city leaders built lavish town halls and prided themselves in the construction of local parks, museums, libraries and schools. In many cities there was desperate poverty concentrated in overcrowded and run-down slums, a stain on the urban landscape of what was still (just) the wealthiest empire in the world. But the glue that kept together the urban society of semi-skilled, skilled and middle-class workers was a network of organisations, clubs and societies. These ranged from trade

unions to working men's institutes; from church, chapel and
Sunday School societies to football, cycling or cricket clubs;
from the Boy Scouts and Boys' Brigade to office, factory and
trade associations; from old boys' groups to craft guilds. For
many Edwardian males, these societies combined local pride
with national patriotism. It was hardly surprising that in the
recruitment fever that swept the country in late August and
September 1914, men from these local groups would want to
stay together and share in wartime the companionship they
had established in peace.

So it was that the 'Pals' battalions came into existence.
The first such battalions appeared in late August at different
ends of the nation. A group of City workers from Lloyds
and the Baltic Exchange in London formed what was called
the Stockbrokers' Battalion. Sixteen hundred recruits who
turned up in top hats, morning coats and Norfolk jackets
were inspected on 29 August and then marched off to the
Tower of London, where they were sworn in. A week later,
the Stockbrokers – now called the 10th Battalion Royal
Fusiliers – were sent to Colchester for training. At the same
time, in Liverpool, Lord Derby, a major landowner, business
chief and chair of the local Territorials Association, was given
permission by Kitchener to raise a battalion of men from
among the business houses of that city. He made an appeal
to 'clerks and others engaged in business' who might want to
come forward if they knew 'they would be able to serve with
their friends and not be put in a battalion with unknown
men as their companions'. Derby was unsure if he would
succeed. But on the evening that his appeal appeared in the
Liverpool Daily Post, 1,500 men turned up at the drill hall.
Derby referred to the unit that was recruited as a 'battalion
of pals', thus giving this distinctive type of unit the name
that stuck.[12]

It was partly because Kitchener had decided to recruit

new battalions for his New Army rather than simply expand the existing Territorial Force that the concept of the Pals battalion spread so rapidly across the industrial cities of northern and Midland Britain, for it was here that the largest reserves of manpower were available. In Liverpool, the response to Derby's appeal was so overwhelming that he ended up raising not one but three battalions as groups of men from the Cunard offices, the Cotton Exchange, the banks and insurance companies volunteered en masse. They were eventually designated the 17th, 18th and 19th Battalions The King's Liverpool Regiment. In Manchester, the Lord Mayor and the city dignitaries rushed to follow suit and on 1 September, 800 men were sworn in, warehousemen and office workers from the same offices being allocated to the same companies and platoons. So many Mancunians came forward that within two weeks four battalions had been raised, one of which consisted entirely of officials from the city corporation, local county and urban district councils and education committees.

Birmingham also quickly got in on the act. Here the local paper asked volunteers to submit their names and 4,500 responded. Officials in the town hall tried to ensure that men from a single firm were asked to come to the recruiting office on the same day. After they had attested they were sent home until being called up to start training. The process was far more civilised and better organised than almost anywhere else. Three Pals battalions were raised this way. Tyneside was another area that saw a rush to join up in September. The local Chamber of Commerce started to enrol men, and the first group had attested before the receipt of War Office approval to raise new battalions. So they were sent to join the 9th Northumberland Fusiliers, who were already in training. When approval came through, two Pals battalions were immediately raised, along with a third over the next couple of months. Initially known as the Tyneside Pioneers, they were later designated the 18th and 19th Northumberland Fusiliers.

In Sheffield, the initiative to form a battalion came from two university students who were attending a course of summer lectures on the war. Recruitment began in the first week of September and was specifically directed at university students, ex-public schoolboys, lawyers and clerks. On 10 September the volunteers formally attested; so many friends wanted to stay together that, as far as possible, the university students, teachers and bankers were assigned to one company, the tradesmen and mining engineers to another and the remaining clerks, teachers, accountants and professionals to two further companies. Many of the young elite of the city and its surrounding districts marched off on 15 September to start their training. The unit eventually became the 12th Battalion The York and Lancaster Regiment.[13]

In Hull, the local Lord Lieutenant, Lord Nunburnholme, printed posters calling for 'clerks and others' to join a new battalion. This became known as the Hull Commercials. It was followed by two more battalions, the Hull Tradesmen and, later in the month, the Hull Sportsmen and Athletes. A couple of months afterwards a fourth battalion was raised in the town; for want of an alternative name, they were known simply as 'T'others'. The four battalions were eventually designated the 10th, 11th, 12th and 13th Battalions East Yorkshire Regiment.

Several influences came together in this fever of recruiting across much of the country in late August and September 1914. The news from France suggested, within the limitations of military censorship, retreat and panic among the units fighting at Mons. Stories of glory and individual heroism were many, but it was clear to most patriots that Britain's small army would soon be overwhelmed by the vastly greater

German forces unless more men rushed to the colours. Moreover, during September came stories of terrible atrocities committed by German soldiers on Belgian civilians. There was real evidence of German violence against the civilian population, who were being encouraged to act as saboteurs behind advancing German lines. The Germans thought this civilian insurgency was a violation of the rules of war. But the genuine evidence was magnified enormously by a press that soon began to speak of the 'wicked' or the 'evil' Hun.[14]

If this provided the motive for many young men to come forward so eagerly, it was the strongly competitive sense of civic pride that made them want to stay together within the military in the associations they were used to. Although the drive to form the Pals battalions came from the local mayors and city elders, eager to show that their locality was as patriotic as the next, it was all approved from above. Battalions were only recruited when they had direct War Office approval, and often this came from Kitchener himself. Aware of the need to get more men into the army as soon as possible, he had realised by the end of August that the existing mechanisms were not up to it. The formation of the Pals battalions by local groupings neatly got around this limitation, while utilising some of the same energies that had gone into the Territorial Force. But the Pals battalions were instead part of Kitchener's New Army, to be trained and readied as he wished.

All this frenzied activity required funding. Here again, local sources enthusiastically came up with what was needed. Not only did young men come forward to enlist but private companies and wealthy individuals provided the funds for clothing, equipping and feeding the volunteers. Often they also made offers of drill halls and open spaces for the men to begin their training. In Manchester the organising committee offered to find £15,000 but in a fortnight had raised £26,701 – the largest donation of £7,000 coming from the Gas Department of the city corporation and £1,000 having been given by a wealthy local businessman.[15] In Birmingham local companies and private individuals raised £17,000 towards the cost of recruiting their local Pals battalions. In mid-September, Kitchener made it a condition that Pals battalions would only be approved if they could raise their own initial funding. These new battalions almost became private citizens' armies. Today it seems extraordinary that so much private charity was offered to fund an official policy of military recruitment at a time of war. But this was, in effect, the last hurrah of the Victorian attitude of self-help in which people did not turn to the state but used their own resources to solve a problem. No doubt the older men were as happy in their giving as the younger men were in stepping forward to enlist. Eventually, in the summer of 1915, the War Office repaid most of the sums that had been raised locally but in some cases wealthy local figures refused to take the money – meaning they had, in effect, personally subsidised national War Office activity.

Recruiting rallies took place across the nation during the month of September. Behind huge banners portraying slogans like 'Duty' and 'Your Brothers Are Calling You' soldiers would march and bands would play. Anthems were sung and speakers recited stories of the dreadful atrocities being committed in Belgium while invoking the nobility of Britain's cause. Pre-war divisions were put aside. Trade union leaders and suffragettes pleaded with men to take up the good fight. Music hall stars sang songs to encourage men to go to war. Women were as eager as their men folk to see the army grow; mothers encouraged sons, sisters told brothers to join up. Indeed, it was during this month that some women started to hand out white feathers in the street to men of enlistment age who were spotted wearing civilian clothes. It might seem strange now that so many men should be so enthusiastic about heading off to the carnage of war, and that so many women should cheer to see their husbands, sons and brothers marching off to their deaths. The fact was, of course, that apart from a tiny number of visionaries who predicted the scale of the destruction that would follow, most people had no sense of what a modern European war would be like. It was assumed that huge armies would fight a couple of battles, the fleets would engage each other at sea, some ground would be occupied and then everything would quickly be over. With so little awareness of the destructive capacity of modern artillery, machine guns, aircraft and bombs, there was barely any dread of war; instead there was real enthusiasm for it, and a desire among the young to be part of it before it was all over.

A photographic appeal appeared on the front cover of the magazine *London Opinion* on 5 September showing a portrait of a moustachioed and uniformed Kitchener pointing his index finger directly out at the viewer above the slogan 'Your Country Needs You'. The image had been designed by Alfred Leete, a commercial graphic artist who had created adverts for brands like Rowntrees, Bovril and Guinness, as well as for the London Underground. Now he brought successful advertising techniques to the business of building a new army for war. In answer to thousands of requests the magazine offered postcard-sized reproductions for 1s 4d per hundred. At the end of September the design was first issued as a poster. It was soon reproduced in huge numbers and in many variations. Before long, Kitchener was staring out from thousands of hoardings, shop windows, buses, trams, railway carriages and vans all over the country. It has become one of the most famous and enduring images of the war, although by the time it appeared as a poster recruitment had already passed its peak.[16]

All over Britain it was the professional and commercial
classes who were the first to respond to the recruitment
campaign, along with many clerks who in the early decades
of the twentieth century formed a growing community of
white collar, lower-middle-class workers in every office and
warehouse.[17] Forty per cent of those eligible joined up – perhaps representing a desire to escape from the monotonous
routines of office life. Most saw war not only as a duty but
also as an adventure, an opportunity for self-discovery and
to attain an intensity of living that was impossible in peacetime. As Rupert Brooke put it,

Now God be thanked who has matched us with His hour,
And caught our youth, and wakened us from sleeping.[18]

About 30 per cent of those eligible who worked in manufacturing – including the railways and transport industries – joined
up, although among this group there were also many unemployed, who were often the first to come forward. But not
everyone responded with equal vigour. In rural areas the
figure was much lower at about 22 per cent.[19] Here there were
no masses of unemployed, and communities were far less
eager to see their young men disappear. Who would take on
their tasks of harvesting and tilling the soil? Animals would
still have to be fed and cared for; dairy cattle would still need
milking twice a day. Women might take over work in offices,
shops and factories but did not at this stage take on heavy,
physical farm labour. Also, as distance from urban conurbations increased, the pull of civic pride became less strong. In
the rural areas of Devon, Somerset and Dorset, for example,
the response rate as a proportion of eligible men was roughly
one-quarter that in the industrial cities of northern England.
Further west in Cornwall, the response rate was half of that
again.[20]

Scotland has traditionally provided some of the bravest soldiers and toughest regiments in the British army. In
Glasgow, three new Pals battalions were formed. The first
consisted almost entirely of drivers, conductors, mechanics
and workers from the corporation's tramways; the second
largely from members of the city's Boys' Brigade; the third
was organised by the Chamber of Commerce from the city's
business houses, from students at the Glasgow Technical
College and from old boys of the Glasgow Academy, the
'Glasgow Commercials'. The three battalions were later
designated the 15th, 16th and 17th Highland Light Infantry.
Between them they would live up to the long Scottish tradition of winning glory for the British army.

In the north of Ireland, there existed before the war a
Protestant army known as the Ulster Volunteer Force (UVF).
This was 90,000 strong, well drilled and armed. It had been
formed to resist Home Rule for Ireland, what was called
'Rome Rule', and by the end of July 1914, civil war appeared
inevitable. But the coming of war in Europe transformed the
situation. Sir Edward Carson, leader of the Ulster Unionists,
felt he had no option but to pledge the province's loyalty
to the union. Carson was reluctant to offer the UVF to
Kitchener's New Army until he was certain the government
would drop plans for Home Rule, but as news arrived of suc-
cessive defeats and disasters, in early September the Ulster
Unionist Council decided to offer 35,000 volunteers to the
War Office. 'We do not seek to purchase terms by selling our
patriotism,' Carson declared at a large meeting in Belfast.
And, in a great gesture of solidarity, he went on, to frantic
cheers, 'England's difficulty is not Ulster's opportunity;
England's difficulty is Ulster's difficulty.' He encouraged the
Volunteers to sign up en masse, saying, 'Go and help to save
your country and to save your Empire . . . Go and win honour
for Ulster and for Ireland.'[21] Five battalions were formed from

the UVF in Belfast; two in County Down; two from Antrim; one each from Tyrone and Derry; one from Donegal and Fermanagh; and one in Armagh, Monaghan and Cavan.[22] They were fully equipped with uniforms and boots at the expense of the UVF and immediately began training under canvas in fields outside Belfast.[23] Together, these battalions formed a single division, the 36th (Ulster) Division, one of the first in Kitchener's New Army.

However, much of the recruitment into the Pals battalions depended upon a local figure with a strong sense of leadership and an ability to inspire. No one fitted this bill more powerfully than Hugh Cecil Lowther, 5th Earl of Lonsdale, one of the country's great eccentrics. Known as 'England's greatest sporting gentleman', Lowther had left Eton after only two years to concentrate on his sporting passions of hunting and horse riding. In 1882, aged only twenty-five, he suddenly inherited the earldom of Lonsdale on the death of his elder brother. Overnight, he became one of the richest men in Britain, owning two castles in Cumberland and Westmorland (today's Cumbria), two houses in London, vast estates in the north-west and the Whitehaven collieries running out under the sea off the west Cumberland coast. Now he had the financial resources to back his hobbies, one of which was boxing. Lonsdale claimed that he had once beaten the American, John L. Sullivan, the heavyweight champion of the world, and on this basis became chairman of the Pelican Club, the aristocrats' sports club. Under Lonsdale's lead, the Marquess of Queensbury laid down a set of rules that became the governing regulations for the sport. Lonsdale later became the first president of the National Sporting Club and he created and provided the 'Lonsdale Belt' as a trophy for boxing champions.

In September 1914 he turned to a new sport, and put up posters across his vast estate calling on men to show their patriotism. Trimmed with his racing colours of red and yellow, the posters screamed 'Are you a Man or Are you a Mouse? Are you a man who will for ever be handed down to posterity as a Gallant Patriot . . . [or] as a rotter and a coward? If You Are a Man Enlist Now'. Miners and shepherds, farmers and estate workers came forward and formed their own Pals battalion, known as 'the Lonsdales'. Two companies were recruited in Carlisle from north Cumberland, a third in Workington from west Cumberland and a fourth in Kendal from Westmorland. The noble earl equipped them with uniforms, appointed their officers and ordered ammunition at his own expense. Before long they were drilling on one of his racecourses outside Carlisle. It took some time for the War Office to catch up, and it was not until December that they were officially recognised as the 11th Battalion The Border Regiment. But they kept their nickname and were ever afterwards widely known as the Lonsdales.[24]

Recruiting the 11th Borders was unusually a combined urban and rural affair. The roll of warrant officers, NCOs and other ranks who joined the battalion shows that in addition to estate workers and labourers from the Lonsdale estate, whom Lonsdale as their landlord no doubt encouraged to join, the volunteers came from a broad range of backgrounds, typical of a region which included large rural and farming communities and several busy industrial and market towns. There were dozens of colliers from Workington, steel workers from Seaton, weavers from Cumberland, farm labourers and those who listed themselves as 'farm servants' from every small village and hamlet in the area. There were clerks from every office and warehouse. It is difficult reading through the roll to see how the shops of the main market towns could have coped with the loss of so many drapers, hatters, grocers, butchers and bakers who responded to the call to arms. Plasterers, blacksmiths, tanners, coopers, wheelwrights,

French polishers, chauffeurs, police constables and school teachers all rushed to join up. In addition there were those who listed their occupations as 'Fish Fryer', 'Skin Sorter', 'Cycle Mechanic' or 'Groom', and two volunteers who put themselves down as 'Hotel Boots and Waiter' – presumably local hotel employees who in addition to waiting at table also cleaned the clients' boots.

Carlisle itself had a famous biscuit factory, Carr's, many of whose workers joined up, and was a town served by seven separate railway companies, each operating with its own engine sheds and engineering works. Several volunteers in the autumn of 1914 were listed as engine drivers, firemen, shunters, signalmen and porters, many proudly listing the companies for which they had worked – including the Midland Railway Company, the London and North Eastern Railway (LNER) and the Caledonian Railway. Those who joined the Lonsdales in the autumn of 1914 formed a perfect cross-section of young, male Edwardian society in a prosperous, mixed region of north-west England.[25]

Pals battalions were formed from Cambridge to Grimsby, and from Accrington to Barnsley. Groups of sportsmen and old boys from the public schools formed four battalions known as the University and Public Schools Brigade, designated the 18th, 19th, 20th and 21st Battalions Royal Fusiliers. By the end of September nearly 750,000 men had volunteered, including 200,000 who had joined the Territorial Force despite Kitchener's encouragement to build his New Army. By the end of the year, 134 Pals battalions had been formed.

The rank-and-file soldiers of the regular army in the nineteenth century did not have a good reputation. Recruits were usually from the unskilled, lowest labouring or working classes, from industrial slums or the impoverished countryside. The vast majority were unemployed who probably joined up to get decent food and lodging, along with regular if basic wages.[26] Men would spend years away, abroad or on the other side of the country, with little chance of family life or of leading a 'genteel' existence. Soldiers were usually perceived as being rough, tough and drunken, and many had difficulty with writing and reading. Even Wellington described the men who had delivered him victory at Waterloo as 'the scum of the earth'. The German ambassador described the British army in 1901 during the Boer War as 'the dregs of the population'.[27] This had certainly begun to change during the Edwardian era and the Territorial Force was far more middle class in its make-up than the regular army. But it was the men who flooded into the Pals battalions who utterly transformed the army's image. The proportion that came from the lower middle classes was far higher than in the regular army; and the middle classes were proportionately far more numerous in the New Army than in the nation as a whole.

Of course, the key feature of the Pals battalions was the simple but fundamental fact that they were made up of *volunteers*. Whether urban office clerk, rural farm worker, miner or railway employee, everyone had chosen to join Kitchener's army. They were keen to learn, willing to obey and eager to serve. They wanted to become soldiers, get out to France and do their bit. They did not boast about what they had done, they just got on with it in an understated, British sort of way. They all had hopes and aspirations for the future: for jobs, for promotions, for friendships and love affairs – some might have been thinking of marriage or of starting a family – but all this was willingly put on hold while they went off to serve their country. Lloyd George summed up the popular view of the new armies when he wrote that they included 'the pick of the youth of the country in physique, brain and character. In every sphere of life all that was best among the young men of the land joined the Army.'[28]

Rudyard Kipling, one of the greatest writers in Edwardian Britain, toured the nation to observe these men drilling in barrack squares and training in country estates and was deeply moved by what he saw. With his own literary finesse he summed the men up: 'Pride of city, calling, class and creed imposes standards and obligations which hold men above themselves at a pinch, and steady them through long strain. One meets it in the New Army at every turn ... The more one sees of the camps the more one is filled with facts and figures of joyous significance, which will become clearer as the days lengthen; and the less one hears of the endurance, decency, self-sacrifice, and utter devotion which have made, and are hourly making, this wonderful new world. The camps take this for granted – else why should any man be there at all? He might have gone on with his business, or watched "soccer". But having chosen to do his bit, he does it, and talks as much about his motives as he would of his religion or of his love affairs.' Kipling foresaw a great future for these volunteers, concluding, 'They are all now in the Year One, and the meanest of them may be an ancestor of whom regimental posterity will say "There were giants in those days!"'[29]

All this adds up to an extraordinary phenomenon that swept much of Britain in the late summer and early autumn of 1914. Recruitment began to decline in late 1914 and by February 1915 had dropped to around 90,000 per month. There were several reasons for this. Stories of chaos in the recruiting offices and bottlenecks in the training camps did not help. But the principal reason was that as requirements for supplies and ordnance from the military created an industrial boom, so the extra demand for labour outmatched the supply. As a consequence wage rates went up. Once the initial patriotic appeal had worn off, many skilled workers who found that for the first time in their life they could earn £2 10s a week in a munitions factory were reluctant to accept barely half of that (with allowances) by taking the King's Shilling. But even so, by the end of 1915 some two million men had volunteered to fight for Kitchener, King, Country and Empire. No other country experienced a frenzy of volunteering on this scale. It has been called the story 'of a spontaneous and genuinely popular mass movement which has no counterpart in the modern English-speaking world'.[30]

In addition, tens of thousands of young women also volunteered and in a demonstration in July 1915, 30,000 women marched past Parliament carrying banners demanding the right to serve. Initially, most women volunteered as nurses, but increasingly they went into a host of other duties ranging from farm work (the Women's Land Army was formed in 1915) to clerical roles in the Women's Army Auxiliary Corps (formed in December 1916) and to the Women's Royal Naval Service (formed in 1917). Some women, like Vera Brittain, gave up the university courses that they had struggled to start out on, to contribute to the war effort just as their brothers had done. Brittain became a Voluntary Aid Detachment nurse, known as a VAD, and summed up her motivation for volunteering very clearly when she wrote, 'Not being a man and able to go to the front, I wanted to do the next best thing.'[31]

It is a great tribute to this generation that so many millions of young men and women willingly came forward. It was the first and last time that it would happen on such a scale. Most of the innocent volunteers of 1914 were ignorant of the horrors they would face. The shock, disillusionment and trauma of modern industrial war, the dreadful losses that scarred a generation, the memory of the trenches, would all have a lasting effect. Britain in 1939 was probably no less patriotic than in 1914. But there would be no rush to join up en masse as there had been in the first weeks and months of the Great War.

But for those eager volunteers who responded to Kitchener's call in September 1914, the progress through Basic Training into army life would be neither smooth nor rapid. On arrival at many military establishments scattered across the country, most recruits found not the welcome they expected but scenes of utter chaos. It would take many months yet to build up even the foundations of a Citizen Army.

2

Training a Citizen Army

Ralph Mottram, like so many Britons, was deeply shocked by German 'treachery' in attacking 'gallant little Belgium'. He had a good job with the promise of an excellent career ahead of him at Barclays Bank and ageing parents whom he felt he should care for. But in a flush of patriotic fervour he decided to follow Kitchener's call and enlist for three years, or for the 'duration of the war', whichever came sooner. Barclays agreed to hold his job pending his return. Mottram had to struggle to join up, waiting for several days because of the crowds at the recruitment office in London. Having finally enlisted, like most recruits he had to attest and take the oath of allegiance and was then given one silver shilling 'to serve the king'. Having been given a date to report to his regimental depot, he began drilling at an assembly ground in Lowestoft, without uniforms or weapons.[1]

The British army was totally unprepared for the avalanche of new recruits that began to arrive at camps across the country in the autumn of 1914. Barracks intended to house 300 men soon had to accommodate five times that number. Thousands were forced to sleep out in the open. Beds and sometimes even blankets were not available. Basic equipment and clothing was non-existent. Sometimes there was no food or rations for men who were forced to find a local pub or café to eat in. Even when food was provided there might be no knives, plates or mugs. In Preston, Fulwood Barracks was the depot for several Lancashire regiments. It had accommodation for about one thousand men but twice that number arrived almost every day. Locals offered recruits bed and breakfast in their own homes to help cope with the overflow, while the loft of the local Tramway power station was turned into a dormitory where hundreds slept every night.

Charles Jones worked in a London solicitor's office, joined up in early September and was sent to the Chichester depot of the Royal Sussex Regiment. He described in a letter to his wife conditions in the barracks, designed for 500 men but now packed with 1,200 raw recruits 'consisting mainly of London roughs and country yokels of the worst description'. After an exhausting first day he was told to sleep in the depot's library, but to his horror the place was 'packed like sardines with one of the noisiest and obscene collections of human beings it has ever been my misfortune to meet, and the smell of them packed into a small building after a hot day was truly sickening.' Men from the middle and lower middle classes were shocked both at the lack of provisions and at the foul language they heard. Jones said the recruits introduced 'Damns and Bloodys etc etc' into every sentence.[2] Men from smart middle-class homes complained at the lack of basic sanitary arrangements. Buckets pressed into use as toilets were soon overflowing. Sometimes several hundred men had to wash in the same basin. Of the first recruits to join up in August and September 1914, the transition from civilian to army life was chaotic, subject to much petty bureaucracy and extremely arduous. It would strain the patriotism of even the most ardent recruit.

Many recruits thought they would be given a rifle and would be over in France fighting the Germans in no time.

In fact what they faced was endless drilling, marching and what a later generation would call 'square bashing'. Not only were there no uniforms but although their instructors told them that an infantryman's rifle was his best friend, there were precious few such weapons to be had. Men trained with wooden sticks. Occasionally, some obsolete Lee-Metford rifles would arrive. But even then there were never enough and it was necessary to pass them around, one company or platoon training with them one day, and another the next. And when there were rifles, there was no ammunition. It was back to drilling, marching with straight backs and square shoulders up and down for hours on end, forming fours, and learning to obey commands without thinking from loud, barking NCOs.

In contrast, for many volunteers from working-class slums, the army would eventually offer a warm overcoat, decent boots, respectable clothing and three hot meals a day. Used as they were to hard physical graft in the mines or dull monotonous jobs for long hours in a factory or workshop, the army seemed to such men to be a marked improvement. Even some middle-class men found that once settled into army routine, they had less to worry about than in civilian life. C.E. Montague, writing after the war, observed that for the average soldier, 'All was fixed from above, down to the time of his going to bed and the way he must lace up his shoes.'[3]

However, such was the spirit of these first eager volunteers that there was little protest at the conditions they had to bear. Mostly, they accepted the difficulties as part of the process of doing their bit for King and Empire. Everywhere men were encouraged by the fantastic public support they received. As they marched through towns, people would come out to cheer them, often giving the recruits tobacco or chocolate as they passed by. For many recruits their biggest concern was that the 'show' would all be over by the time they got to

France. Harold Macmillan, who after Eton and two years at Oxford had joined the Artists' Rifles and began drilling at the Inns of Court in central London, wrote, 'Our major anxiety was by hook or by crook not to miss it.'[4]

Some of those who had joined the Pals battalions had a slightly easier time of it. If they were training locally, many of them were allowed to sleep at home for the first few weeks or even months. In Salford, for instance, the local Tramway Committee laid on free trams for men living outside town to get in to barracks for morning parade at 8 a.m. The Baths Committee provided free baths and the Parks Committee offered open spaces for drilling and training. Such arrangements were in line with the idea that these were local battalions supported by local charity and municipal funds. In Sheffield, the City Pals were offered free passes to travel from home to their training ground. With so many men scattered across the city and its suburbs, communication was always going to be difficult, so daily orders were printed in the local papers. The battalion started its training at Bramall Lane football ground. Photographs show the volunteers training in their civilian clothes, often in shirtsleeves during what proved to be a hot summer. Soon the men moved on from Bramall Lane, as the turf had to be prepared for the new season. Drilling continued in local parks. An ex-Guardsman remarked that the bright, enthusiastic recruits had learned more in three weeks than most recruits would pick up in three months. This comment was reported in the local paper and many thought that meant the battalion would soon be in France. Great was the disappointment when it was realised this was not the case.[5]

The Lonsdales, recruited in the north-west, had started their training at the Blackhall racecourse outside Carlisle, given over for this purpose by the Earl of Lonsdale himself. The local men went home at night, but with volunteers coming in from all over the hills and dales of Cumberland and Westmorland, the grandstand was converted for use as a temporary dormitory. In addition, huts were urgently needed as barracks. Carpenters were brought in, wood supplied and construction began, again much of it funded by the noble earl. He also provided basic outfits for the men to train in, some in his estate colours, some in grey, the colour of the old Cumberland Volunteers. The battalion history noted: 'From early morning to dusk physical training, preliminary manual drill and movements were practised. The training was handicapped, however, by the lack of rifles, even of those for drill purposes only.' As the autumn weather got cooler and the War Office had still not provided greatcoats or blankets, Lonsdale personally bought one thousand of each in London for the men to use. He also supplied an ambulance wagon, a water cart, two pairs of black horses and thirty mules for transport. The training of the battalion brought together the feudal concept of the local lord raising his own troop of soldiers with the new idea of locally raised and funded Pals battalions.[6]

What sort of army did the hundreds of thousands of volunteers in the summer and autumn of 1914 find themselves joining? In the first decade of the twentieth century the army was an organisation going through a period of dramatic and sometimes difficult change. The Victorian army had been tiny, a volunteer army geared to fighting colonial wars, mostly against tribal forces with little modern technology. It was an army that put great emphasis upon tradition and the regular repetition of the same practices. The Boer War had revealed dreadful failings as the army of the world's most powerful imperial nation struggled for three years to defeat a group of Boer irregulars. Changes were clearly necessary.

Reform came in the Edwardian era, when the radical Secretary of War, Richard Burton Haldane, gave the army a thorough shaking up. Haldane was a passionate believer in the primacy of science. He tried to apply scientific principles to the organisation of the army and to the defining of its strategic objectives. From this, he believed, all else would follow. At the heart of the reforms he implemented was the decision to send a mobile expeditionary force to continental Europe to support Britain's ally, France, in the event of that country's invasion by a hostile Germany. The ancient local militias and county yeomanry forces were disbanded and regrouped into the Territorial Force. As we have seen, the Territorials' principal purpose was to provide home defence when the regular army travelled to fight on the continent.

Haldane also appointed a new Imperial General Staff to co-ordinate the strategic direction not only of the British army but also of the armies of the Dominions, to ensure that the Empire would act as a coherent, unified entity. The professional head of the army would be the Chief of the Imperial General Staff (CIGS), effectively the Empire's senior army commander. Haldane encouraged the introduction of a more technical, professional approach. This coincided with the development of various new items of military technology, for instance the short Lee Enfield rifle, heavier quick-firing artillery, the Vickers-Maxim machine gun and the aeroplane.[7] Each of these new technologies unleashed a debate within the senior echelons of the army as to its value and effectiveness. This not only created tensions but also tended to produce something of a division between officers who embraced change and the new technologies on offer, and those who were happy with the traditional methods of fighting a war. Many senior figures were deeply suspicious of change and of anyone who tried to apply new ideas or new learning to the traditional craft of soldiering. Field Marshal Lord Wolseley had summed up this Victorian point of view when he wrote in 1897, 'I hope the officers of Her Majesty's

Army may never degenerate into bookworms. There is happily at present no tendency in that direction, for I am glad to say that this generation is as fond of danger, adventure and all manly out-of-door sports as its forefathers were.'[8]

The army, like most other national institutions in Edwardian Britain, reflected the society out of which it came. The officer class was drawn from the gentry and upper landed classes and had been almost entirely educated at the public schools. This educational system put much more emphasis on learning Latin and Greek than it did on understanding physics or chemistry. As a consequence most senior figures in Edwardian Britain knew a lot about classical history and literature but were almost entirely ignorant of scientific method or of new developments in physics, chemistry or engineering. At a conference in May 1916, several leading figures in British science lamented the bias in the educational system. Pointing out that the headmasters of thirty-four of the top thirty-five public schools were classicists and that not a single college at Oxford University had at its head anyone with scientific training, they described the hostility towards science in the British public schools as 'truly deplorable'.[9]

Senior figures in the army shared the outlook and assumptions of other leading figures in the Edwardian establishment, including most politicians, City bankers and senior civil servants. So while the Royal Military College at Sandhurst, where most senior officers had begun their army careers, taught military history and specific skills such as ballistics, it did not have a single course on science.[10] In evidence to an enquiry into the education and training of officers in 1902, senior figures within the army lined up to stress the value of sports like hunting and polo to the building of character. Lieutenant-Colonel Murray, Assistant Commandant at Woolwich, went on record to say, 'We would rather have a classically educated boy than one who has given up his mind very much to Electricity and Physics and those kind of subjects. We want them to be leaders in the field first ... Power of command and habits of leadership are not learned in the laboratory ... Our great point is character; we care more about that than subjects.'[11]

The public schools were particularly strong on trying to develop 'character'. They emphasised values like group loyalty, obedience to the existing hierarchy, hostility to intellectual debate and a preference for healthy, outdoor team sports. Gentlemanly virtues did not usually include a vigorous enthusiasm for new ideas and technologies. Socially, meanwhile, the army was deeply conservative, and for officers army life revolved around a pleasant set of fixed rituals based on loyalty to a battalion or regiment. Officers had servants to look after them, just as they would in civilian life. In the higher echelons of the army most senior officers felt they were professional soldiers who knew what they were doing, had been doing it for some time and saw no good reason to change. Moreover, there was an embedded hostility to the idea of imposing a prescriptive doctrine across army activities. Emphasis was put on the individual taking his own decisions on a pragmatic basis, not relying on a pre-existing theory. In many ways this made a virtue out of a belief in 'muddling through'.

Within this framework of thinking, those who were trying to encourage a more technical frame of mind were always going to struggle. But society was being transformed by new technology and the applications of new scientific ideas. The changes were evident for every Edwardian to see. Electricity lit up the streets of every town and city and enabled the intro- duction of a range of new domestic and commercial products, from the telephone to the vacuum cleaner. Chemical industries transformed many industrial processes, enabling the mass production of such items as paint, cement and agricultural fertilisers along with the development of new cleaning compounds, drugs and pharmaceuticals, as well as explosives. Inventions like the internal combustion engine, radio, cinema and powered flight all provided challenging alternatives to traditional military technology. The army simply could not ignore these changes and senior figures were aware that other nations' armies were changing the way they made war. The Japanese army and navy had achieved victory over the Imperial Russian forces in their war of 1904–5 in part by the effective use of new technologies like the machine gun and the torpedo. Some senior officers were certainly keen to embrace new military technologies. But old values died slowly.

A great exponent of a new form of technocracy was H.G. Wells, one of the most popular authors of the day. Wells made his reputation with such hugely successful works of science fiction as *The Time Machine* (1895), *The Invisible Man* (1897) and *The War of the Worlds* (1898). But in 1902, a year after the death of Queen Victoria had symbolised the end of one era and the start of another, Wells published what was, for him, an unusual book. *Anticipations* was an extended essay in which Wells envisaged a world run by technocrats and engineers, a world in which some nations had adapted to new technologies and others had not. He was one of the great critics of the public school ethos, writing: 'The nation that produces in the near future the largest proportional development of educated and intelligent engineers and agriculturists, of doctors, schoolmasters, professional soldiers, and intellectually active people of all sorts ... will certainly be the ascendant or dominant nation before the year 2000.'[12] In a core section of the book, Wells imagined with extraordinary prescience how the wars of the future would be fought. He anticipated the end of generals riding about on horses and carrying a sword, for they would be replaced by engineers, as all wars would involve the use of new technology. He foresaw the coming of 'total war', in which the old divisions between combatant and non-combatant would disappear. He anticipated trench warfare in vivid detail. He predicted the development of the tank as an attempt to overcome the stalemate of the trenches, calling these new machines 'land ironclads'.[13] He even anticipated aerial warfare – and he was writing a year before the Wright Brothers' first successful powered flight. He went so far as to anticipate the development of aerial bombing, and predicted with haunting accuracy that the next war would bring an appalling number of casualties: 'thousands and thousands of poor boys will be smashed in all sorts of dreadful ways and given over to every form of avoidable hardship and painful disease.'[14]

Wells did not get everything right. He thought the submarine had no future and he imagined that aircraft would have giant steel battering rams at their front. But he was absolutely clear in his prediction of a future society in which science would rule supreme, and that unless Britain adapted others would take over. He concluded, 'the power of the scientifically educated, disciplined specialist ... [will be] provably right. It may be delayed, but it cannot be defeated; in the end it must arrive – if not today and among our people, then tomorrow and among another people, who will triumph in our overthrow.'[15]

It is unlikely that *Anticipations* was read much by senior figures in the army, but many younger officers were perhaps concerned by his predictions. Winston Churchill, then a young MP and not yet in office, read the book avidly and responded by sending Wells an eight-page critique in which he disputed some of its conclusions.[16] The book certainly had an impact, contributing to the extensive debate in Edwardian England about the role of science and technology in a changing world. Some new independent schools were founded with a mission to teach scientific subjects. The whole debate started up again when in July 1909 a Frenchman, Louis Blériot, and not an Englishman, made the first flight across the English Channel. A xenophobic uproar followed in the press, while Wells argued in the *Daily Mail* that this was not only a failure to take up a new technology, but was also a failure in education that showed other nations were moving ahead.[17]

Yet although the British army was not at the forefront of the scientific debate that gripped the age, there was much discussion of future technologies and new tactics. Traditionally, the army had taught that the 'charge', often by cavalry, was the tactic that led to final victory on the battlefield. But how could this be translated to an era of massed firepower when to cross open ground would be suicidal? There was fierce debate about such questions at the Staff College, the Camberley institution where ambitious officers went to study, train and prepare for high command. For instance, the technology of the machine gun was widely accepted, but how was the weapon to be best used? Was it a device for use by the artillery or the infantry? The artillery rejected its use. But the infantry found the early Maxim machine gun to be large, cumbersome and slow to mount on its heavy tripod. In the Boer War it took a team of ten men and almost as many horses to transport, set up and operate a heavy machine gun. In the decade before the First World War it was the man at the top, the CIGS, General Sir William Nicholson, who was pressing for the wider employment of heavy machine guns, while it was still unclear exactly how they would be used in combat and whether they were primarily a defensive or an offensive weapon. There was also debate about the use of automatic rifles and what would later be called light machine guns. The new Lewis gun, much lighter and easier to fire than a heavy machine gun, was in use in the navy and in military aircraft, but the infantry had not yet found a role for it.

While such matters were the subject of active debate, however, it was still possible for an influential figure like Brigadier Sir Lancelot Kiggell (who would be Haig's chief of staff later in the war) to pronounce that despite the firepower that could be brought to bear on the modern battlefield it was the individual soldier who would still determine the outcome of battle. 'Victory is won actually by the bayonet, or by the fear of it,' he said at a military conference in 1910.[18] Clearly, change was very slow to come.

The use of aircraft was also a topic that generated much discussion. At first Nicholson proved to be hostile to the new technology and was opposed to the use of aircraft until the highly fragile contraptions of the pioneer aviators had become more reliable and were powered by better engines. In April 1909, the reforming Haldane established an Advisory Committee for Aeronautics. He appointed some of the finest physicists and scientists in the land to advise the army on topics including 'the mathematical investigation of stability', 'the effect of rudder action' and the 'materials for aeroplane construction'. In this way, Haldane hoped to bring science to bear on the activities of the small group of enthusiastic but often amateurish pioneers.

Still some senior army figures were sceptical. After watching a flying demonstration one senior commander was overheard saying, 'These playthings will never be of use in war.'[19] However, after the French had successfully used aircraft for reconnaissance in their annual manoeuvres in 1910, Nicholson changed his mind. Realising that the British army would be left behind unless it began serious experiments with different aircraft types, he started the process that led two years later to the establishment of a new unit within the army, the Royal Flying Corps. The RFC was set up to train pilots and observers, to develop the appropriate technology and to create up to eight squadrons of trained fliers for active service. By the advent of war, the RFC would put a squadron of aircraft into the field to support each infantry corps of two divisions.[20]

Many of the era's contradictions are represented in the thinking of General Sir Douglas Haig. A Lowland Scot, Haig had attended the Staff College in 1896–7, when he was in his mid-thirties. Studying military history, largely from the era of Napoleon and Wellington, Haig had come to some conventional conclusions about strategy: that the primary purpose of the artillery was to support the infantry; that an enemy had to be confronted head-on and when worn out was to be defeated by the deployment of one's own reserves; and that the cavalry were to exploit the success of the infantry and make a victory decisive. He was taught that it was the morale and discipline of the individual soldier and his commander that brought victory. These values and assumptions were those of the nineteenth-century army.

However, after many years of service in India and the Empire, and after making a name for himself in the Sudan War of 1898 and in the Boer War a few years later, Haig began to update his ideas. Thanks to his excellent social connections which, through his wife, went right up to the royal family, he became Director of Training. In 1907 Haldane selected him as Director of Staff Duties, and he was placed in charge of drawing up a new set of Field Service Regulations summarising the changes in tactics, strategies and command of the army. The new Regulations were an attempt to bring together many of the technology-led changes that were taking place. As his recent biographer has pointed out, Haldane the science-led army reformer would not have put his faith in Haig to carry out such a central task if he were simply 'a well-connected duffer'.[21]

While remaining politically and socially conservative, Haig had become one of the reforming group within the army. In 1911 he supposedly dismissed aviation, saying 'Flying can never be of any use to the army,' but as aircraft improved in capability he very soon came around and by 1914 was an enthusiast for their use. At times he was almost over-confident in the use of prototype and unproven technology. This would manifest itself later on the Western Front. As an individual, Haig in many ways represented the contradictions within the British army in 1914. New ideas and support for new technologies were bubbling away within an all-embracing philosophy that emphasised the validity of tradition and a dislike of doctrine.

The medical service, the Royal army Medical Corps (RAMC), was part of the wing within the army that actively embraced modernity, in an effort to bring it up to date with the immense advances of early twentieth-century medicine. The RAMC had been formed in 1898 largely due to pressure put on the War Office by the British Medical Association to renew its medical services and bring them more into line with the services available to civilians. Before then, army medical staff had suffered from low status within the army; as non-combatants, military doctors were often seen as unwelcome outsiders and sometimes were even excluded from army messes. Many within the medical profession also looked down on military medicine, and in Victorian times it was extremely rare for the brightest young medical students to go into the army. The joke about army doctors was that they were ruled by the principle of NBR – 'No Bloody Research'. The new military medical corps would change all that, giving doctors and surgeons military status right up to a newly invented rank of Surgeon-General.

Almost immediately after its creation the RAMC faced the challenge of the Boer War. The performance of the brand new medical corps was variable, and the lack of trained military doctors meant that the army was forced to call upon hundreds of civilians with no military experience to go out to South Africa to offer their services. Typhoid fever was rampant within the armed forces in South Africa and the lack of sanitary provisions caused a public outcry. But overall the new medical service provided a marked improvement, roughly halving from the previous major conflict the proportion of casualties who died of their wounds.[22]

After the Boer War, a royal commission was set up to recommend reforms in the provision of medical services for the army and this ushered in a decade of change. Haldane's army reforms and his belief in scientific progress also profoundly affected the RAMC. The old Army Medical School at Netley on the south coast near Southampton (created under pressure from Florence Nightingale after the debacle of the Crimean War) was closed. A new, modern Royal Army Medical College opened in Millbank in 1907, just behind what was then the brand new Tate Gallery. In a further attempt to bring military medicine up to speed with the rapid developments taking place in the civilian field, this was given the status of a postgraduate medical college affiliated to the Faculty of Medicine at London University.

The RAMC's Director General was the energetic and ambitious Sir Alfred Keogh. From a leading Anglo-Irish family, Keogh was tall, with a large forehead, and had a genuinely commanding presence. A brilliant young physician, he had unusually chosen to specialise in military medicine. Having impressed the high command with his ability to get things done during the Boer War, a rapid series of promotions brought him to the top job in the RAMC in 1905 and he saw eye-to-eye with Haldane on the need for reform.

Keogh had suffered from mild typhoid fever during the Boer War, and so with reforming zeal he set about improving the deficiencies in military sanitation. He opened a School of Hygiene at Aldershot, while a new manual on *Military Hygiene and Sanitation for Soldiers* in 1908 proclaimed that 'disease prevention is synonymous with military efficiency'.[23] Meanwhile, Sir William Leishman, Professor of Pathology at the new Military College, developed a form of inoculation against typhoid that would prevent this ancient scourge of armies in the field from becoming endemic in the next war.[24]

Keogh also tried to improve the standards in base hospitals and to equip them with modern operating theatres and the latest medical technology. He introduced new field ambulance units to speed up the provision of advanced medical care between the front-line regimental aid post and the general hospitals in the rear. Furthermore, he encouraged civilian consultants to join the Territorial Force, bringing their expertise within the remit of military medicine in an attempt to ensure that if civilian reinforcements were needed in a future war, then there would be a pool of those with some military experience. The British Medical Association gave Keogh full support in this initiative and called for 1,200 medical officers (MOs) and 12,000 NCOs and men to join the medical reserve. In 1910, Keogh left the RAMC to become Rector of Imperial College, London, but the reforms he had unleashed continued to transform military medicine. Keogh had shown what a committed reformer with energy and vision could achieve, even when operating within the conventional structure of the traditionally minded War Office.

There was one area, however, in which no developments took place within the new RAMC. Although well established in continental Europe, psychology was still a relatively young science in Britain. In the early days of the RAMC army doctors had to take courses on anatomy, physiology, general health care and the use of antiseptic dressings, as well as more specialised sessions on tropical diseases, malaria, dysentery and cholera. In addition there was a course of six lectures on 'lunacy', what today would be called psychiatry. But in the Boer War there were few cases of nervous trauma. The only reported cases were of officers who, under the stress of command, suffered from anxiety or 'panic attacks', the cure for which was usually a period of rest and a quiet talk with the padre.[25] As the RAMC addressed and updated many of its medical practices it did nothing to review its understanding of or concern for mental illness, no doubt reflecting a general view in Edwardian Britain that such illnesses were a sign of weakness or character deficiency. Mental patients in early twentieth-century Britain were consigned to long periods cut off from the rest of society and shut away in lunatic asylums. Like the rest of British society, the RAMC preferred to, as it were, sweep the problem of mental illness under the carpet. Although a medical congress in Germany in 1907 had included a session on *Kriegsneurosen* (war neuroses), based on the study of the nervous breakdown of Russian officers in the war with Japan, there was no equivalent interest in Britain. Partly this was because with a small, volunteer army it was thought to be unnecessary; only 'the right sort of chap' would join up and he would never be in need of psychiatric help.[26] As a consequence, observers noted in the early months of the Great War, there was not a single specialist in mental or nervous diseases within the ranks of the RAMC.[27] It was simply not regarded as a subject worthy of pursuit; there was no need in military medicine for trained psychiatrists. It was with this attitude that the military medical services approached the impending war.

The army that, in 1914, faced its first general European war in a hundred years was therefore an institution torn between the rituals of tradition and the challenges posed by new technologies and reforming ideas. It was small, unlike the vast armies of the continental powers. While the British army did not exceed 200,000 men, the German army could call on over five million; the French and Imperial Russian armies could mobilise four million each. Britain's army now had to face the unique challenge of growing in size twelve-fold while fighting a war that no one seemed to have seriously anticipated. The strains would soon begin to tell.

There had been no planning for how the army's procurement system might prepare for the scale of recruitment that took place in the autumn of 1914, with three-quarters of a million men volunteering by the end of September. The textile companies that manufactured army uniforms produced only on a small scale. Now that mass production was needed, the War Office took some time to find ways to scale up manufacturing output. One problem was that many of the dyes needed, particularly khaki, were produced in Germany before the war. That nation had by far the most advanced chemical industry in Europe. Since it would take time to produce the hundreds of thousands of new khaki uniforms needed, battalions received temporary uniforms made out of other materials. Having waited until November for their first uniforms to arrive, the Sheffield Pals, for instance, were horrified to find that they were not the khaki that they could wear with pride, but blue-grey. The men felt they looked like an army of postmen. It was not until mid-1915 that they were fully kitted out in khaki.[28] Nor was there enough webbing kit available. New webbing was manufactured by Hepburn, Cole and Ross of Bermondsey and was known as 1914 Pattern. Instead of five pouches on each side of the waist belt, there was only one slightly larger pouch. It could not carry as many rounds of ammunition as the standard pre-war issue, but it was easier to mass produce and would do for now.

In line with the size of the army, the armaments and munitions industries in Britain were also only small in scale. In 1914, 80 per cent of army orders for guns and shells came from a small number of government-run ordnance factories. Most rifle production was carried out at the Royal Small Arms Factory in Enfield, north London. It was here at the end of the nineteenth century that the Lee Enfield rifle (named after the designer of the rifle's bolt system, James Lee, and the site of the factory) was first produced. This bolt-action, magazine-fed weapon soon became the standard issue rifle of the British army and would remain so throughout the two world wars. The government factory at Enfield doubled its weekly production to 3,000 rifles by November 1914, but at that rate it would still take six years to equip all the new volunteers.

Production of shells was centred on the Royal Arsenal in Woolwich. Here too, production was only small in scale to meet the relatively low pre-war demand. Shell production expanded by 90 per cent but the British army, like those of all the protagonists, soon found itself desperately short of shells. The production of rifles, guns, shells and other components was eventually contracted out to several other companies. Big arms companies in Britain, like Vickers and Armstrong, were keener on large-scale shipbuilding for the navy. There was more profit in building one dreadnought battleship than in manufacturing hundreds of separate artillery pieces and rifles. All this would change in May 1915 when the shells crisis brought about the creation of the Ministry of Munitions. But that was in the future, and the problem in the first months of war in creating a mass army was far more the supply of materiel and munitions than finding manpower.[29]

If there were problems in feeding, equipping and arming Kitchener's New Army, finding sufficient officers to lead it presented another immense challenge. It was estimated that 30,000 new officers were needed. Each battalion that went to France in August 1914 was told to leave a few officers and NCOs behind. While their fellow officers went into battle with the Germans, those left in Britain chafed at having to run depots and manage the hordes of new recruits. But they played a vital role in organising the New Army and were sometimes the only regular soldiers available to begin training the volunteers.

In addition, officers who had retired in the years before the war were recalled into active service. They were known as 'dug-outs', having been dug out of retirement. Some did an excellent job. Many, however, were too old or too unfit to take command of units that were completely different in nature from those they had led many years before. It was reported that every time one large and elderly 'dug-out' went on a route march, he became so exhausted that he would hail a passing motor car with a shout of 'On His Majesty's service' and demand to be driven back to camp.[30] In addition to the 'dug-outs', several officers who had served in armies around the empire were called upon to lead the new Pals battalions. Kitchener ordered 500 officers who were home on leave from service in India not to return, and made a direct appeal to the Commander-in-Chief in India: 'We want officers badly. Let me know privately if you can spare any.'[31]

The lack of trained and experienced officers affected every level of the army. As the new divisions of Kitchener's army were formed, so brigadiers received promotion to the rank of major-general. Many rose successfully to their new responsibilities, like Brigadier Ivor Maxse, Commander of the 1st (Guards) Brigade, who was recalled from France to lead the newly created 18th Division. He went on to bring new ideas to the thinking of the high command on the Western Front for the rest of the war. Other promotions were not so successful; men experienced in commanding brigades of about 4,000 were not necessarily up to the challenge of commanding a division of around 20,000. Several would be removed later.

However, the huge number of volunteers that came forward from the industrial heartlands of the country revealed another facet of the nation's economy. Although hundreds of thousands of workers and clerks willingly volunteered, there was a marked lack of the middling sort who would have made up a managerial class. So, when it came to finding junior officers, an appeal went out to Officer Training Corps around the country. All universities had OTCs, although they were of doubtful military value. Recruits spent a great deal of time on shooting, horse riding and drill, very little on tactical training. Nevertheless, thousands of men with some limited experience gave up their university education to join the army. Most public schools and some grammar schools also had OTCs, and many of the older boys from the major public schools came forward to join up. In the first eight months of the war, 506 junior officers volunteered from Marlborough, 411 from Charterhouse, 403 from Wellington and 350 from Eton.[32] This recruitment process was clearly elitist. Any boy from a top public school was automatically offered a commission. Pupils from less well known schools were not. R.C. Sherriff, just 18 years old, later recalled his attempt to obtain a commission in August 1914. '"School?" inquired the adjutant. I told him and his face fell. He took up a printed list from his desk and searched through it. "I'm sorry," he said, "but I'm afraid it isn't a public school."' Mystified, Sherriff explained that he had been to a top grammar school founded by Queen Elizabeth in 1567. 'I'm sorry,' the adjutant responded. 'But our instructions are that all applicants for commissions must be selected from the recognised public schools, and yours is not among them.'[33]

It was two years before Sherriff got his commission in the 9th East Surreys; he would serve with distinction at Vimy Ridge and at Ypres, where he won an MC. However, by March 1915 at least 20,000 volunteers had come forward from the universities' and schools' OTCs.[34] The army could be sure that the special education these public school boys had received would give them a sense of superiority that would be invaluable in commanding men and equip them well for leadership. And for the first years of the war, at least, by selecting its subalterns from this limited and privileged pool the army could preserve its tradition that an officer would also be a gentleman.

However, at first, the problems were immense. The 7th Royal Scots started its training with only one officer in command of 900 men. The 15th (Scottish) Division had only five regular officers per brigade. The 36th (Ulster) Division, having been drawn from the working-class districts around Belfast and the Ulster countryside, was not able to find public school OTC boys from its recruitment area, so officers were drafted in from across Britain. Commanding officers of the new battalions and divisions were often able to select the names of men they wished to commission. But the commanding officer of the 16th (Irish) Division, formed by recruiting many Irish nationalists who had been part of the National Volunteers before the war, rejected every officer nomination from anyone who had been in the nationalist militia. He preferred Englishmen with more conventional and privileged backgrounds. John Kipling, the son of the author, had tried many times to join up but had been turned down by the medical boards because of his very poor eyesight. When his father helped him finally to wangle a commission it was to the 2nd Battalion The Irish Guards that he was assigned, although he had no connections with Ireland or the Irish.

Battalion commanders devoted much time and energy to trying to find the right officers with military experience. Again, the story of the Lonsdales battalion, the 11th Borders, is revealing. The officer appointed by Earl Lonsdale to command the battalion was highly qualified. Lieutenant-Colonel Percy Wilfred Machell was a 'dug-out', having come out of retirement, aged fifty-two, to take command. Much of his service had been with the Egyptian army; he had fought in several campaigns through the 1890s and had raised and commanded a Sudanese battalion. In 1898 he was appointed military adviser to the Ministry of the Interior in Egypt, a senior position in what was effectively a British colony. He received many Egyptian decorations and had excellent connections through his wife, Lady Valda, the daughter of one of Queen Victoria's nephews, Admiral Prince Victor of Hohenlohe-Langenburg. Machell was not only an experienced military commander but also a fine administrator and a whirlwind of energy as he sought to bring his newly raised battalion into fighting order. When he took command in October 1914, there were no officers from the regular army in the battalion and for two months he had no adjutant to carry out day-to-day administrative duties. None of the officers appointed had any regular military experience.

The battalion history notes that 'Every detail had to be taught by him [Lt-Col. Machell], for the officers, with very few exceptions, knew no more than the men, and had to be taught themselves before they could teach ... He organised the feeding of the men ... he arranged for the hutting, the clothing, the water supply, the lighting and conservancy of the Camp ... These things alone would have occupied the activities of six ordinary men, but in addition to all this the C.O. was constantly on parade, training and smartening up both officers and men, drawing up the programmes of work and seeing that they were carried out.' Machell himself added, 'I have to act drill-sergeant and buck and bark vociferously to get up a high standard ... Men take the talking very well. It is much better than punishing ... Far better to make a man than break him.'[35]

In addition, Machell clearly spent a great deal of time trying to appoint the right men as officers. When he heard that the son of one of his friends, a Mr Whitehead, was returning from Burma and had come up from the ranks to become an officer he tried to persuade him to join the battalion. He wrote to the boy's father on 2 November, 'I am not anxious about the numbers [of volunteers], but I have scarcely any officers, and do not see where they are to come from. The men are of excellent class and are all very keen, besides being of fine physique.' Machell was clearly revelling in his new task and concluded the letter by adding, 'I hope all is well with you – I was never better myself, and I have not found my years to put me at any disadvantage so far.'

Later that same month he wrote to young Whitehead himself to encourage him to join the battalion. 'Your father is a great friend of mine ... It is a difficult job to get any officers and I have no adjutant. It's lucky I like work and know how to run my own show but I shall be glad of a little help ... I have nothing but OTC boys [as officers].'[36] It seems that young Whitehead did join the battalion, although only temporarily. But the exchange is illuminating in showing how difficult it was to find suitable officers and how hard commanding officers of the Pals battalions had to work to train up their volunteers into fighting units.

The result of putting so many gentlemen-officers in charge of hundreds of men from the working or lower middle classes was something of a surprise. In many instances it seems that 'nicely raised young men from West Country vicarages or South Coast watering-places came face to face with forty Durham miners, Yorkshire furnace-men, Clydeside riveters, and the two sides found that they could scarcely understand each other's speech.'[37] But, contrary to expectations, a firm bond slowly began to grow between these social groups brought together almost for the first time in 1914 and 1915. Sharing the comradeship of the trenches created a further mixing of dialects and cultures. Many new swear words became almost respectable in upper-class language.[38] Thousands of young officers grew to admire and respect men from massively disadvantaged backgrounds who still showed great courage and humanity under the pressures of war. Siegfried Sassoon, for instance, described how his life was changed by the trust he felt the men he commanded had put in him.[39] Harold Macmillan gained an insight into the lives of his men that contributed to his lifelong sympathy for working-class people.[40] The result of this mingling was one of the least expected social revolutions of the twentieth century.

If the junior officers grew to admire the men whose welfare they were now responsible for, this was certainly not the case with the senior officers of the regular army. They had a very different view of the New Army that by the end of 1914 was busily drilling and training up and down the land. The senior officers reflected the attitudes of their class and many felt a level of contempt for the urban working classes. They thought they were generally unpatriotic, out to pursue their own interests, and that they could not be trusted. Some officers had expressed the view before the war that the working classes would be the first to crack under the pressure of war or the threat of invasion. The Boer War had revealed the scandal of the lack of physical fitness of recruits from the industrial slums of Britain, many of whom did not measure up to the basic physical requirements needed to join the army. The proportion of recruits who attained the height requirement of 5 foot 6 inches was lower in 1900 than it had been in 1845, giving rise to much talk about the 'degeneration' of the race. In 1914, on the eve of war, Major-General Sir Walter Knox picked up on this theme and wrote of the 'physically deteriorated race of town-bred humanity' that he believed was 'the flaw in our armour' as a nation.[41]

Not everyone, then, was impressed with the tremendous

response to Kitchener's appeal. When Kitchener created an entirely new army from volunteers, most of whom had no military experience coming from families without any military background, some of the most senior figures in the army dismissed the whole venture. General Sir Henry Wilson, pre-war Director of Military Operations at the War Office, was in August 1914 appointed deputy chief of staff to the commander-in-chief of the expeditionary force, Sir John French. Some months after the declaration of war, Wilson said of Kitchener's New Army, 'Under no circumstances can these mobs ... take the field for two years.' He described the New Army as 'ridiculous and preposterous' and 'the laughing stock of every soldier in Europe'.[42] Another senior officer wrote to his wife describing them as 'a roughish lot with hardly a gentleman among the officers'.[43] Even for a young subaltern already serving in France in the spring of 1915, rumours about general inadequacies were rife. Lieutenant Robert Graves wrote in a letter home, 'The general impression here is that the new army divisions can't be of much military use.'[44]

While Kitchener was establishing the New Army in Britain, the BEF began fighting its first battles in France. The stories of these battles are well known. The four divisions of the BEF were positioned on the French left (according to pre-war planning the BEF was supposed to consist of six infantry divisions and one of cavalry, but Kitchener was persuaded in August 1914 to keep two divisions back in England as he had little faith in the Territorial Force to defend the homeland and fears of an imminent German invasion were rife). The BEF was up against troops of the German First Army led by General von Kluck. This army was advancing at the rate of ten miles per day, an extraordinary achievement for an infantry force that largely marched on foot, supported by 84,000 horses that needed two million pounds of fodder every day.

The first engagements with the BEF took place around the Belgian mining town of Mons on 22 and 23 August when the advancing Germans walked straight into the British line. The BEF performed well. The infantry had been trained to fire their Lee Enfields at the rate of fifteen aimed rounds per minute and this they did, inflicting three times as many casualties on the Germans as they suffered themselves. The rapid German advance came to a temporary halt, but their howitzers were soon deployed and rained down a withering fire on the British positions. The French Fifth Army on the British right started to withdraw under the relentless momentum of the German advance. When Sir John French, the commander-in-chief, realised that the troops on his flank were pulling back he ordered the BEF to withdraw. What followed became known as the 'Retreat from Mons'. The British army alongside the French retreated continuously for thirteen days, covering a distance of 200 miles in the summer heat. There was only a single, temporary delaying action fought at Le Cateau on 26 August. As the Germans approached the French capital, the government withdrew from Paris to Bordeaux. Finally, with some of his forces only twenty-five miles from Paris, the French commander-in-chief, General Joseph 'Papa' Joffre, ordered both armies to stand and fight. The resulting Battle of the Marne was one of the turning points of the war.

The German commander, General Helmuth von Moltke, constantly varied the implementation of the Schlieffen Plan laid down by the General Staff before the war. Having marched through Belgium, rather than encircling Paris from the north, he decided to wheel south to the east of the city. Joffre spotted that this was the moment to counter-attack and began to create an additional army, the Sixth, on the British left. But Sir John French wanted time for the BEF to rest and recuperate after its long withdrawal. Kitchener himself rushed to France and, wearing his full field marshal's uniform, ordered French to stay in line with Joffre. After a fierce battle along the Marne, the situation was still undecided when on 9 September the Germans themselves began to withdraw to the north. Paris had been saved, at least for now.

The German plan to destroy the French army in the west before the Russians had fully mobilised in the east had failed. When the Russians attacked around Königsberg and Tannenberg in the forests and lakes of East Prussia in late August and early September, the Germans were faced with what they most feared, a war on two fronts.

In the west there began what was misleadingly called the 'race to the sea'. Neither side particularly wanted to reach the sea; each wanted simply to outflank the other. The French army confronted the Germans first on the river Oise, then around Albert and subsequently at Arras. When neither side succeeded in breaking through, the armies moved further north into Flanders. The BEF was ordered to stop the German advance at the medieval Belgian cloth town of Ypres in late October. Haig's I Corps bore the brunt of the fighting. Both sides fought an intense and bitter engagement and the British line nearly broke at the Messines ridge to the south of the town. But more and more British troops were rushed in to plug the gaps. At one point there were no reserves left. Around Ypres, the professional British army experienced some of the most severe fighting it had ever engaged in.

As it looked as though they could not turn the allied flank, the Germans began a process their engineers had trained for many times for on manoeuvres, digging in and protecting their trenches with thick lines of barbed wire. Exhausted, the Allied armies quickly followed suit. The two sides dug a network of trenches, the Germans seeing them as a permanent feature. Wherever they could, the Germans took the higher ground and began entrenching deeply, building fortified positions defended by nests of heavy machine guns. The devastated villages of France and Belgium provided strongpoints in the German lines as the remains of houses and cellars could be well fortified. The British and the French on the other hand took the view that their lines were only temporary defences and the German army would soon be expelled from the land it had occupied in Belgium and France. The new German Chief of the War Staff, General Erich von Falkenhayn, realised that the battle to outflank the Allies was lost and reported to the Kaiser on 9 November that it was no longer possible to maintain the offensive in Flanders because 'the barbed wire cannot be crossed.'[45] Further digging in produced a line of trenches extending from the English Channel to the Swiss border.

Incredible as it seems, the War Office had not prepared for the scale of losses that British forces would suffer in a full-scale European war. Each front-line battalion was to have its own regimental aid post near the scene of combat. But events in the first months of the war moved with such speed that these advanced dressing stations were often little more than a temporary treatment centre in a barn or a crater a few hundred yards behind the fighting. Many miles further back were a series of well-equipped base hospitals, constructed first at St Quentin and later at Le Havre, Boulogne, Amiens and Rouen. The wounded were to be evacuated from the front to these base hospitals as quickly as possible. But here was the problem. Although the latest plans within the RAMC included the use of motorised lorries as field ambulances, Sir Henry Wilson had decided they would not be necessary and that horse-drawn ambulances would prove sufficient. The result was that in the first actions it proved impossible to evacuate the wounded quickly enough. As the Retreat from Mons began, some wounded were taken away by horse-drawn ambulance wagons; others remained behind, exposed to shell fire and to capture by the enemy. As one orderly in the RAMC put it, we 'took 2 wagon loads of them [wounded men] with us leaving two wagons for cases which might crop up along the road ... I was sorry to have to leave 14 men behind in the barn, but there was nothing to do as we had no room for them.'[46]

Medical officers struggled near the front to cope with the numbers of casualties. In addition to the army medical services, various titled ladies came forward to raise funds and even to organise their own private hospitals along the French coast. The Duchess of Westminster set up one such hospital in the old casino at Le Touquet. Out went the gaming tables, and in came two medical wards, a fully equipped operating theatre, an X-ray unit, a pathological laboratory and beds for 260 patients. The hospital was staffed largely by volunteer doctors and surgeons from St Bartholomew's Hospital in London, with the support of 60 orderlies from the St John's Ambulance Association. Many upper-class ladies, friends of the Duchess, came to visit and were seen helping to prepare bed linen and bandages. It seemed to provide an opportunity for the wealthy and titled to do their bit to help the war effort. However, there were inevitable tensions with the RAMC, who before long took over and incorporated these private charitable hospitals into the military system.

The French and German armies were the first to experience the shock and awe of modern firepower in August 1914. The French armies who attacked across open fields in Alsace and Lorraine, wearing their blue jackets, bright red trousers and white kepis, were mown down by German machine guns in vast numbers. In a single day, 22 August, 27,000 French soldiers were killed. By the end of the month, the French had lost 260,000 dead and wounded. The German army also suffered terribly in the bloody month of August, having lost about 265,000 men by the time of the Battle of the Marne.

It was at Mons that the British army first encountered the horror of modern firepower. One officer recalled: 'It was as if a scythe of bullets passed directly over our heads about a foot above the earthworks. It came in gusts whistling and sighing ... It seemed inevitable that any man who went over the bank must be cut neatly in two.'[47] In fact British losses at Mons were relatively light at 1,850. During the minor action at Le Cateau, the BEF's II Corps under General Horace Smith-Dorrien suffered 7,812 casualties and held up the German advance for only a few hours. In the series of running battles later called the First Battle of Ypres in October and November, the BEF suffered 54,105 casualties. The battle would be remembered for the destruction of much of the regular professional army. Eighty-four infantry battalions of about 1,000 men at full strength had gone to France in August. After the Battle of Ypres, seventy-four mustered less than 300 men and eighteen of these had fewer than 100 men. By the end of November, total British losses amounted to 89,964 out of an original army of about 100,000 men.[48] Brigadier John Charteris, Haig's intelligence chief, wrote in his diary in early November, 'The horrible thing about these last few weeks has been to see our battalions dwindling, and no reinforcements arriving to fill the gaps. What we want here now is more men and more ammunition ... the casualties are enormous. We can't go on forever, we must have men.'[49] The British, like the Germans and French, now dug trenches and tried to replace the huge numbers scythed down in the first terrible confrontations of the war.

The war in the west had turned to stalemate. Lord Kitchener wrote to Sir John French in January 1915 that 'the German lines in France may be looked on as a fortress that cannot be carried by assault and also cannot be completely invested.'[50] The British army had gone to war in 1914 planning for a war of manoeuvre and of dramatic flanking movements. But they now found themselves on a static, defensive battlefield with an enemy front line akin to a fortress running for 450 miles from the sea to the Alps. For the first time in its history, there was no flank for the army to turn. The Allies could lay siege to the German lines, but they would find it nearly impossible to assault them successfully. This type of warfare could have been predicted from previous conflicts like the Russo-Japanese War and possibly even the American Civil War. But it had not been. Both sides now had to get used to facing a foe equipped with massed artillery and machine guns by settling down in deep, sometimes waterlogged trenches. This would be a new experience for the armies of Europe and would bring unexpected consequences. The medical authorities were almost immediately faced with an extraordinary challenge that hardly anyone had anticipated.

3

The Shell Shock Enigma

In late October 1914, the 1st Battalion Royal Fusiliers, an elite unit within the regular British army, were out of the line in rest billets near Armentières in north-eastern France. They had been through a period of fierce fighting in the so-called 'race to the sea' and had taken part in digging the first trenches that would bring the stalemate characteristic of the next few years of war. One morning a company commander alerted his medical officer to the fact that one of his sergeants was 'out of sorts'. The MO, as he later wrote, found the sergeant 'sitting staring into the fire. He had not shaved and his trousers were half open. He seemed a morose fellow; I could get nothing out of him.' His company commander did not want the sergeant sent away from the battalion sick, as he did not appear to be ill and the company could not afford to lose an experienced NCO at a critical point. But the next day, when the rest of the battalion were moving back up to the front, the sergeant took a revolver and 'blew his head off'. The battalion was immediately involved in more intense fighting and the MO wrote, 'I thought nothing of this at the time; it seemed a silly thing to do. I knew nothing then of the tricks war can play with men's minds. In those early days . . . we did not bother about men's minds; we did what we could for their bodies. We did not ask if a man was wearing well or if he would last. Of course he would last, why shouldn't he.'[1]

Throughout November and December 1914 the situation grew more puzzling as an increasing number of men with strange and bizarre injuries began to arrive in the Casualty Clearing Stations (CCSs) behind the newly dug trenches of the Western Front. The men showed no visible signs of physical wounds. They had not been hit by machine gun bullets, nor had they been struck by shrapnel. They did not have damaged limbs. They had no apparent wounds to the head. Some of them had minor cuts and bruises but nothing more severe. But they all seemed to display similar strange symptoms that mystified the MOs. Most were suffering from peculiar forms of paralysis. Many were described as having 'the shakes'. Some could not stand up or walk normally. A few did not appear to be able to speak coherently and were stammering badly. Others had been struck completely dumb and could not speak at all. Most appeared to be in a state of stupor and a few had completely lost their memory. Others seemed to find it difficult to see clearly. Many had lost their sense of taste or smell. Some vomited repeatedly.

The MOs who tried to attend to them had not seen such strange symptoms before and were not sure how to respond. As many were sent back to England with 'nervous and mental shock', the War Office began to grow alarmed at the numbers of men being evacuated home. The British Expeditionary Force had already lost a high proportion of its strength and could not afford to lose otherwise fit men due to nervous problems.[2]

It was the mysterious physical symptoms that seemed so puzzling. One MO described what he witnessed: 'The eyes pop out of their sockets, the expression becomes fixed and glassy, the facial skin loses all of its red colour, the skin becomes yellow, the cheekbones protrude. The lips are shut tight and sticky spittle tacks up the tongue to the roof of the mouth. The heart works in short, convulsive beats, breathing becomes slower ... From time to time a cold shudder runs through the body and the teeth chatter.'[3] Another physician attached to a hospital in London wrote that 'Men in this state may break down in tears if asked to describe their experiences at the front.'[4] This was decidedly unsoldierly behaviour. How was the army to react to this strange new phenomenon that no one seemed to understand? The RAMC had no experts in this field. They had to find someone to explain what was happening.

The army assumed at first that the men were suffering some form of epileptic fit. So the War Office asked Dr Aldren Turner to go to France as a 'consultant' to investigate. Turner, a highly regarded neurologist from the National Hospital for the Paralysed and Epileptic in Queen Square, London, was a doctor in the Territorial Force. An expert in epilepsy, he had given a major series of lectures on the subject in Edinburgh in 1910 and had written a textbook on nervous diseases. Turner confirmed that from the Battle of Ypres in October 1914 onwards a stream of men had come out of the line suffering some form of paralysis under shell fire. But after a couple of months he had to return to his practice in London. To try to treat these men further the army turned to a doctor who was already in France, working as a volunteer in the Duchess of Westminster's former hospital at Le Touquet.

Dr Charles Samuel Myers was an unlikely figure to come to the aid of the British army. He was from a family of wealthy Jewish cloth merchants and had grown up in Bayswater, west London. He never fitted easily into the commercial world into which he was born and, having inherited from his mother an interest in music and culture, he became a gifted violinist. He resisted pressure to go into the family business and instead went up to Cambridge to read Natural Sciences in 1892. There he became a pupil and an admirer of William Halse Rivers, a pioneer of experimental psychology in Britain. After Cambridge Myers went to St Bartholomew's but did not go into medical practice. Instead, in 1898, he decided to join an anthropological expedition to the Australasian islands of the Torres Strait with a group of Cambridge friends including Alfred Haddon, William McDougall and his tutor William Rivers. It was a strange decision, but the expedition was groundbreaking in trying to find a scientific basis to record the psychology, the music and the cultural rituals of the local population. At its heart the expedition's purpose was to study the anthropology and psychology of the locals to investigate if there was a difference between the brains and intelligence of these 'natives', as they were then called, and 'civilised' men.

After nearly a year abroad Myers caught a fever in Borneo and returned home to take up his post as house physician at St Bartholomew's. But he soon decided to return to Cambridge and to pursue the study of psychology alongside Rivers. He wrote a standard textbook on the subject in 1909 and raised funds to open a new experimental laboratory for psychology at Cambridge in 1912, the first of its kind in Britain.[5]

When war was declared, Myers was at work in his laboratory in Cambridge studying phonographic recordings of ethnic music produced by Australasian tribes. But before long he could no longer concentrate on the task and decided that he must put his professional skills at the service of the army. However, the War Office turned him down, not wanting to recruit medical officers over the age of forty (Myers was forty-one). So he pulled some strings with his contacts at St Bartholomew's and got the job of registrar in the Duchess of Westminster's war hospital at Le Touquet. When the RAMC decided to bring the hospital under its own wing in

November 1914, Myers was commissioned in the corps as a captain. While he was at Le Touquet, three soldiers were brought in suffering from various forms of war neuroses. As someone who had devoted his life to the study of the mind, he was the obvious doctor to treat these sad cases. Other doctors turned psychiatric cases away; Myers welcomed them. As he later wrote, 'it was clear to me that my previous psychological training and my present interests fitted me for the treatment of these cases.'[6]

The first cases treated by Myers included a soldier who had been trapped for several hours in the barbed wire of No Man's Land. While he was stuck on the wire, several eight-inch shells had burst nearby. The man, who had been cheerful and positive before this terrifying experience, was eventually brought back to the British lines in a pathetic state, crying and shivering in a cold sweat. His mates described his escape as 'a sheer miracle'. He appeared to be suffering from blurred vision and felt a burning sensation in his eyes, making him panic that he was going blind. Myers concluded that although the soldier was not physically wounded, he had suffered some form of physical concussion from the proximity of the shell explosions and that 'the high frequency vibrations' from the shell had caused 'an invisibly fine "molecular" commotion in the brain'.[7] Myers believed that the man was now displaying the symptoms of this physical damage. When he wrote about this and the two other cases in the doctors' journal *The Lancet* in February 1915, he described the condition, adopting a term used by the soldiers, as 'shell shock'.[8]

This first use of the term 'shell shock' in medical circles suggested that the cause of the mental disorder was concussion of the brain from the bursting of a shell nearby – *physical* damage to the nervous system is exactly what the words 'shell shock' were intended to signify. However, the term was soon in use to describe a wide range of physical symptoms that doctors could not easily explain. It was a simple term but one that had instant resonance for those who saw the strange cases coming in from the front, and doctors began using the words to describe almost every sort of nervous breakdown, trauma or anxiety neurosis. Although the stalemate of trench warfare had only existed for a few months, the military authorities quickly realised that this form of immobile war was a new phenomenon. Men cowering in a trench with shells constantly landing all around them, unable to exercise the instinctive human response to run away, were suffering from extreme forms of anxiety or stress. The shells were far more lethal than those used in previous conflicts, consisting of high explosives that could be fired in rapid succession from miles away. Sudden, horrific, seemingly random death or mutilation became a feature of trench life that every soldier had to live with.

Almost everyone who went through such a bombardment during the First World War described in similar terms the effect it had on them. Gerald Brenan was typical of most when he later wrote of being caught in a German barrage: 'I do not think anyone who has not lived through one of these can form a conception of what they were like. The earth appears to rock and tremble. The air is filled by a persistent rushing sound, broken by the crash of explosions. The mind cannot think, the arms and legs tremble automatically, and the tough man is the one who recovers quickest.' After enduring a particularly heavy barrage, Brenan looked at the soldiers in the trench around him and 'saw the shattered looks of the men who had survived, and heard the moaning and the sobbing of a poor fellow who had broken down'.[9]

Tom Pear, a young academic psychologist who had studied under Myers at Cambridge, wrote a few years later that conditions in the trenches were unique, claiming, 'Never in the history of mankind have the stresses and strains laid upon body and mind been so great or so numerous as in the present war.'[10] But it was not only the younger generation of psychologists who attributed the high incidence of shell shock to the unique conditions of the Great War. General Horne, commander at the time of an infantry division in France, agreed with this view and claimed that shell shock 'became a serious factor in this war owing to the peculiar character of the war [in contrast to previous conflicts].' He concluded that shell shock could be put down to the high level of 'explosives and bombardments [that] had never been known before'.[11] A medical officer from the Western Front later said that 'acute breakdown ... occurred especially during bombardments when the men, sometimes in large numbers, lost their heads and lost their control.'[12]

Now that this strange new phenomenon had a name, the army needed to know how to shape its response. However, the problem for the military was that there was no agreement as to how to treat the many different conditions and neuroses labelled as 'shell shock'. Myers' diagnosis and use of the term began an intense debate within the medical community in Britain about the nature of shell shock. The study of 'nervous diseases' had become fashionable within the medical profession in the twenty years before the Great War. Indeed it had been written in 1909 that 'Nervous breakdown is the disease of our age'; this was put down to the speed of modern life and the stresses and strains generated by the 'wear and tear' of the urban and industrial environment with the 'constant struggle for a livelihood'.[13]

However, in the Edwardian era a fundamental class divide emerged between the treatment of 'poor lunatics' in mental asylums by psychiatrists on the one hand, and the treatment of wealthy clients by neurologists, on the other. There had been a big increase in the number of registered lunatics in the second half of the nineteenth century, so that by 1913 there were estimated to be 165,000 men and women in largely Victorian mental asylums that were now horribly overcrowded. Relatively little treatment was available for the poor individuals in these wretched places, where each psychiatrist (known as an 'alienist') had between 400 and 600 patients at any one time. As a consequence, being sent to an asylum was often a life sentence. The early twentieth-century lunatic asylum has recently been described as 'a storehouse for incurables'.[14] Certainly in the public view admittance to an asylum was a cause for intense shame. The Victorian asylum system had been partly created to lock away and out of sight those who were classed as 'imbeciles', regarded as being unable to contribute to society. The doctors who did study these patients concluded that mental illness was frequently hereditary, and it was usually perceived as some sort of weakness. Much debate took place in late Victorian and Edwardian Britain about what was called the 'degeneracy' of the race, the growth in the number of lunatics being cited as proof of this. And most people felt that lunacy was incurable. 'Once a lunatic, always a lunatic' was a phrase used by London County Council in a report on its mental asylums in 1914.[15] This was not a message of hope for the impoverished insane or pauper lunatic.

On the other hand, growing numbers of the wealthy patients who suffered from some sort of nervous disorder were diagnosed as having 'psychoneuroses' like 'neurasthenia' and attended the growing number of specialist neurologists in Harley Street and elsewhere around the country. The terms used to describe their mental problems sounded far more scientific and serious. In London, Dr Aldren Turner was only one of many neurologists based at the National Hospital for the Paralysed and Epileptic in Queen Square, often combining part-time work at the hospital with private practice. A third kind of treatment that was new at the time was psychotherapy, in which doctors talked through the core problems with their patient and, sometimes using hypnosis, tried to unlock the key emotional issues that lay at the root of his or her mental disorder.

The specialists coming out of the universities in Britain where psychology was studied, Cambridge and Manchester, regarded the situation with respect to the treatment of nervous diseases in the country as 'deplorable'. They despaired at the lack of treatment for those sent to lunatic asylums and at the complete absence of psychiatric clinics, places 'exempt from any stigma' to which patients could go for advice and counselling that might help them avoid admission to an asylum. They saw the lack of psychiatric training in Britain as the root cause of the problem. Training could help medical practitioners realise 'the vitally important fact that mental disease is curable'. Although medical science had witnessed great advances in the treatment of heart disease, tuberculosis, diphtheria, tetanus and other common ailments, and great improvements in the use of antiseptics and anaesthetics and in the science of bacteriology, it was argued that there had been 'little or no progress' in fifty years when it came to the treatment of mental illness.[16]

In Europe the treatment of mental ailments was far more advanced than in Britain. In Germany, almost every university medical department had a psychiatric clinic attached to it. Paris had two major schools of neurology. At the Salpetrière Hospital, a vast complex on the site of an old gunpowder factory, Prof. Jean-Martin Charcot became known as the founder of modern neurology in the late nineteenth century. He helped to identify the causes of many mental disorders including epilepsy, stroke and hysteria. The word 'hysteria' derives from the Greek word for the womb, and it was often seen as primarily a woman's condition until

Charcot showed that men could display the same symptoms. By using hypnosis, Charcot was able to treat forms of paralysis of, say, the arm or leg that were put down to hysteria. His successor, Jules-Joseph Dejerine, believed that through conversations with his patients he could discover the cause of their trauma and cure it.

At La Pitié Hospital in Paris, Dejerine's great rival, Joseph Babinski, used a very different technique. A specialist in treating hysteria, he believed that much hysteria was caused by suggestion – that the patient convinced himself he was suffering from the disease and consequently developed its symptoms. Babinski argued for the efficacy of forceful persuasion to try to reverse the emotional process that had caused the hysteria. The physical symptoms the patient displayed would then disappear. Sometimes this included forcefully telling the patient that he or she could easily recover. This much harsher treatment (known as *traitement brusqué*) also included the use of electric shock therapy to treat the patient's symptoms.

Meanwhile, in Vienna, Sigmund Freud had taken psychotherapy one step further. The aim of psychoanalysis was to try to uncover memories or emotions that had been repressed and hidden in the 'unconscious' mind. Freud argued that many of these repressed emotions dated from childhood and were sexual in origin. Only when they had been discovered and brought to the surface of the conscious mind could a patient be cured and restored to normal mental health. All these European developments had their groups of advocates in Britain before the war, but they remained few in number and very much in the minority.

In confronting the mental problems of its soldiers, the army itself had a problem. Conventional military thinking held that a soldier was either fit and capable, in which case he was available to fulfil his duties; or he was sick or wounded, in which case he would be treated by military doctors until his recovery enabled him to return to the ranks. In the very few cases where a soldier had a nervous problem he was either classed as a malingerer and so would be subject to military discipline, or as a lunatic – in which case he was dismissed from the service and dispatched into the public asylum system. The idea of a man suffering from a nervous condition and needing treatment to recover so as to be able to return to his unit was alien to military culture. As has been seen, the RAMC had no expertise in the area of psychiatric medicine. And most senior figures in the army would have held the view that all soldiers, whether officers or from the rank and file, were supposed to put up with difficult or harsh conditions, to show a stiff upper lip and bear up. The large numbers who now appeared to be suffering from some form of mental breakdown vastly complicated this simple way of perceiving things. And the army was completely unprepared for the avalanche of shell shock victims that now faced them. Before the war, the only provision made for hospital care for soldiers suffering from mental or nervous breakdown was a single ward, 'D' Ward, in the Royal Victoria Hospital at Netley. Here, there were only 124 beds for an army of 200,000 men.[17]

During 1915 and the early months of 1916, Myers toured the CCSs and base hospitals and examined some 2,000 patients. Throughout these months the debate continued to rage about the causes of the multitude of psychosomatic conditions under the 'shell shock' label. Frederick Mott, a leading figure in neurology before the war and an adviser to London County Council, had spent some years studying the brains of lunatics in mental asylums. He was well known for taking the traditional line that heredity was a major factor in cases of insanity. During the war, he did not work at the front but studied victims of shell shock evacuated to the newly built

Maudsley Hospital in south London. Carrying out a series of microscopic examinations of the brains of soldiers killed by blast, he identified cerebral lesions which he concluded were the cause of shell shock in patients who had survived the explosion of a nearby shell. He argued in a series of lectures that exposure to shell fire caused a pathological effect on the body's nervous system, brought about by concussion to the brain from the impact of an explosion.

Mott agreed that psychological factors played a part and that a man's state of mind before an explosion might well affect his reaction to it. However, as he saw more and more cases, he modified his line and accepted that there were soldiers with a fine record for bravery and no history of a 'neuropathic tendency' who also succumbed. Some people were more disposed to suffer from the horrors of trench life than others, Mott concluded. This helped reconcile him to the fact that many apparently healthy young men were going down with shell shock. He argued that fear was a biological instinct and the anticipation of death or mutilation was a major cause in what he called the 'neuroses of war'.[18]

An alternative view came from Harold Wiltshire, an experienced physician who worked at a base hospital in Rouen, France for a year before concluding that the symptoms of shell shock were entirely of psychological rather than physical origin. He observed that men who had lost limbs from being hit in shell explosions did *not* suffer from shell shock. In hospital they were often cheery and supportive of the medical and nursing staff. This contrasted with the morose gloom and lack of hope of patients in a shell shock ward. He believed that men suffering from shell shock had been worn down by the prolonged strain of trench warfare into a position in which a sudden psychological shock could tip them over the edge. 'Gradual psychic exhaustion from continued fear is an important disposing cause of shell shock,' he wrote. 'Horrible sights are the most frequent and potent factor in the production of this shock. Losses and the fright of being buried are also important in this respect.'[19] He cited the example of a soldier who suffered from mental shock because he was ordered to clear away the remains of a number of men who had been blown to pieces by a shell. Wiltshire located the causes of shell shock firmly in the realm of psychology.

It was becoming clear to those working with patients that 'shell shock' was, as Myers himself later admitted, 'a singularly ill-chosen term; and in other respects … a singularly harmful one'.[20] In the vast majority of cases, Myers accepted, shell shock had psychological and not physical causes. But by this point, the term was well established. Pears and Grafton Smith agreed that it was a 'popular but inadequate title for all those mental effects of war experience which are sufficient to incapacitate a man from the performance of his military duties'.[21] But the use of 'shell shock' as a term was by now too prevalent to be abandoned.

The existence of so many different medical attitudes towards nervous disorders meant there was no consensus for the army to draw upon in formulating its approach to shell shock. But something had to be done in the attempt to treat and classify the numbers of men coming out of the lines suffering from paralysis neuroses. So the military accepted both of the very different attitudes within the medical profession about shell shock, adopting two principal divisions from the start. First, there was a class-based distinction between officers and men. The rank and file were diagnosed as suffering from shell shock, often seen as a form of hysteria. The condition manifested itself in physical symptoms of deafness, blindness and paralysis. Mott concluded that soldiers converted their mental distress into physical signs of hysteria.

On the other hand, it was believed that officers suffered from neurasthenia, the cause of which was understood to be a prolonged process of breakdown, and the result of the extra responsibility they had to bear. The anxiety neuroses of officers were more likely to produce symptoms like exhaustion, loss of concentration, bad nightmares or depression. Officers, it was argued, were used to being more active, to giving orders and to being in command, and as they traditionally repressed their emotions with the so-called 'stiff upper lip' attitude, they were gradually 'worn down' by the anxieties of command in the trenches. The men, however, were used to taking a more passive position, to obeying orders, and were therefore thought more likely to suddenly 'snap' under pressure in the trenches. As Myers put it, 'The neurasthenic remains an intact, though worn out individual whereas (more or less recognisably) the personality of the hysteric has changed. The breakdown in the neurasthenic is due to persistent wear and tear; in the hysteric ... this is avoided by a sudden snap or fission.' He concluded that the reasons for the difference between the condition affecting officers and that from which men suffered were not difficult to find. 'The forces of education, tradition and example make for greater self control in the officer. He, moreover, is busy throughout a bombardment, issuing orders and subject to worry over his responsibilities, whereas his men can do nothing during the shelling but watch and wait.' Bizarre though these distinctions might seem today, they were commonly accepted during the war.[22]

In addition to this class-based divide, doctors took either a 'soft' or a 'hard' line in recommending how the army should treat this strange new condition. Those who were more sympathetic to the existence of emotional or psychological problems within otherwise perfectly normal and healthy individuals believed that the emotional basis of their condition could and should be identified and cured. Others, who saw all nervous and mental disorders as a symptom of some sort of weakness of character, or even mental degeneration, took a harsher line and were more likely to want to bully the men back to their fighting units as quickly as possible.

Underlying much of this was the suspicion among many senior officers, and also plenty of medical officers, of malingering, that many of those who claimed to be suffering were simply pretending to have shell shock as a means to escape the horror of the trenches. Either that or they were weaklings who did not have the moral fibre to stand up to the duty that was expected of them. In army parlance they were called 'skrimshankers and malingerers'. Medical officers complained to Myers, 'We have seen too many dirty sneaks go down the line under the term "shell shock" to feel any great sympathy for the condition.' '"Shell shock" should be abolished' was another response. Later, Myers himself would be in 'hearty agreement' with these views, accepting that there were several instances of soldiers swinging the lead and trying it on.

Shell shock had quickly attained a certain cache of social approval. The subject received wide coverage in the newspapers, provoking a broadly sympathetic response to its sufferers. For the relatives of soldiers back home, it came as a source of relief if a man was diagnosed as suffering from shell shock. It gave him a certain dignity worthy of respect, like a soldier who had lost an arm or a leg. Fit men would turn up at an aid post, and when asked what was wrong with them would proudly boast, 'Suffering from shell shock, sir.' Myers believed they would never have wanted to be labelled as suffering from mental breakdown or 'nervous shock'.[23] Hence the army clearly had one major priority in its approach to shell shock: to pick out the malingerers and return them to their units.

Myers, in the main, took a 'soft' line in treating the first cases he came across. As a psychologist, he believed not only that he understood some of the causes of the various neuroses he treated but that he could help to cure them. As an army doctor he realised he had to accept that his responsibility was to treat wounded men and return them to the fighting line as soon as possible. In March 1915 he was sent to the base hospital at Boulogne. Within days of arriving he was dealing with several extreme cases. At times Myers used hypnosis to try and cure patients. One young soldier was convinced he was still in the trenches and spent his time dodging shells while hiding under his bed. Other men had dreadful stoops and could not walk straight. Myers treated a man who had been struck mute by a dreadful experience in the trenches and within days was able to restore his power of speech. Myers brought to his new role an almost evangelical energy. He was thoroughly committed to showing that if the causes were understood, shell shock could be treated successfully, and he was able to return about one-third of his patients to duty.[24] Although the army high command was still deeply suspicious, they put up with Myers as long as he delivered a reasonable success rate in returning men to their battalions, and he was promoted to lieutenant-colonel.

Much medical thinking about shell shock in the early phases of the war emphasised the fact that men with previous experience of nervous conditions were more likely to be affected than those who had never suffered before. Myers observed that 'Previous emotional disorder, worry, insomnia and above all, a psycho-neurotic predisposition favour the onset of the [shell] shock.' This notion was also fundamental to Mott's belief that a hereditary link to insanity was the reason why most people suffered from nervous conditions. An American doctor working for Mott at the Maudsley researched the heredity of 100 shell shock victims and found that 74 per cent had a family history of neurotic disease (as against 10 per cent of the general wounded). This seemed to prove to Mott that most nervous conditions were hereditary and he wrote that his views were 'now based on statistics'.[25]

Even Myers was not averse to describing this in moral terms. He said such victims could be divided between the 'good and the bad: the former, often a highly intelligent person, keeping full control over his highly sensitive nervous system; the latter, usually of feebler intellect, having little hold over his instinctive acts to escape danger, the emotions which impel him to them, and the resulting conflicts'.[26] Once again, in this delineation of men into those who are 'highly intelligent' and those of 'feebler intellect', a clear class division appears. Most officers would belong to the former category and men from the rank and file, of course, to the latter. It is easy to see why, in this climate of thinking, some senior military officers were sceptical that shell shock was any sort of legitimate medical condition and not just a case of men with 'weak' or 'feeble' minds suffering from the strains of war.

The situation grew worse as 1915 advanced and more men were reported to be suffering from some form of shell shock or neurasthenia. After a few months, 7–10 per cent of officers and 3–4 per cent of other ranks in the main hospital at Boulogne had been sent home to Britain to recover from 'the effects of nervous and mental shock'.[27] The fact that many of these men came from good backgrounds with no experience of previous mental disorders, and had excellent military careers, made it more difficult for the military to dismiss shell shock as simply a condition experienced by 'misfits' of one sort or another. Some officers, however, came up with a simple explanation. They saw the phenomenon as a sign of the transition from a trained and professional army to a volunteer or previously part-time army. Lieutenant-General

Sir John Goodwin said after the war that he had known no cases of shell shock in the original BEF that went to France in 1914. He emphasised the importance to regular soldiers of the 'inculcation of an *esprit de corps*, loyalty, pride in himself and his unit, and the old history of the regiment to which he belongs', something it was essential to instil in training.[28] Like many other pre-war officers who took a similar view, Goodwin was demonstrating once again the disdain felt by the regulars towards the Territorials and Kitchener's New Army.

However, the issue of shell shock was not of concern to the army alone. The press eagerly picked up the question of the mental state of the country's soldiers and during 1915 it became a subject of great public interest. In the main, both the press coverage and the public debate were sympathetic to men who had broken down under the intolerable pressure of modern warfare. *The Times*, for instance, in May 1915 had a feature on 'Battle Shock' in which it tried to explain to its readers about 'The Wounded Mind and Its Cure'. Arguing that 'wounds of consciousness' should receive 'the same serious attention as wounds of flesh or bone', the article explained how 'a brave man' could be brought down by 'the effects of severe shell fire'.[29] Physical wounds were as old as war itself, but mental disorders among soldiers seemed to most people to be a uniquely modern form of injury.

By the early twentieth century, moreover, the idea of a 'civil society' in which individuals, organisations and the state had both rights and responsibilities was beginning to take root. The Workmen's Compensation Act of 1897 had recognised the responsibility of employers for accidents to their workers. In its social welfare reforms, the pre-war Liberal government had introduced old age pensions in 1908 and three years later made (limited) provision for workers' health care and unemployment benefits. And by 1914, both soldiers and their families were beginning to regard medical treatment in the army as an entitlement, as their right. Kitchener's New Army was a citizen army and modern concepts of citizenship, justice and good health care were increasingly widespread. It was therefore seen as the duty of the army to provide appropriate health provision, in return for the agreement to serve; all wounded men were entitled to modern and efficient medical treatment.

But the public became particularly sympathetic to the sad cases of men who had broken down under the pressure of war. They did not want them consigned as 'incurable' lunatics, they wanted them treated and returned to active service. In a typical article in April 1915, *The Manchester Guardian* reported that 'the appalling conditions of modern war' had played havoc with the nervous systems of 'hundreds of men'. It reported one soldier as saying 'Shell fire is damnable. Most of us will face any amount of rifle fire without a murmur ... but we fairly get the wind up when shells begin to drop.' The newspaper noted that a breakdown was usually only temporary and that 'the mental disorder arising from war shock usually vanishes with good nursing and perfect rest. It is clearly the duty of the State to ensure that these shall be forthcoming quickly, fully, and under the most acceptable conditions.'[30] In this small but significant way, the debate about shell shock helped advance the case for the welfare state.

By early 1915, as the conflict in the west ossified into a static war along the trench lines of the Western Front, the armies on both sides developed systems of medical care that relied upon evacuating wounded men from the front line to an established hierarchy of medical aid positions. In the British army, any man with an ailment would go first of all to his regimental aid post or advanced dressing station. This was usually only two or three hundred yards behind the front line, situated where possible in an old farm building, in the cellars of a village house or in a large dugout. Each battalion in the army had its own medical officer, a qualified doctor who worked in the aid post with a small group of orderlies.

The MO was a familiar figure in each battalion, living with the men in the trenches and dealing with daily issues relating to soldiers' health, like regular colds, fevers and specific problems like trench foot. In addition, he was the first port of call for the wounded. Being so close to the front, regimental aid posts were frequently exposed to enemy fire and were only marginally safer than the front lines themselves; as a consequence more than a thousand medical officers were killed during the war.[31] During a major offensive, the situation in the aid posts would become chaotic as large numbers of wounded were brought in. There were often only minimal supplies of clean water and rarely enough space. But the intention was that every injured man would be examined and cleaned up. If possible a wound would be dressed, sometimes by coating it with iodine, or by setting a fracture in a splint.

When it came to nervous disorders, there was universal agreement on one thing as the war progressed: that the battalion MO played a vital role. First, he would probably know each man and be able to distinguish between malingerers and those with genuine symptoms. Second, a soldier was likely to treat with respect anything his MO said to him, for the men usually held such professionals in high regard. A good MO could calm a man down, give him rest, and get him out of the firing line for a few days; all of which could greatly help with recovery if the nervous disorder was mild. In fact treatment for most victims of shell shock did not go much beyond this. A man was given plenty of rest, along with good and regular meals; a doctor or his MO would then tell him that he did not have a disease and should pull himself together and get back to his battalion. The treatment was simple but effective, and 'it not infrequently ended in the man coming forward voluntarily for duty, after having been given a much needed fortnight's rest in hospital.'[32]

Lieutenant-Colonel Rogers, MO of the 4th Black Watch battalion, outlined his approach after the war: 'A good deal depends on the Medical Officer; in fact I think most depends on the MO attached to the battalion – his knowledge of men in general and his knowledge of the men in his unit in particular. He ought to know the men personally and take an interest in them. There is no reason why he should not have an elementary knowledge of psychology ... and if you are able to explain to him [a patient suffering from neurosis] that you have investigated his condition and that there is nothing really wrong with him, give him a rest at the aid post if necessary and a day or two's sleep, go up with him to the front line, and when there see him often, sit down beside him and talk to him about the war or look through his periscope and let the man see you are taking an interest in him, you will not get nearly so many cases of anxiety neurosis.'[33] Rogers saw his role almost as that of the friendly, wise, local family doctor.

Myers added something else to this approach. He came to believe that doctors should attempt to treat minor shell shock victims without delay and as near the front as possible, if there was to be any hope of returning men to their units quickly. He argued that dealing with cases of mild shell shock near the front line was far better than sending a man down the line to a field ambulance unit or a CCS, both of which were equipped more like small hospitals, with operating theatres, wards and specialist surgeons, out of range of the enemy's artillery.[34] Myers tried to persuade the army to set up specialist wards only a few miles from the front. But traditionalists in the army were hostile to the idea; their view was that there was no place for men with mental problems near the front line, more earthily expressed in the statement that it did not want to be 'encumbered with lunatics in Army areas'.[35] Even though approaches to the treatment of victims varied enormously, Myers at least had some success in establishing specialist centres for more serious cases of shell shock, in what came to be known as 'forward psychiatry'.

Regimental medical officers did not usually have the scientific language to assess or describe conditions that came under the 'shell shock' heading. William Tyrrell was an MO on the Western Front from 1914 with the 2nd Battalion Lancashire Fusiliers. In describing a man's store of 'nervous energy', Tyrrell used the easily understood analogy of having a current and a capital account in a bank. After dealing with hundreds of shell shock cases, he summed up his position: 'A man instinctively masks his emotions almost as a matter of routine. In trifling everyday affairs this is involuntary and automatic with a negligible expense of nervous energy ... This expenditure is usually out of his current account, consequently it is not missed and has no untoward effect.' However, Tyrrell believed, major crises drew upon a man's capital account of nervous energy, and as he tried to cover this up and camouflage it, it drew deep on his reserves. 'A continuous series of great crises without intervals for replacing spent energy ultimately exhausts the capital account and you get a run on the bank, followed by loss of control, hysteria, irresponsible chattering, mutism, amnesia, inhibition of the senses, acute mania, insensibility, etc, with the diagnosis of nervous breakdown or "shell-shock".' Tyrrell put shell shock down to fear and the 'fear of being found afraid. Any emotion which has to be repressed or concealed', he believed, drew upon a vast 'output of nervous energy'.[36]

Charles Wilson, MO with the 1st Battalion Royal Fusiliers, expressed this in similar terms: 'A man's courage is his capital and he is always spending. The call on the bank may be only the daily drain of the front line or it may be a sudden draft which threatens to close the account. His will is perhaps almost destroyed by intensive shelling, by heavy bombing or by a bloody battle.' Changing his metaphor, Wilson wrote that 'men wear out in war like clothes.'[37]

Of course, treating more serious battlefield neuroses was beyond the capacity of the over-stretched MO and the front-line regimental aid post. Without question it was necessary to send severe cases down the line for specialist care. Here too, however, the class attitude prevailed. While it was regarded as acceptable to send cases of neurasthenia (mostly officers) home to Britain for care, most specialists argued that cases of hysteria (rank and file) should be treated in France. Again, the emphasis was on providing rest, sleep, regular meals and a calm environment. A specialist medical officer treating these men should not only have a training in psychology and psychotherapy, but according to Myers 'should possess enthusiasm, confidence, cheerfulness and tact, with wide knowledge of the failings of his fellows and an ability promptly to determine whether a policy of persuasion, analysis, intimacy, sternness or reprimand should be adopted. Only the experience of such a man can lead to the successful treatment of individual patients, the detection of the malingerer, and the avoidance of injustice to genuine cases.' Myers added that no specialist medical officer should ever have more than 75 cases to deal with at one time. He argued that if these conditions were met then recovery was possible; otherwise, if psychiatric casualties are simply 'herded together and left to themselves, they are almost sure to go from bad to worse'.[38]

This was a feature on which both senior military figures and the medical fraternity agreed. Shell shock and anxiety neuroses were likely to spread rapidly. Charles Wilson reported to the post-war Committee of Enquiry that shell shock was 'very contagious, like measles'.[39] A man display-ing signs of strain, whether simply a case of the shakes or something far more severe like hysterical paralysis, deafness, dumbness or blindness, could both upset those around him and encourage others to simulate the condition. Behind this, partly, was once again the fear of malingering. If a group of soldiers saw a man whose nerves had 'gone' being taken back down the line for rest, recuperation and respite from the hor-rors of the trenches, then they would be encouraged to want the same. But there was also agreement as to how unsettling a man in a bad nervous state could be on the others in his section or platoon. Bombardier Harry Fayerbrother of the Royal Field Artillery was in a gun crew at Ypres when one of his team suffered a serious attack of shell shock. 'He upset all of us,' Fayerbrother later recalled. 'There were just five or six of us in the dugout and every time a shell come over he went haywire, shouting and screaming as if he wanted to tear the place to pieces, and tear us to pieces too. We just couldn't put up with it, so I grabbed him by the scruff of the neck and took him down the duckboard track to the dressing station.'[40] One officer summed this up succinctly by reporting that 'jumpy men make others "jumpy"'.[41]

The contagious nature of shell shock touched on the larger issue of the need to keep up morale within a unit. As a conse-quence, patients with nervous conditions were almost always segregated from the rest of the wounded. When transported by ambulance train they usually travelled in separate locked carriages and were always the last to disembark when the rest of the wounded had been taken away. At Denmark Hill station in south London, next to the Maudsley Hospital, tem-porary platforms were built to allow shell shock patients to be admitted direct to the hospital out of sight of observers or other patients.[42] A young VAD nurse, Claire Tisdall, later recalled the shame associated with these tragic victims. She was collecting a group of patients from an ambulance train when another train appeared unexpectedly. The second train was totally closed up, with all the windows barred and shut. 'What's this ambulance coming in?' she asked an orderly. 'Haven't we done the train?' 'No, sister,' came the reply. 'This is for the asylum; it's for the hopeless mental cases.' The young nurse later wrote, 'I didn't look. They'd gone off their heads. I didn't want to see them. There was nothing you could do and they were going to a special place. They were terrible.'[43]

When the War Office enquiry gathered evidence in 1922, several witnesses confirmed that in some units shell shock had been contagious and had resulted in the loss of many men, whereas in others the incidence had been low or even non-existent. General Horne specifically put the high inci-dence of shell shock within a unit down to 'poor morale', which was 'due to the failure in training to the proper state of efficiency'. In addition to the ordinary sources of morale, such as 'justice of cause, pride in regiment, and supremacy in the use of weapons, there is one thing that assists morale very highly – good food and good care taken of the men.' As Horne concluded, it was not only 'bad morale but physical conditions that influence shell shock'.[44]

Sir John Goodwin, an army surgeon all his professional life, had ended the war as Director General of the Army Medical Service. He observed that if there were two battal-ions side by side in the line and one suffered from a high incidence of shell shock and the other did not, then he 'would look to the officers to see what their influence was with the men and how they were looking after them; how close they were to their men and how much they believed in their men'. He would also 'look to the medical officers as to how much they knew and understood their men'. A poorly led

battalion was more likely to suffer from shell shock than a
well officered one because 'in a well-trained, well disciplined
regiment, no matter what the stress is, there is comparatively
little in the way of breaking down.'[45]

Colonel Fuller, who had been a director of training at the
War Office in the first half of the war, claimed that a 'bad
battalion' with a high incidence of shell shock cases could
'infect' a good battalion alongside. He cited a case where a
Guards battalion at Ypres refused to go into the line beside
another battalion, saying they would prefer to take over that
section of front line themselves rather than 'go in with that
battalion.' Fuller regarded an excess of shell shock cases as
a 'discredit to the regiment', a sign that 'the commanding
officer and officers of the regiment have not established in
the men a sufficiently high morale' and that there was 'something wrong with the training and organisation of the unit'.[46]

It was this linkage with overall unit morale that made shell
shock, in the eyes of such officers, so dangerous. The cohe-
siveness of a fighting unit was dependent upon maintaining
a high level of morale. Being so contagious, shell shock and
war neuroses could easily bring a whole battalion down. If
this got out of hand, it would be fatal to the fighting spirit of
the whole army in France.

It became clear that there was no single cause for the
variety of symptoms described under the catch-all term
shell shock. That was why the military was so puzzled as to
how to respond. Many men felt a considerable sense of guilt
and shame in being diagnosed, that they had let their peers
down. This added to victims' anxiety. Some men would hold
on as long as they could, but the accumulated stress would
finally get to them.

One anonymous officer who gave evidence to the War
Office Committee of Enquiry into Shell Shock in 1922 had
a remarkable story to tell. According to his account, it was

'the repression of fear, the repression of the emotion of being afraid' that made 'the greatest tax' upon his 'mind and strength'. This officer survived the almost total destruction of his battalion three times in heavy fighting during the Second Battle of Ypres in the spring of 1915 but nevertheless carried on. Then he was in a dugout that received a direct hit. Three of his comrades were killed but miraculously he was left visibly unhurt, although his hair was slightly singed. He busied himself burying his comrades and once more carried on. Then he was buried by debris for several hours after a shell landed nearby. Having been dug out, he still continued in command. It was only when the quarter-master brought up a string of horses, not knowing that all the officers for whom they were intended had been killed, that the witness said, 'I broke down and cried.' He cried continuously and was helpless for a week. It was the cumulative effect of the horrors of trench life that did for this officer. Although in this case, remarkably, he returned to his unit six months later and fought on the Somme, saying of this experience, 'I had no difficulty whatever in controlling myself – not the slightest.'[47]

In its typical way, the army decided to categorise cases in order to make the problem easier to deal with. Victims who had suffered from the explosive shock of a nearby shell were classed as 'Shell Shock W' (for Wounded). This reflected the original sense of the term shell shock as some sort of physical injury sustained by proximity to an explosion. Men in this category were acknowledged as being wounded as a result of enemy action.

Those who were thought to be suffering from some sort of hysterical response, a temporary breakdown of the nerves, were classed as 'Shell Shock S' (for Sick). The two words 'Wounded' and 'Sick' signified a lot more in First World War army parlance than might be obvious today. Being classified

'Wounded' meant that a man had been injured as a consequence of enemy action. He could wear the blue outfit of a
wounded soldier and would be accorded the dignity which
came with this. A man might be regarded as 'Sick', however,
if he had dysentery or flu, something from which he could
recover quickly with the correct treatment. When it came to
Shell Shock 'S' this category included men who had congen-
ital nervous instability or had become unstable or hysterical
in the trenches. They were not classed as genuine wounded
caused by enemy action and were to be returned to their
units after a period of rest, relaxation, regular meals and
time in a positive environment. The final category, usually
reserved for officers, was Neurasthenia, caused by prolonged
mental strain and manifested by symptoms of chronic
fatigue, headache and the loss of appetite.

This classification did little to improve the already confused situation. The distinction between 'W' and 'S' was
artificial and arbitrary. It did however succeed in helping to
make the problem look less serious by allowing a large proportion of men suffering from shell shock to be categorised
as simply being 'sick'. Just like those suffering from flu, they
would not then be listed as battle casualties.

No doubt the RAMC congratulated itself that at a stroke
it had made shell shock seem less acute. However, obvious
inequities soon became apparent. Men suffering from a genuine breakdown were not always given proper treatment.
Others with similar or even less serious symptoms were
evacuated to England. Charles Samuel Myers noted the case
of an artillery officer whose battery came under heavy bombardment, during which he tried to keep going for as long
as possible before eventually collapsing. He was diagnosed
with a nervous complaint and categorised 'Shell Shock S'.
Two of his men who had given way as soon as the bombardment began were categorised as 'Shell Shock W', having

suffered according to regulations from the 'effects of an explosion due to enemy action'. According to Myers, the two soldiers, 'by giving way immediately, became entitled to rank as wounded and wear a wound stripe'; the officer, by bravely carrying on, was sent down stigmatised as 'nervous'.[48] This was clearly inappropriate and unfair; nor would it help solve the core problem of how to treat nervous diseases.

This was the rather confused state of affairs within the army concerning shell shock by early 1916. But while the doctors argued about causes and treatments and senior officers looked on in puzzlement, large numbers of men suffering from war neurosis kept coming in from the front. Care arrangements had been simple at first. A specialist treatment unit dedicated to shell shock victims had been set up at the base hospital at Etaples. At first no more than a small wooden hut segregated from the rest of the hospital, in late 1915 and early 1916 the unit had been overwhelmed with patients and had increased in size to over 2,000 beds. By this time the battalions of the New Army were arriving in France in large numbers. Senior officers were already sceptical about the training of these new battalions and the quality of the men recruited into them, most of whom had no military background. But over the next few months the army would face the biggest test it had confronted in its history. In the summer of 1916, with the beginning of the Battle of the Somme, what had been a frustrating and troublesome medical issue was suddenly transformed into a problem that threatened to undermine the fighting capability of the entire British army.

4

The Big Push

By the beginning of 1915, the German military leadership had decided that the war on the Western Front was to be primarily defensive. They turned east, sensing an opportunity to defeat the Russian armies and to knock Russia, the weakest of the Allied nations, out of the war. The German armies achieved real success here, forcing the Russians out of most of Poland and overrunning Serbia. Meanwhile, along the Western Front the German army entrenched and created formidable defensive lines, protected by acres of barbed wire with huge concrete redoubts in support, and hiding well-situated machine gun posts backed by seemingly endless batteries of artillery.

Trench warfare in the west became a matter of routine. 'Stand To' came just before dawn, when officers would rally their men and put them on alert. Then followed several hours of lookout and sentry duties, broken up sometimes by hot meals and the constant need to repair and rebuild trench walls and fortifications or pump water out of them. The men would doze along the fire step or in any cubbyhole they could find; officers slept in dugouts domesticated by photos, books and parcels from home. On most 'quiet' days there was still shelling and the constant need to avoid exposing oneself to sniper fire. But often the only action came at night when raiding parties went out, trying to claim dominance over No Man's Land and to capture prisoners or gather intelligence from the other side. Most battalions were on the front lines for anything between three days and a week; in the reserve or second line for about the same length of time, often endlessly carrying supplies back and forth along congested communication trenches; then, for a similar period, on rest duty, behind the lines and usually out of artillery range. Here, the men would go through more training or drilling and usually enjoy some sport; officers would attend courses, catch up with administration and spend evenings in the local estaminet or bar. Then, back up to the front and the routine would start all over again.

In addition to the regular rhythms of trench life, the Western Front saw considerable offensive activity during 1915. In March, the British attacked at Neuve Chapelle; the French, two months later, in the Artois region. Initially the Neuve Chapelle attack was successful and British soldiers breached the German lines. But, as so often happened in the First World War, the reserves were inadequate and were not sent forward in time. The Germans were able to counter-attack and reoccupy the lost ground. More seriously, the assault at Neuve Chapelle revealed a huge shortage in the supply of shells. No one in the War Office had anticipated a war of this sort in which such vast numbers of shells would be required. The armaments factories were far too small and were not producing anything like enough.

All the nations at war experienced similar crises in 1915, but Britain's was particularly severe. It tipped the political balance between those who thought the war would be short, that Britain's liability would be limited and the country could ride it out on the strength of its navy, and those who held that the nation needed to mobilise far more efficiently to fight a

modern, industrial European war. The crisis led to the fall of
Herbert Asquith's Liberal government. It was replaced by a
Coalition government of Liberals and Conservatives, although
Asquith remained Prime Minister. The fall of the government
also led to the creation of a Ministry of Munitions to coordi-
nate and dramatically improve the supply of ammunition. At
its head was David Lloyd George – the radical Welshman who
firmly believed the war needed to be run on more professional
and scientific grounds.

In April 1915, the Germans carried out their one offensive
act in the west that year when they launched an attack at
Ypres to try to break through to the Channel ports. It was
in this attack that they first resorted to chemical warfare,
releasing chlorine gas from canisters, letting it drift in the
wind over the Allied lines. The gas attack caused panic and
created a gaping hole in the French lines, but the Canadians
on the flank were able to hold on and this time it was the
Germans who failed to follow up swiftly enough. The Allies
loudly condemned the Germans for their use of chemical
warfare as an abhorrence, a violation of the terms of war;
and then quickly prepared to use gas themselves. Haig soon
convinced himself that this was a war-winning technology
and wrote to the War Office saying that decisive results 'are
almost certain to be obtained' by the 'very extensive' use of
gas.[1]

In September the French and British made their first
full-scale joint attack – the French in Champagne and the
British at the industrial town of Loos. Six British divisions
participated; again the initial assault was successful but the
British bungled the use of their reserves. British casualties
amounted to 59,000 men, including more than 2,000 officers.
The French bore the brunt of the fighting, but their attacks
also failed with the loss of 191,000 men. And these dreadful
losses resulted in negligible territorial gain.

At the end of 1915, therefore, both sides looked at a war that had gone way beyond anything they had anticipated in 1914. All the armies had suffered massive casualties. The French had lost 1.43 million killed and wounded by the end of 1915. The Germans had lost more than half a million men on the Western Front alone in what was supposed to be a quiet year. The British, meanwhile, had tried to bypass the war in France and Belgium by attacking Germany's ally Turkey, first by a naval campaign in the Dardanelles then with an amphibious landing on the Gallipoli peninsula supported by French, Australian and New Zealand forces. Amphibious operations are some of the most complex an army can attempt, and British forces were not up to it. The command and planning was appalling. The Turks were well led and fought ferociously. The result was further stalemate and dreadful loss of life, the number of British, Allied and ANZAC dead and wounded amounting to 132,000. All sides needed to consider new tactics for 1916.

At the beginning of December 1915, at a conference held at Chantilly, the Allied war leaders agreed on a joint attack in the early summer of 1916. The Russians would attack on the Eastern Front. The Italians, who had joined the war on the Allied side, would attack in the south, in the Alpine region. The French and British armies would attack on the Western Front. While the planners realised that none of these actions would be likely in themselves to bring a decisive breakthrough to victory, together they would put immense strain on the German army and its weaker ally, the Austro-Hungarians. It was a good strategy. And it was a case of 'combined thinking' long before this was common.

At the end of 1915 two key changes took place in the British army. First, Sir William Robertson was appointed Chief of the Imperial General Staff in London. Unusually for the British army, Robertson, known as 'Wuffy', had risen right through the ranks from private to field marshal. He had a reputation for plain speaking – and for dropping his aitches. A convinced advocate of the need to defeat Germany on the Western Front, he would bring renewed commitment to the importance of that theatre. Accordingly, the expedition to Gallipoli was ended and the troops were evacuated from the peninsula.

Second, of even greater significance, Sir John French had proved to be inadequate as commander-in-chief of the British army in France. He was unable to cope emotionally with the level of losses the army was experiencing and had fouled up the use of the reserves at Loos. Prime Minister Asquith, after some manoeuvring, demanded French's resignation. He was replaced by Sir Douglas Haig, then aged fifty-five. Having worked closely in the mid-1900s with the reforming Secretary of War Richard Haldane and rewritten the army regulations for the infantry, also playing a key role in the creation of a new War Staff to oversee the planning of strategy, Haig definitely belonged to the modernising wing of the British army. In August, he had gone to France as commander of I Corps – consisting of two divisions totalling around 40,000 men. His men had fought at Mons and on the Marne, and had heroically held the line in the First Battle of Ypres. At the end of 1914 he was promoted to commander of First Army – with up to fifteen divisions, or over 200,000 men. During 1916 he would take command of a little more than fifty divisions, or more than one million men and growing. Moreover, he had commanded the two major British assaults in 1915 at Neuve Chapelle and Loos. Of all British generals in 1916, Haig appeared well equipped to be commander-in-chief.

However, he suffered from being extremely inarticulate, almost shy, with strangers. He liked to surround himself with familiar figures he had known and worked with before – and this was not always the best way to bring out new ideas and strong leadership. He felt tongue-tied and awkward when he met the press, which he hated doing. In this way he was very unlike a general of the early twenty-first century, who has to be media savvy and good with soundbites, whether in messages to his men or to a waiting television reporter. But Haig possessed a strong faith. This was partly a religious conviction – he was a committed member of the Church of Scotland and much enjoyed Sunday sermons – but he also had great confidence in his own abilities. At times this manifested itself as a conviction that he had a divine mission, was acting as God's instrument, and that God was on his side. However, he was no fanatic. He was thorough, intelligent and utterly professional. He recognised the complexity of the machine he led and realised the importance of getting the logistics right. And, for his day, he looked the part of a great general: tall, blue eyed and moustachioed, always immaculately turned out, determined and strong. Most people thought he had the necessary qualities to command an army in the field that was struggling to understand a type of warfare that had never been expected.

When Haig took command of the British Expeditionary Force in France, Kitchener gave him written instructions on his role. His 'governing policy' was to achieve 'the closest co-operation between the French and British as a united army'. However, Kitchener further wrote, 'I wish you distinctly to understand that your command is an independent one, and that you will in no case come under the orders of any Allied General further than the necessary co-operation with our Allies referred to.'[2] Thus, from the start, Haig's brief suggested the complexity of his command. He was to co-operate fully with the French as part of a coalition army but to act as an independent force and not to follow French orders. Meanwhile he also had political masters in London who had not signed up to the idea that warfare on the

Western Front should continue when it seemed to bring no clear victories but generated endless and long casualty lists. Sir William Robertson warned Haig in January about 'deplorable' politicians who 'fight and intrigue against each other ... They have no idea how war must be conducted in order to be given a reasonable chance of success, and they will not allow professionals a free hand.'[3] In carrying out his command, Haig would have to balance pressure not only from Paris but also from Westminster.

The military strategy that Haig inherited was for all the Allied armies to grow their strengths and to prepare for a combined offensive in the east, south and west, to take place in the middle of 1916. Haig showed initial enthusiasm for attacking around Ypres in Flanders, where the capture of the Belgian channel ports of Ostend and Zeebrugge offered a clear strategic objective. But in discussion with General Joffre, the French commander-in-chief, he was persuaded to take part in a joint Anglo-French offensive at the point where the British and French lines met in Picardy along the river Somme. Haig agreed to this strategy in mid-February. Like all the best military plans, however, it was soon blown aside by events.

On 21 February, the Germans launched a full-scale offensive against the French positions at Verdun. The German generals knew the French would not surrender the city, which had great symbolic significance for them as one of the fortress towns that had held out in the war against Prussia in 1870. An intense siege of Verdun began, the Germans amassing heavy artillery to fire on French lines that were then assaulted by storm troopers. None other than the Kaiser's son, Crown Prince Wilhelm, commanded the German Fifth Army at Verdun. General Philippe Pétain, in command of the French defences, brought up artillery and seemingly endless reserves of infantry. In the first three months of the battle, forty French divisions took part in the defence of Verdun. The determination of the French lived up to German expectations and their defiant catchphrase became '*Ils ne passeront pas*' (They shall not pass). By the end of March the French had suffered nearly 90,000 casualties. Field Marshal von Falkenhayn, Chief of the German War Staff, later said that he hoped the Battle of Verdun would 'bleed the French army white'.[4] He nearly succeeded in doing so.

In March, French commanders came back to the British, pleading with them to help relieve German pressure at Verdun. Haig ordered British divisions to take over twenty miles of the Western Front from the French so their troops could be sent to relieve Verdun. But as the butchery of the French forces continued, Joffre met with Haig at his headquarters on 26 May, and told him that French losses at Verdun would amount to 200,000 men by the end of the month. He asked when Haig would be ready to launch his offensive; between 1 July and 15 August, Haig replied. At the mere mention of the later date, according to Haig's diary, Joffre 'got very excited and shouted that "The French Army would cease to exist, if we did nothing till then."' Embarrassed by this 'outburst of excitement', Haig immediately agreed to launch the attack on 1 July or thereabouts.[5]

Instead of the offensive being a 50-50 joint venture, however, Haig now realised that he must bear the greater part of the attack. Joffre's initial plan had been for the French to attack on the Somme with thirty-nine divisions supported by 1,700 heavy guns. By the time the attack took place, this had been reduced to twelve divisions and 688 guns. For the first time, the British army would dominate a joint Anglo-French military enterprise. Soon the upcoming offensive would be widely referred to as 'the Big Push'.

The area selected for the great Anglo-French offensive was far from favourable. A low chalk ridge, known as the

Thiepval ridge, ran from north-west to south-east. The German front line ran along the west-facing slope of this ridge, incorporating a line of villages whose names would come to acquire iconic status in British military history – Serre, Beaumont-Hamel, Thiepval, Ovillers, Pozières, La Boiselle, Fricourt, Mametz. British troops were to attack up the slope of this ridge, where the Germans had not only dug a network of defensive trenches but also deep dugouts penetrating thirty feet and more into the chalk, most of them interconnected by tunnels and linked to more than one trench. Several were lit by electricity and some were even carpeted. The front was also defended by a series of formidable bunkers or redoubts, where well-protected machine guns were able to direct fire not only across No Man's Land itself, but down into the territory behind the British front line. At the north end, the small marshy valley of the Ancre river cut through the ridge, and further north still was a German salient protruding into the British line at the woods of Gommecourt.

To the south of the ridge was the valley of the Somme itself. Here the British line ended and the French line took over. The terrain here was flatter and much more favourable to the attacking force. The battlefield was dissected by a long straight road, Roman in origin, that ran from the small town of Albert, behind British lines, due north-east to Bapaume, well behind German lines. The full width of the battlefield from Gommecourt in the north to the Somme in the south was about fifteen miles, although the winding front line ran for about eighteen miles. Along the top and to the east of the ridge was a series of woods at Mametz, Delville and one known simply as High Wood.

Along the high ground, roughly two miles behind their front line, was the German second line, invisible from the British guns as it was on the eastern, reverse slope of the ridge. But this second line was almost as strong as the German front line, while, two or three miles further behind, German engineers had started to dig a third line. However formidable these defences might appear, not everything was stacked in favour of the defender. The German forward positions on the western slope of the chalk ridge were in full view of the Allied artillery and provided a clear target for barrage fire. And Falkenhayn had made it clear that any ground lost was to be recaptured immediately, requiring counter-attacks across heavily cratered and intensely con-tested ground which would lead to heavy casualties among German defenders to add to those of the Allied attackers.

Finally, although the Somme always receives much attention as a quintessentially British battle, it must not be forgotten that this was an Allied offensive in which French troops, although reduced in number from the initial plan, still played a substantial role in the southern sector of the battlefield. They were commanded by 65-year-old General Ferdinand Foch. Too young to have been involved in the defeat of 1871, Foch had gone into the artillery. He was an unusual, eccentric figure. A small, grey-haired man, he would speak and even shout in short sentences that some-times he did not finish, constantly gesticulating with his hands. But although his subordinates often mimicked his almost comic style, he was a highly competent general who had first taught at and then commanded the Ecole Supérieure de Guerre (the French Army Staff College) before the war. His academic mind had led him to think hard about the nature of industrial warfare. In the true French military tradition he believed wholeheartedly in the offensive spirit, but he realised this had to be supported by a superiority in materiel, most particularly in artillery pieces and ammunition. Trying to learn the lessons of 1914 and 1915, Foch had concluded that what was required was 'Lots of artillery, few infantry.'[6] He believed in delivering a series of hard punches against the enemy by using heavy artillery to prepare the way, before small numbers of mobile troops launched focused attacks at the enemy's weakest points.

Reporting to Foch was General Marie-Emile Fayolle. Like his boss, Fayolle was an artilleryman who had taught at the Ecole Supérieure de Guerre. He too believed in the powerful concentration of heavy artillery to clear the way for an infantry assault. He had been called out of retirement into the French army in August 1914 and had been given command of a brigade. He had risen rapidly and was now in command of Sixth Army, which adjoined the British where the two armies met at the Somme. A down to earth, calm and highly effective commander who today would be called 'a soldiers' general', he liked to walk in the front trenches and had frequently been under fire. Like Foch, Fayolle was quite clear about the nature of modern industrial warfare. He wrote in his diary that this was a war 'not merely between two armies but between two nations. It will continue as long as they have resources.'[7] Foch and Fayolle worked closely with the British units alongside them to the north, and their tactics would prove a great success in the early stage of the battle to come.

The lion's share of the British offensive on the Somme was fought by the Fourth Army. Its commander was Lieutenant-General Sir Henry Rawlinson, known to his friends as 'Rawly'. An infantryman who had gone from Eton and Sandhurst into the elite Coldstream Guards, he was fifty-two years of age in 1916. Most of his experience had been in colonial wars in India and Burma, Sudan and South Africa. At the beginning of the war he had commanded a division; in 1915 he was promoted to command a corps, and in early 1916 he was put in command of Fourth Army. As Haig's subordinate at Ypres, Neuve Chapelle and Loos, he had built up a good working relationship with his commanding officer. He had also developed his own view of how to conduct a modern battle in the trench warfare of the Western Front. He believed in attacking at the weakest point, capturing German lines and then defending them from counter-attack, a tactic he called 'bite and hold'. He described this simply: 'Bite off a piece of the enemy's line ... and hold it against counter-attack. The bite can be made without much loss, and if we choose the right place and make every preparation to put it quickly into a state of defence, there ought to be no difficulty in holding it against the enemy's counter-attacks, and inflicting on him at least twice the loss that we have suffered in making the bite.'[8] This was the classic justification of a battle of attrition. According to this approach, Rawlinson had no expectation of breakthrough, just a plan to draw in the enemy and exhaust him.

Haig had a different vision of the battle, although he was never clear or consistent. Sometimes he spoke of a breakthrough. But it is unlikely he believed wholeheartedly in such an outcome. Mostly he spoke of putting immense pressure on the German army and of relieving Verdun. His initial, very ambitious plan was for a short artillery bombardment to precede a surprise attack across a broad front to capture the German first line, as well as the second line along the reverse of the Thiepval ridge, on the first day. This involved the infantry advancing between two and three miles, depending upon the distance across No Man's Land. There would then follow an assault upon the German third position. This would open up the opportunity to use the cavalry to get behind (in the jargon of the day to 'roll up') the main German lines, to capture the town of Bapaume and then move north towards the city of Arras.

The cavalry were not the sabre-wielding Victorian force of popular imagination. In the era before tanks and armoured cars, they were the nearest to mobile troops any commander had. They could be used either as mounted riflemen or as shock troops to seize key points behind enemy lines and hold them until the infantry caught up – a little like airborne troops in the next war. As a former cavalryman, Haig was keen to use his preferred force, and he put three cavalry divisions under a separate commander, Lieutenant-General Sir Hubert Gough, known as 'Goughy'.

Gough, at forty-five, was the youngest of the senior commanders on the Somme – seven years younger than Rawlinson and ten years younger than Haig. He came from a well-known military family and his father, uncle and brother had all won VCs. He was Haig's protégé and his rise, from brigade commander at Mons in 1914, had been meteoric. He was now given command of what was called the Reserve Army, although without a full general's rank. The cavalry and two divisions of supporting infantry in this army were to wait until there was a big enough gap in the German lines to charge through and begin a period of mobile warfare that Haig was confident he could win.

Rawlinson was unhappy with Haig's plan, and in accordance with his 'bite and hold' doctrine argued that each of the German first and second lines should be taken separately. Time should be allowed for the enemy to weaken himself by counter-attacking before the next line was captured. Rawlinson knew the landscape well and was perhaps concerned by the thought of having to advance up the slope of the ridge.[9] He put great faith in the ability of the artillery to completely smash the German defences and destroy the barbed wire but, he contended, this would take time. In a paper on 19 April, he argued against Haig's plan for a short artillery bombardment because 'effective wire cutting cannot be carried out in five or six hours'. It would take, he said, 'at least three days ... for there is a very large amount of wire to be destroyed ... far more than was the case at Loos'. He argued for 'a long, accurate bombardment which will pulverise strong points one by one' and give the enemy 'no chance of sleep'; he would then be sure to 'break down under the strain'.[10] Rawlinson also argued that the effective range of the artillery – that is the range at which they could be certain of ensuring accurate fire – was a limiting factor. It was possible to fire accurately on the German first line, but not on their second until there was time to move the batteries and observers forward.

Haig and Rawlinson therefore had fundamentally different views about both objectives and tactics in the upcoming Big Push. Haig conceded several vital points to Rawlinson. He accepted the need for a long artillery bombardment and the pair agreed this should last five days. He also compromised over the capture of both first and second lines on the opening day. North of the Albert–Bapaume road, where the German second line was close to the first, the objective would be to capture both lines on the first day. South of the road, where the German second line was further back, the objective would be to seize only the first line. But the confusion in the overall purpose of the battle was never resolved. Was it to be a sudden, powerful and decisive thrust to bring the enemy to his knees, thus opening the way for a breakout that the cavalry were to exploit? Or a slow, artillery-led assault, line by line, grinding the enemy down, drawing in his reserves until his resistance broke?

Haig still believed that speed was of the essence. The lesson he had drawn from Loos was that it was necessary to rush reserves in quickly and that the decisive blow should create a gap in the German lines in the first couple of days. Rawlinson and Foch were believers in taking the advance stage by stage, redeploying one's artillery at every step. This difference of attitude continued until the very day of the offensive. As one historian has put it, was it to be 'bite and hold' or 'rush and hope'?[11]

It might be thought that such confusion over both the overall objective and the tactics needed to achieve it was strange, an indication that the army high command was dysfunctional. Certainly, Haig should have taken a firm grip on the situation but did not. He did not have the personality to overwhelm his subordinates. In addition, he had continually to react to French demands to advance the start of the offensive before he felt he was ready and to redefine the shape of the battle as the French commitment to it dwindled. Also, without raising impossible expectations, he had to 'talk up' the prospects of victory to the politicians at home. It was not until April that he received even lukewarm political support for the Somme offensive from the Cabinet's War Committee in London. Rawlinson, on the other hand, did not have complete confidence in the plan he was now to carry out, although he dutifully wrote, 'I have told DH I will carry out his plan with as much enthusiasm as if it were my own.'[12]

Despite the differences between Haig and Rawlinson, the commander-in-chief maintained his confidence in his army commander throughout and largely delegated the more detailed tactical planning to him. This was indeed how the British army functioned, by downwards delegation of tactical decision making. Rawlinson himself let corps and divisional commanders decide their detailed plans according to local circumstances. This was clearly sensible, as it encouraged initiative and the adaptation of plans for specific strengths and weaknesses in the field. However, it could also mean failure to work through the overall strategy consistently.

In addition to the main assault, Third Army was to organise a diversionary attack to the north. The commander of Third Army was General Sir Edmund Allenby, known as 'the Bull', another cavalryman and probably the only senior commander who was seen as a rival to Haig. He was ordered to attack at the woods of Gommecourt where a German salient protruded into the British line, and to make the preparations for the assault as obvious as possible in order to divert German forces from the main zone of the battle. Although not keen on the concept he ordered his relevant corps commander to make appropriate plans. He decided to use two Territorial divisions, one each from the Midlands and London, to attack on both sides of the wood. If successful they would meet up behind the enemy's lines and cut off the German salient.

The plan Haig and Rawlinson had argued over was then passed on to the six corps commanders who would partici-pate in the battle. Their staff officers worked on the detail and in turn passed on orders to the seventeen divisional commanders involved. Reconnaissance aircraft took tens of thousands of aerial photographs of the German trenches, enabling the production of photo mosaics and, from them, detailed maps of the German lines for distribution to the commanders. It was from aerial photos that interpreters were able to follow the construction of the German third line, four or five miles behind the front.[13] Each division was to attack on a front of approximately one mile with two brigades in the line and one in reserve.

Divisional staff officers began to plan for and amass the nec-essary resources. Huge supply dumps were set up to assemble shells, ammunition and every sort of munition. Workshops were built to service the guns, and stables constructed for thousands of horses. Reservoirs and water pipelines were installed. Vast supplies of food, clothing and equipment were gathered in depots – each division required 200 tons of sup-plies every day, equivalent to four trainloads. Hospitals, CCSs and field ambulance units were made ready. What today is called 'logistics' was then known as 'administration', and a great deal was needed to prepare for a First World War battle of this scale. And so the brigade staffs received detailed plans, which they passed down through the chain of command. One brigade commander was astonished to receive a document of 76 pages outlining the plan of attack to which divisional staff officers had added 365 supplementary instructions.[14] Eventually, each battalion commander was to receive dozens of pages of typed orders, along with photos and maps. To most of the officers involved it seemed that everything had been prepared for, that every detail had been considered and that never had plans been so well drawn up for an operation.

In June, however, there was yet another change of mind. The Russian offensive in the east, led by General Alexei Brusilov, proved against all expectations to be a great success. The Russians advanced across a vast front one hundred miles wide and smashed the Austro-Hungarian armies, forcing the Germans to come to the rescue of their allies. Meanwhile, German forces at Verdun, while having given the French a massive pounding, had themselves suffered great losses. By the end of June the French had lost just over 250,000 men; but by that time German casualties had reached 224,000. Haig's intelligence chief led him to believe that German forces in the west had been substantially reduced and that units were being withdrawn to shore up the Eastern Front. Having left Rawlinson to draw up detailed plans with his corps commanders for a slow, attritional offensive, Haig decided that perhaps a decisive breakthrough was possible in the west after all and issued a new set of orders only two weeks before the battle was due to commence. He ordered Rawlinson to make some of his day-one objectives more ambitious and to prepare to order the cavalry to break out towards Bapaume, about ten miles behind the German front line. Rawlinson was baffled by the last-minute changes but did what he could to implement them. It was yet another illustration of what have been called 'the ambiguities inherent in the British concept for the Somme'.[15]

Both commanders, however, were agreed on one point. The battalions of the New Army had arrived in massive numbers in France during late 1915 and early 1916. Haig was now in command of fifty divisions. Because nine of the seventeen divisions taking part in the assault were from Kitchener's New Army, the generals did not expect much of the assaulting infantry. Indeed, even the surviving regular and Territorial divisions were by now largely reinforced with battalions from the New Army, and their commanding officers were aware that they too were packed with novice soldiers. It has been estimated that 97 out of the 143 battalions destined to attack on the Somme – that is two-thirds of the attacking force – were made up of volunteers.[16] Haig and Rawlinson were in command of a citizen army whose men only eighteen months before had been clerks, railway workers, dockers, teachers, waiters or miners. They had received basic training but they had no experience of fighting or war.

Disdain for the New Army among officers of the regular army was still apparent. Haig wrote in his diary in March 1916, 'I have not got an army in France really, but a collection of divisions untrained for the field.'[17] Rawlinson wrote, 'The fact that a very large part of the troops to be engaged are new troops with little experience, and among whom the standard of discipline, leadership and tactical training of company commanders is not what obtained in our troops of a year ago ... [means that] disorganisation will appear more quickly.'[18]

Coping with a twelve-fold growth of Britain's army in the field brought a vast array of challenges. In terms of leadership, no one in the senior ranks had any previous experience of command at the level they were called upon to perform on

the Somme. Of the twenty-three divisional commanders in
the field, only three had even commanded a brigade before
the war.[19] To both Haig and Rawlinson, this was particularly
damaging when it came to the lower levels of command.
The public schoolboys from school corps, the university
men from the Officer Training Corps recruited as company
or platoon commanders lacked nothing in enthusiasm, but
there had been insufficient time for them to develop or learn
tactical skills. Haig noted during the Battle of Loos that the
army lacked 'junior officers with some tactical knowledge' to
take the right decisions at the right time.[20]

   Haig and Robertson's solution was simple. The attacking
force should not be asked to show any initiative or to do
anything tactically complex. When the barrage ended, on
command, they should climb up wooden ladders out of the
trenches and walk slowly, in straight lines, across No Man's
Land. Each man should be two or three yards from the men
on his right and his left. This way, if one man should waver,
the others would reassure him. The second wave should
follow the first, 50 to 100 yards behind, the third behind this,
with a fourth to follow. They should not run or charge at the
enemy line as this might break their formation, but should
walk forward at a steady pace. Both the German and French
armies were experimenting with the use of storm troops
to rush into the enemy lines within seconds of the barrage
ending. But this was thought to be too difficult for the men
of the New Army. Of course, some local commanders chose
to vary this plan, while others, like General Poulteney at III
Corps in the centre of the assault, kept to it rigidly. At a lower
level, some brigade commanders told their men to crawl into
No Man's Land and to shelter in craters or sunken roads
until the artillery ceased fire. They would then have less far
to walk before reaching the enemy front line. But this was to
be relatively rare.

On arriving at the German front line, the advancing infantry were told simply to jump into the enemy trench and, using bayonet, rifle or bombs, to flush out any traumatised survivors. They would then occupy the line and prepare to defend it from counter-attack, known as consolidating the line, waiting for the next unit to come up, leapfrog them and move on to the next objective. Fourth Army drew up a set of Tactical Orders specifically to make all this clear for inexperienced junior officers. Every company and battalion commander received a 31-page printed pamphlet outlining the spacing of the lines of attacking infantry, the number of waves ('four or more'), the need for 'a steady pace' not a rushed advance, how to consolidate trenches, and so on. A great deal was left out, for example how to respond to machine gun fire and how units should react to delays or hold-ups among adjoining battalions. Nor was there any suggestion that where an initial attack had failed because of heavy resistance, further attacks should be called off or, better still, redirected to a point at which resistance was less fierce. The result, according to the *Official History*, was that the 'plan of the battle was too rigid' with a 'uniform strength all along the front, although parts of it were obviously more difficult to deal with than others'.[21] This rigidity was the consequence of the senior commanders' belief that untrained troops could not be asked to show local initiative.

Moreover, each man was carrying a minimum of 66 lb (30 kg) of supplies. These were intended to last for up to two days, as resupplying men who had occupied the German lines was regarded as impossible in the first instance. Most men were therefore carrying a pack that included their personal kit, including a spare pair of socks, water bottles, a day's rations, two gas masks, a field dressing, 220 rounds of spare ammunition, two hand grenades (known after their inventor as Mills bombs), and an entrenching tool. Some also carried bombs for trench mortars, extra shovels or spare barbed wire to defend the captured trenches. The men with this additional equipment might have been carrying up to 85–90 lb (approx. 40 kg). With all this on their backs while holding their rifles with bayonets fixed, it was thought that most men could do no more than walk forward slowly in line.

Of course, it would only be possible to walk steadily across No Man's Land if the barbed wire had been destroyed, and the enemy strongpoints and machine gun nests totally pulverised. The five-day artillery barrage was eventually extended by heavy rain for two further days. Nearly 1,500 guns fired just over 1.6 million shells in this preliminary bombardment, ranging from trench mortars and 18-pounder field artillery pieces, through the 4.5-inch heavy guns right up to giant 15-inch howitzers. On average there was a gun every twenty-one yards along the entire front. They fired in continuous eighty-minute bursts on sections of the German line, then paused and after a couple of hours started up again on another section. For the first two days the gunners concentrated on destroying the barbed wire. Then they shelled the German lines and fortified strongpoints. Every night they fired on the communication lines to prevent supplies from being carried up. At times the shelling would pause and gas was released. Then the shelling would start up again. It was the heaviest bombardment carried out by British gunners so far in the war.[22]

There was complete confidence from the top down that the barrage would utterly destroy the German positions. At a conference of corps commanders, Rawlinson made it clear that '"nothing could exist at the conclusion of the bombardment in the area covered by it" and the infantry would only have to walk over and take possession.'[23] Most of those who witnessed this tremendous, relentless shelling of the enemy front line believed that nothing could survive it. Captain Cuthbert Lawson was a forward observation officer with the 29th Division near Beaumont-Hamel. He wrote: 'Armageddon has started today. I get a wonderful view from my observing station and in front of me and right and left there is nothing but bursting shells. It's a weird sight, not a living soul or beast, but countless puffs of smoke, from the white fleecy ball of the field gun shrapnel, to the dense greasy pall of the heavy howitzer high explosive.'[24]

Charlie Campbell May, an engineer before the war, had been among the first to join one of the Manchester Pals battalions. At twenty-seven he was now a captain and a company commander in the 22nd Battalion Manchester Regiment. On 29 June, he expressed in his diary the confidence so many men felt: 'We are all agog with expectancy, all quietly excited and strung to a pitch but unhesitatingly I record that our only anxiety is that we will do our job well. That is but natural. This is the greatest thing the battalion or any of us have ever been in.'[25]

In the last week of June, as the guns thundered, the roads behind the lines and the British communication trenches were packed with men moving slowly up towards the front. They were in good spirits, singing songs, cheering and waving every time they saw a camera. Divisional and brigade commanders came out to watch them pass by. One called out to a Leeds Pals battalion, 'Good luck men. There is not a German left in their trenches, our guns have blown them all to Hell.'[26]

Many of those about to go over the top wrote letters home that were only to be sent if the writer did not survive. One of these was later published in the press as a tribute. The officer, writing to his parents, began: 'I am about to take part in the biggest battle that has yet been fought in France, and one which ought to help to end the war very quickly. I never felt more confident or cheerful in my life before, and would not miss the attack for anything on earth. The men are in splendid form, and every officer and man is more happy and cheerful than I have ever seen them.' He continued on a more philosophical level, 'It is impossible to fear death out here when one is no longer an individual, but a member of a regiment and of an army. To be killed means nothing to me, and it is only you who suffer for it; you really pay the cost. I have been looking at the stars, and thinking what an immense distance they are away. What an insignificant thing the loss of, say, 40 years of life is compared with them!' He concluded, as many did, by writing, 'This letter is going to be posted if ... Lots of love, From your loving son.'[27]

On the evening of 30 June, in his headquarters at Querrieux, Rawlinson surveyed the situation in a document that recorded his thoughts on the eve of battle. He noted that he was in command of 519,324 men and 'the spirit of all ranks is splendid.' He recorded that 'The corps and divisional commanders are the best we have got ... All know their job.' He was pleased that the 'artillery work done during the bombardment, and the wire cutting, has been well done', and went on, 'The Russians are on the move ... The situation at Verdun is critical, and we cannot wait any longer if it is to be saved. So, the issues at stake in tomorrow's battle are as great, if not greater, than in any which has been fought during the war. What the actual results will be no one can foretell, but I feel pretty confident of success myself, though we shall only get it after heavy fighting.' The argument about whether the battle would lead to a breakthrough that could end the war, or would be just another stage in a long, continuing attritional conflict between nations, was resolved at least in Rawlinson's mind, but he was ready for any outcome. He concluded his survey, 'That the Boche will break, and that a *debacle* will supervene, I do not believe; but if that should take place I am quite ready to take full advantage of it.'[28]

A few miles away in Montreuil, at GHQ, Brigadier Charteris, Haig's intelligence chief, also reflected on what would happen on the following day. 'We do not expect any great advance, or any great place of arms to fall to us now. We are fighting primarily to wear down the German armies and the German nation ... The casualty list will be long. Wars cannot be won without casualties. I hope the people at home realise this.'[29]

That evening, in his advanced headquarters at Chateau Valvion north of Albert, Haig wrote in his diary, 'The weather report is favourable for tomorrow. With God's help, I feel hopeful for tomorrow. The men are in splendid spirits: several have said they have never before been so instructed and informed of the nature of the operation before them. The wire has never been so well cut, nor the artillery preparation so thorough. I have seen personally all the Corps Commanders and one and all are full of confidence.' In a separate letter to his wife, Dorothy, he spoke of his sense of divine mission: 'I feel that everything possible for us to do to achieve success has been done. But whether or not we are successful lies in the Power above. But *I do feel* that in my plans I have been helped by a Power that is not my own. So I am easy in my mind and ready to do my best whatever happens tomorrow.'[30]

The *Official History* summed up the view felt by many. 'No braver or more determined men ever faced an enemy than those ... who went "over the top" on the 1st July 1916. Never before had the ranks of a British Army on the field of battle contained the finest of all classes of the nation in physique, brains and education. And they were volunteers not conscripts. If ever a decisive victory was to be won it was to be expected now.'[31]

Dawn came up on Saturday 1 July with a light mist. But

as the sun rose higher it soon burned this away to leave a beautiful, clear, sunny summer day. Charlie May wrote a few words in his diary an hour or so after dawn that morning capturing the combination of optimism and anxiety that many must have felt. 'It is a glorious morning and is now broad daylight. We go over in two hours time. It seems a long time to wait and I think, whatever happens, we shall all feel relieved once the line is launched. No Man's Land is a tangled desert. Unless one could see it one cannot imagine what a terrible state of disorder it is in. Our gunnery has wrecked that and his front-line trenches all right. But we do not yet seem to have stopped his machine guns. These are pooping off all along our parapet as I write. I trust they will not claim too many of our lads before the day is over.'[32]

May was right to be concerned about the German machine gunners 'pooping off'. All the commanders had got it wrong. The barbed wire had not been cut. The German trenches had not been smashed. After building up to a final crescendo all along the 18-mile front, the British barrage lifted. The gunners readjusted their ranges and, according to the artillery plan, began firing on the second German line over the ridge. Then, at exactly 7.30, officers blew whistles and led their men over the parapets. In the German lines the sentries sounded the alarm and men came scampering up from their deep dugouts to man the machine gun posts and line the fire step. The result was a massacre. Within a couple of hours the cream of Kitchener's New Army were lying in No Man's Land. The Pals battalions, quick in their forming but long in their training and so high in their hopes, were cut down in minutes. When the tallies were done and the numbers counted there had been 57,470 casualties, of whom 19,240 had been killed or would die of their wounds.[33] It was the greatest loss ever sustained in a single day in the history of the British army. But this was not the end. It was just the beginning.

5

Epidemic

Gerald Brenan was an artillery observer in the 5th Battalion Gloucester Regiment, located opposite the village of Serre. In his observation post about a mile from the village, he watched events across No Man's Land on the morning of 1 July through a telescope as men tried to advance up the slope towards the German lines. Like everyone else, he had been enormously impressed with the Allied artillery bombardment 'that shook the air with its roar and sent up the earth on the German trenches in giant fountains. It seemed as if no human being could live through that.' From a relatively safe distance, Brenan saw what happened next.

'Our men climbed by short ladders onto the parapet and began to move forward, shoulder to shoulder, one line behind the other, across the rough ground. They went slowly because each of them carried a weight of 66 pounds. A moment later the German barrage fell on our trenches, and their machine guns began to rattle furiously. Clouds of blue and gray [sic] smoke from the bursting shells, mingling with a light ground mist, hid the general view, but through the gaps I could see the little antlike figures, some of them keeping on, others falling, creeping, writhing, lying still ... But as the hours passed, I could not see that any of them had reached the German support line, and later I knew why: the Boche machine gunners had come out of their deep dugouts and were mowing them down.'

To Brenan it was clear that after the slaughter caused by the German machine gunners, it was the artillery that had created mayhem in the British ranks. 'All this time the barrage that had fallen on our shallow assault trenches had continued and was churning up the earth all around ... Slowly the sun rose higher and higher in the sky, and the heat of that scorching day grew and grew; but I could detect no movement on the slope in front of me except that here and there a wounded man could be seen creeping toward a shell hole. It became clear that our attack had failed ... The pick of our young men, the first to volunteer for the war, were dead and on our corps front not a yard had been gained.'[1]

What had gone wrong? The artillery that had so impressed everyone had not been as effective as it appeared. A storm of steel had been fired at the wire and the German lines, but the British artillery was desperately lacking in heavy guns and the damage caused by the 18-pounder field artillery was far less severe than it looked. Furthermore, even the placement of a gun every few yards along the front did not achieve the concentrated fire that the commanders had intended. The shell fire was actually less intense than had been available along the shorter front at Loos. And there had been little counter-battery work, no real attempt to knock out the German artillery. Everything had been concentrated on destroying the wire and smashing the German trenches. The German batteries were able to return fire and were already ranged and sighted, in case of an attack, to shell No Man's Land and the assembly trenches. As soon as the Allied barrage lifted, the German guns, almost untouched, opened fire on the British assault, as Brenan witnessed.

Nor had the barbed wire been cut. To do this with artillery involved the use of high explosive (HE) shells, which exploded into a number of sharp-edged fragments. The French used this type of shell and had been successful in destroying the wire in front of their lines. However, the British artillery was short of HE so, instead, used shrapnel shells which exploded shattering hundreds of small round metal pellets into the vicinity. These were far less effective in cutting through barbed wire that in places was twelve belts thick. Officers looking out through periscopes from the front trenches could see that the wire had not been cut. According to Charles Howard of 93rd Brigade, not far from Serre, his corps commander had told the men that the wire was blown away and the troops could walk straight to the German lines, but 'we could see it standing strong and well'. Second Lieutenant Ian Grant of the 46th Division also reported that the artillery had failed to cut the wire as they 'were not competent to do it properly', and that as a consequence wire-cutting patrols had been sent out into No Man's Land.[2] But because they did not meet expectations, these reports were simply not believed higher up the command chain. Only optimistic reports were allowed to filter up the system. The higher up the command ladder one stood, the less realistic was one's understanding of the effectiveness of the bombardment.

There were also many defects in the shells fired. The expansion of Britain's munitions factories had been dramatic but quality control was still poor. The army of newly trained workers were working long hours, but too few of them were skilled and flaws were slipping through. The fuses of the 9.2-inch howitzer shells regularly fell out in flight and the battlefield was littered with dud shells which had landed and failed to explode. Minute fractures in the steel casing of some of the shells led to premature explosions, that is the shell would explode soon after leaving the barrel of the gun, which was very dangerous to the gunners. The 4.5-inch howitzer batteries suffered from so many 'prematures' that at one point they were known as 'suicide clubs'. The high explosive chemicals in some of the shells oozed out through their casings in the hot weather.[3] It was later estimated that somewhere between 25 and 30 per cent of shells failed to explode properly.[4]

The German trenches had certainly sustained damage, but the vast numbers of troops had sheltered safely in their deep dugouts, undamaged by shrapnel and secure against everything but a direct hit from one of the biggest shells. Trench raids had revealed the depth and sophistication of the dugouts but somehow this, also, had not been registered. On 5 June, troops of the 29th Division carrying out a raid had discovered deep dugouts between the German front line and the support line, with tunnels opening into both. General Rawlinson had been informed and had expressed his concern but had done nothing. In the days before the attack, according to a report based on the interrogation of German prisoners, 'the dugouts are still good. The men appear to remain in these dugouts all the time and are completely sheltered.'[5] Again, nothing had been done in response.

A week of almost continuous bombardment had certainly affected the nerves of the defending soldiers. Stephan Westmann, a medical officer in the German line just south of Beaumont-Hamel, recalled, 'For seven days and seven nights the ground shook under the constant impact of the shell fire. In between the bombardments the gas alarms would sound and we could hardly breathe ... The pounding never ceased. Fresh supplies of food or water never reached us.' Many men suffered from severe shell shock. Westmann again: 'Below the ground, men became hysterical and their fellow soldiers had to knock them out to prevent them from running pell-mell into the deadly hail of shell splinters. Even the rats panicked. They sought refuge in our flimsy shelters, running up the walls and we had to kill them with our spades.'[6]

The survivors were only too pleased to come up out of their dugouts when the barrage ended. Westmann recalled that the British 'did not expect anyone on the enemy side to have survived their bombardment. But German machine gunners and infantrymen still managed to crawl out of their holes. In fact, it was a kind of relief to be able to come up from the trenches, even into air filled with smoke and the smell of cordite. With inflamed and sunken eyes, faces blackened by fire and uniforms splashed with the blood of their wounded comrades, they started firing furiously. The intense German fire produced frightful losses on the British side … before the whole mighty offensive ground to a halt. The British and French generals had not yet learned that it was useless to send human beings to run against machine-gun and intense infantry fire, even after a week of so-called "softening up".'[7]

Lieutenant Fritz Cassel of the 99th German Infantry Reserve Regiment recalled the dugouts as being '18–20 steps deep, that is like two storeys of a house. They had an earth cover of circa 3 metres. Most were connected with each other or had two exits.' He vividly described the events of that morning: 'On 1 July at 7.30 am, the shout of the sentry "They are coming!" tore me out of apathy. Helmet, belt, rifle and up the steps. On the steps something white and bloody, in the trench a headless body. The sentry had lost his life by a last shell, before the fire was directed to the rear, and had paid for his vigilance with his life. We rushed to the ramparts, there they come, the khaki-yellows, they are not more than 20 metres in front of our trench. They advance fully equipped slowly to march across our bodies into the open country. But no boys, we are still alive, the moles come out of their holes. Machine gun fire tears holes in their rows. They discover our presence, throw themselves on the ground, now a mass of craters, welcomed by hand grenades and gun fire, and have now to sell their lives themselves.'[8]

In many sections of the front it came down to a race, when the barrage lifted, between the advancing British infantry crossing No Man's Land, and the German defenders surging up from their dugouts. Who would take charge of the parapet first? But the British soldiers had been told to walk and not run. As they slowly made their way towards the enemy lines the Germans rushed to man their machine gun posts and started to mow down the Tommies. On too many occasions, the British lost the crucial race to the German parapet. It has been argued that the British infantry lost the battle on 1 July only 'by a matter of seconds', that is the interval between the lifting of the artillery barrage and the arrival of the first wave at the German trenches.[9]

Surveying Fourth Army's progress on 1 July, from north to south, many Pals battalions from the industrial cities of northern Britain were gathered in the 31st Division outside Serre. The volunteers from Sheffield, Leeds, Bradford, Barnsley, Accrington and Hull went forward and tried to advance up the slope of the ridge against German lines they were told had been utterly destroyed. To their astonishment they proved to be very well defended. A German rifleman wrote of the Sheffield and Accrington Pals: 'When the English started advancing we were very worried; they looked as though they must overrun our trenches. We were very surprised to see them walking, we had never seen that before ... The officers were in front. I noticed one of them walking calmly, carrying a walking stick. When we started firing we just had to load and reload. They went down in their hundreds. You didn't have to aim, we just fired into them. If only they had run they would have overwhelmed us.'[10] The Pals battalions did not stand a chance. The division lost 3,600 men and achieved none of its objectives.

A little to the south, in the area around Beaumont-Hamel, the commander of VIII Corps, Lieutenant-General Sir Aylmer Hunter Weston, decided to detonate a huge mine under the German positions at the Hawthorn Redoubt at 7.20 a.m., before the time fixed for the general advance. This gave the Germans ten extra minutes to recover and prepare. It might not sound like much, but it was enough to allow German troops to race to the lip of the crater and set up their guns; they were waiting even before the British 29th Division began its assault. The 29th was a rare unit on 1 July as it was an experienced division that had fought hard at Gallipoli, where it had acquired a reputation as the 'Incomparable 29th'. But that did it little good on the first day of the Somme battle.

A secondary assault here, timed for 9.05, was bungled when the 29th divisional commander, Major-General Henry de Lisle, ordered in the reserves believing all the first objectives had been successfully taken. But they had not been. The men of the 1st Essex could not get through the congested communication trenches to their starting point. But no one told the 1st Battalion Newfoundland Regiment, who began the attack anyway and soon came under withering machine gun fire. Unfaltering, the men advanced until nearly 700 of them and all of their officers had been shot down. This sacrifice led to no meaningful gain and the 'Incomparables' lost a total of 5,240 officers and men, mostly in the two front-line assault brigades.

Further south, Lieutenant-General Sir William Pulteney, who led III Corps, adopted the 'steady pace' method of attack laid out in the Tactical Notes. This resulted in very high losses. The 8th Division, an old regular unit heavily reinforced with New Army battalions, had to cross a wide stretch of No Man's Land towards Ovillers village and took heavy casualties. Again, small groups of soldiers did succeed in reaching the German lines but were forced to withdraw later in the day. At La Boiselle, two huge mines were set off at 7.28 a.m., the bigger at Lochnagar leaving a crater ninety yards wide and seventy feet deep. Among the 34th Division, which tried to advance here, were some of the most famous Pals battalions including the Tyneside Irish, the Tyneside Scottish, the Edinburgh City Battalions and the Grimsby Chums. Many were shot down as they struggled across No Man's Land, although some small groups penetrated as far as the German second line before being wiped out. The 34th had the dubious record of suffering the highest casualty rate of the day, losing 6,380 men. Its commander, Major-General Edward Ingouville-Williams (known by the men, inevitably, as 'Inky Bill'), was himself killed by shell fire later in the month.

The popular view of 1 July is thus one of unmitigated disaster and sacrifice in which most Allied soldiers were shot down before they had even been able to cross No Man's Land. Certainly that is true of this section of the front, where VIII and III Corps made no progress at all and suffered immense losses. All along the front, the Germans had placed their machine gun nests in powerful positions that could rake the landscape with enfilade fire, usually from at least two different angles. Some reserve British battalions were shot down behind their own front line as they assembled and began to move up. Additionally, battalions that found the barbed wire had not been properly destroyed tended to bunch together at the gaps in the wire and proved a perfect mass target for the machine gunners. Many of the best-known images of the day came from this section of the front, where one of the two film cameramen who recorded events that day, Geoffrey Malins, was operating. He filmed the explosion of the mine at Hawthorn Redoubt and memorably captured on film a group of 1st Lancashire Fusiliers in a sunken road halfway out into No Man's Land, waiting for the order to go over the top. Their anxious, nervous faces reveal the fear and tension that tens of thousands of men must have felt that morning. When ordered to advance they were simply mown down by the German guns.[11]

However, the full story of 1 July was more variable and on parts of the front the day proved to be a resounding success. From the far north at the diversionary attack at Gommecourt, to the very south, British and French troops succeeded in many places in reaching the German front line, sometimes in force. But the Germans were swift to respond. Their artillery fire was brutally accurate and men who tried to consolidate the captured German positions soon found themselves cut off. Reinforcements were unable to get through the shell fire. Small pockets of brave troops held out for much of the day with dwindling supplies of water and ammunition. The men who had lodged themselves in the German lines and fought until being overcome, usually by late afternoon, won several VCs and even more MCs, often posthumously.

Nor did all units advance slowly in lines, walking across No Man's Land towards the German guns. Some battalions had been told to get out into No Man's Land and to wait, crouching perhaps 100 yards from the German front trench, until the barrage lifted at 7.30. In general, they tended to do much better than their fellows, as they were often able to reach the German trenches before the defenders had time to drag the heavy machine guns up from their dugouts and assemble them for firing.

Broadly speaking, the fighting on that first day of the Somme battle fell into a story of two halves. In the northern half above the old Roman road from Albert to Bapaume, it was a disaster. In the southern half, below the road and including the French positions, it was a great success, although one whose potential was not realised. In the far southern sector along the Somme valley, the French Sixth

Army under General Fayolle performed brilliantly. The artillery bombardment had been far more concentrated and successful here than in the British sector. The heavy French howitzers had been well targeted and the 75mm field guns had used HE to successfully destroy the barbed wire and to strike accurately at the German positions. In the final hours of the barrage, trench mortars had poured down a hail of explosives on the enemy front lines. When the lightly equipped French infantry moved out of their trenches at 7.30 shouting '*Vive la France*,' they found precious little resistance. They advanced through the first German line and on to the second; before long they had reached the third. By mid-morning, the French XX Corps had taken most of their objectives and had captured 2,500 stunned and dejected prisoners. French losses had been slight. The Germans did not think the French could mount an offensive while the Battle of Verdun was draining so many of their men, so without doubt this part of the line was less well defended. Nevertheless, it was a triumph for French arms and a sign that many of the lessons both from 1915 and from Verdun had been learned.

To the immediate left of the French, the British units in XIII Corps under Lieutenant-General Walter Congreve VC were also successful that morning. Again, the barrage had been far more effective here and the Germans had withdrawn from parts of their front line, so badly had it been mauled. The Manchester and Liverpool Pals battalions advanced quickly across No Man's Land to capture their first objective, Dublin Trench, by 8.30. Next to them General Ivor Maxse's 18th Division was held up by one or two isolated but well-sited German machine gunners, who could sweep vast areas of the battle zone. However, they were eventually overwhelmed and by lunchtime British troops had captured the village of Montauban, which formed an important part of the German second line. German soldiers could be seen fleeing back towards their third line.

Further north, Lieutenant-General Henry Horne's XV Corps were coming up against much more determined resistance. Captain Charlie May, who had worried about the German machine guns 'pooping off' in the early morning, was killed as he led his company of Manchester volunteers towards a defensive line known as Danzig Alley. The villages of Mametz and Fricourt, meanwhile, were also proving tough nuts to crack. At Mametz a fortified machine gun post at a shrine in an old cemetery caused dreadful losses in two Devonshire battalions as they tried to advance across a section of No Man's Land about 650 yards wide. At Fricourt, the bombardment by the heavy 9.2-inch howitzers had failed to destroy the German defences as so many of the shells had been duds. The 10th West Yorkshires took the highest battalion casualties of the day, losing 22 officers and 688 men. By nightfall Mametz had fallen, but Fricourt still held out and losses had been considerable.

One of the problems in most First World War battles was that of communication between the front and rear, which ceased to exist the moment an assault began. After the subalterns blew their whistles and went over the top with their men, the fog of war descended. Heavy shelling filled the vast battlefield with smoke, so that line of sight, where it existed at all, was always unreliable. For similar reasons, the use of flags or rockets to signal the position of troops was rarely effective. There were no portable radios available in the First World War and while telephone lines could be laid out, the intense shelling usually destroyed cables as quickly as they were laid. In one day alone at Verdun, ninety miles of cables were needed to repair broken telephone lines.

The situation was similar on the shell-pocked battlefields of the Somme. Aircraft observers could provide useful information, but sometimes they misinterpreted what they were seeing. Also, it was difficult to get reports back quickly enough to those who needed to know. Often the only reliable form of communication was through the use of runners. But these men had to cross open ground and traverse packed communication trenches. It could take hours for a runner to get a message back four or five miles to headquarters, by which time the information was likely to be well out of date. The further back from the front the information had to travel, the longer it took for those in command to receive it, and the less accurate it was by the time it arrived. As far as their commanding officers were concerned, when the infantry advanced they passed out of sight and out of communication into an unknown space. First World War battles were hence often said to be 'platoon commanders' battles': they were the only officers who could influence the course of events once the whistles had been blown and battle had commenced. It meant that the use of reserves was nearly always delayed, with fatal consequences for the outcome of the battle; or the reverse, that attacks were continued when they had become quite pointless, leading to massive and unnecessary loss of life.

This was not the case in the southern sector on the afternoon of 1 July. Having carried out a recce of his front, General Congreve of XIII Corps, it seems, telephoned his commanding officer, General Rawlinson, to tell him that his men had achieved all their objectives and he believed there were no substantial enemy forces ahead of him. He told Rawlinson that he had a reserve infantry division and the 2nd Indian Cavalry Division available and asked if he could deploy them and try for a breakthrough. However, according to Rawlinson's plan, the main thrust that day was to come further north, and Congreve's advance in the south was a holding operation to cover the flank. Rawlinson, an infantry man, never had much faith in the use of the cavalry, and denied Congreve permission to deploy his reserves. He was simply too inflexible, unwilling to adapt his plan only a few hours into the assault. Ironically, in front of Congreve's troops, the Germans could only muster a few scratch reserves and were busy marshalling cooks and clerks to provide a makeshift defence.[12]

Of course, it can never be known what would have happened if the cavalry had gone in and got behind the German positions. But there was certainly a possibility of capturing some ground at the southern end of the Thiepval ridge, an area that would be fought over bitterly and with massive loss of life in the following weeks and months. Rawlinson appears to have made a disastrous decision in not exploiting the opportunities in the south.

The German army had displayed its experience and superiority in many ways during the course of the long and bitter fighting on 1 July. It had selected the better ground for defence and had positioned its nests of machine guns and concrete fortresses accordingly. Its communications were far better, especially with the firing of flares by the infantry to signal to the artillery where a barrage was needed. And the artillery was more accurate, and was consequently able completely to cut off groups of British troops that had lodged themselves in German lines or strongholds. The German leadership reacted swiftly to events on a changing battlefield, calling in reserves, shoring up defences, improvising where needed and striking back in force when the opportunity appeared. But more than anything, despite seven days and nights of horrific bombardment, the German infantryman still fought with determination and courage when called upon to do so. The real victor of that day was the German soldier.

On the other hand, the heroes of 1 July were the British

infantrymen who, believing what they had been told about the destruction of the barbed wire and the enemy trenches, went forward willingly and enthusiastically. Never in history had such optimism as that of Fourth Army, packed as it was with Pals battalions and volunteers for the Territorials, come up against such a cruel reality. Today, the horror of that day looks very much like a massacre of the innocents.

The fighting on the Somme that began on 1 July was to last for 140 days. It was the most intense and long-running battle the British army had ever engaged in. By comparison, the Battle of Waterloo was over in less than a day. The Battle of Loos in September 1915, the biggest the British had so far been involved in since the start of the war, had lasted just twelve fighting days. Although the German machine guns had inflicted many of the casualties in the first hours of the attack from 7.30 on the morning of 1 July, it was the artillery that then started to inflict its dreadful carnage and a vast number of casualties after that opening morning were from the intense artillery barrages.

From day one of the Battle of the Somme there was a massive increase in the incidence of shell shock. Assessing the numbers of those affected is immensely difficult from the available evidence, which does not distinguish between different categories of wounds. And the categories to which shell shock victims were assigned, Shell Shock 'W', Shell Shock 'S' and Neurasthenic, were only sometimes included in the lists of wounded. For example, the *Official History of the Medical Services* records that there were 16,138 battle casualties in France from shell shock in the months July to December 1916, over four times more than in the previous six months; and more than ten times greater than in the six months from July to December 1915. Although this gives an indication of the rate of increase in the incidence of shell shock, it does not convey anything like the real numbers involved; it only includes Shell Shock 'W' and not Shell Shock 'S', nor does it include all of those diagnosed with Neurasthenia. The total number of cases of shell shock was more likely to be in the region of 53–63,000.[13] Shell shock was transformed from a disease into an epidemic almost overnight.

The *Official Medical History* notes that the two principal factors that contributed to the cause of nervous disorders were 'prolonged fighting and heavy bombardment', and that 'the type of warfare practised during the Somme battles of 1916 provided ideal conditions for the development of these disorders.' Artillery duels between British and German gunners 'frequently lasted several hours or days, and during this period of waiting the nerves of all were kept on edge. Then after the attack came the reckoning of the losses amongst comrades.' After a short respite, the whole process would be repeated again. 'Little by little men became worn down by such experience'. Before long, dozens and then hundreds of men started to suffer from their nerves, 'a gradual change would be noticed in the demeanour and behaviour of the patient, and he would eventually reach hospital with the report that he was "quite useless in the line."' The *Official Medical History* notes that other men would be faced 'with an experience of inexpressible horror' and that this would cause a complete and sudden breakdown of their self-control. 'Such men have said afterwards, "It made me feel I had lost my senses."'[14]

The *Official Histories* of the First World War were researched and written in the decades following the war not by independent historians but by senior military figures. The authors usually understated problems and tended to be moderate in their views or criticisms, when they expressed them at all. However, the two authors of the *Official Medical History* did not mince their words when it came to shell shock, nor did they attempt to play down the scale of the problem. The *Official*

Medical History freely admitted that 'nervous disorders' now 'assumed importance as a cause of wastage' and that from the first days of the Somme the problem 'became acute'. It went on, 'In the first few weeks [of the battle] several thousand soldiers were rapidly passed out of the battle zone on account of nervous disorders, and many of them were evacuated to England.'[15]

However, the first problem to engulf the medical services from 1 July was the treatment of the conventionally wounded. There had been much detailed preparation for the Big Push and hospitals had been cleared to cope with the anticipated casualties. By the beginning of July, Fourth Army had fourteen Casualty Clearing Stations at its disposal. Each CCS was effectively a small hospital a few miles behind the front, out of range of the enemy's artillery, and each could accommodate between 500 and 1,600 wounded men. There would be a minimum of ten medical officers in a CCS, supported by orderlies and a few female nurses. This was as far forward as the army allowed women during the war. The CCSs included several wards for different types of patient, modern operating theatres, a laboratory, X-ray machines and a full medical supply depot. They were usually located at central points near road junctions or the siding of a railway line. Some were made up of large buildings requisitioned for the purpose; others existed in rows of marquees and temporary wooden huts laid out across green fields.

Before July, the RAMC had made preparations to evacuate up to 10,000 men per day. Six motor ambulance convoys and three fully equipped ambulance trains were on standby. But in the first days the scale of the casualties overwhelmed the regimental aid posts, the field ambulance units and Casualty Clearing Stations. More than 38,000 wounded men required treatment on 1 July alone. The front-line aid posts and dressing stations were the first to be inundated. Private Frank Ridsdale of the 89th Field Ambulance captured in his diary the chaotic scenes at his aid post: 'First wounded arrived 8am very busy, wounded coming in by hundreds, the road to the hospital like the way to a football match, a pathetic sight, the men lined up 4 deep to be dressed ... working all night, terrible wounds – doing dressings in a dug out by the aid of a candle. Very tired ... terrible bombardment all night shaking the place, never to be forgotten night.'[16]

By the end of the day, the field ambulance units had admitted 14,672 casualties and of these a little more than half, 7,764, had reached the CCSs. This was itself a remarkable achievement. But not even half of the wounded were yet accounted for and thousands of wounded men were in regimental aid posts or, worse, still stuck out in No Man's Land, where it was impossible for stretcher bearers to reach them. Many wounded men lay in the mud and the water-filled craters for several days. One poor man of the 56th (London) Division at Gommecourt lay in No Man's Land for fourteen days before being brought in. Miraculously his wounds did not turn septic and he survived. On the evening of 1 July and over several subsequent days, local truces were agreed with the German troops to allow stretcher bearers to go out and bring in the wounded. Captain Carden Roe, MO with the 1st Royal Irish Fusiliers, described a truce as late as lunchtime on 5 July when a 'large Red Cross flag' was raised above the parapet of the British trench. When after a few minutes the Germans had fired no shots, 'two MOs stood up on the parapet beside the flag. Still the enemy held their fire. The two officers then advanced across No Man's Land with the flag. A mass of curious heads appeared above the German parapet and a German MO and some orderlies came out to meet ours. The officers of both sides stiffened to a ceremonious salute. The Germans carried our wounded from near their wire to the middle of No Man's Land and handed them over to our bearers. This great work of humanity went on until all the wounded were collected. Then, again, the officers saluted. Not a word had been exchanged all afternoon.'[17] As in many such cases on the Somme, the truce had been respected but there had been no fraternisation.

By the evening of the first day of the offensive, the whole medical system – but most especially the CCSs – were suffering from 'acute congestion'.[18] This was exacerbated by a foul-up with the deployment of the ambulance trains. Only one of those allocated had arrived. Through the night thousands more men were brought in for medical care. By early morning of 2 July, a single CCS at Gézaincourt, in the northern sector where the casualties had been particularly bad and which had a narrow-gauge railway link to the front, had received 5,346 casualties. It had been constructed to cope with 1,000 wounded. The overloading of the CCSs was reaching crisis point.

Howard Somervell was a surgeon at Vecquemont at the southern end of the battlefield. One of the largest CCSs, it had prepared for 1600 patients. Somervell was twenty-six and had only qualified as a doctor at University College Hospital, London, in 1915. On qualifying he volunteered and went straight into the RAMC. On 1 July, Vecquemont like the other CCSs was quickly overwhelmed. A line of ambulances a mile long waited patiently to unload their human cargoes. Somervell wrote that 'the whole area of the camp, a field of five or six acres, was completely covered with stretchers placed side to side, each with its suffering or dying man upon it.' Working in one of the four operating theatres, Somervell had the chance occasionally to take 'a brief look around to select from the thousands of patients those few fortunate ones whose life or limbs we had time to save. It was a terrible business.' He learned quickly the principles of military surgery: 'we rapidly surveyed them to see who was most worthwhile saving. Abdominal cases and others requiring long operations simply had to be left to die. Saving life by amputation, which can be done in a few minutes, or saving of limbs by the wide opening of wounds, had to be thought of first.' Writing nearly twenty years later, Somervell recalled, 'Even now I am haunted by the touching look of the young, bright, anxious eyes, as we passed along the rows of sufferers. Hardly ever did any of them say a word, except to ask for water or relief from pain. I don't remember any single man in all those thousands who even suggested that we should save him and not the fellow next to him ... There, all around us, lying maimed and battered and dying, was the flower of Britain's youth – a terrible sight if ever there was one, yet full of courage and unselfishness and beauty.'[19]

On 2 July, the head of Medical Services in France, Lieutenant-General Sir Arthur Sloggett, ordered the immediate dispatch of extra doctors and surgeons from the quiet sectors further north in order to carry out more urgent operations, and he hastened the arrival of three more ambulance trains. By the end of that day, the CCSs had received 14,416 wounded men. By now, the evacuation of wounded from the CCSs to the base hospitals was at last working more efficiently and 11,299 men were taken back by train, motor convoy or barge. By 3 July, the operating theatres in the CCSs had dealt with roughly 10 per cent of patients, double the usual percentage. By this time, the numbers of wounded being moved on from the CCSs actually exceeded the number of new patients arriving. From 3 to 6 July, as more and more casualties were gathered into the system, just over 30,000 wounded were evacuated by hospital ship back to Britain.[20] Crowds gathered at Victoria and at Charing Cross stations to cheer the wounded as trains bearing the men offloaded their sad cases for distribution to hospitals around London. The RAMC had finally caught up with the colossal tragedy of 1 July.

With battalions scattered in various places along the front, with so many men stuck in No Man's Land and with such dreadful losses among officers, it took some time to calculate the full extent of the numbers of dead and wounded on the first day. Even by 3 July, Rawlinson believed the total was not much more than 14,000, less than one-quarter of the actual figure. On that day, he concluded, 'I do not think that the percentage of losses is excessive.'[21] However, as the battle continued and the full scale of the losses on 1 July became apparent, the nature of the wounds that were reported began to change. The machine gun battle on the morning of 1 July became the artillery war that predominated for the rest of the conflict. The losses began to average 2,500 per day and remained at that level for the next twenty weeks. And the incidence of shell shock victims shot up. With this, the higher echelons of the army became increasingly worried.

Commanders firmly believed that shell shock was contagious, that steady, reliable men would be upset by nervy men; that soldiers with symptoms of hysteria would infect the troops around them. They were also concerned that men would see shell shock as an easy way of getting out of the army, the old fear that malingering would increase. As one historian has written, 'commanders feared that an epidemic of hysteria would sweep the army.'[22] With the casualty lists growing, army commanders became concerned to reduce what was now called 'wastage', that is the loss of men who had not suffered physical wounds. If a modern industrial war inevitably led to high rates of injuries from bullets and shell fragments, other forms of 'wastage' must be kept to a minimum.

The Times, like all the major national newspapers, filled its columns with long lists of the dead and wounded. And it had a special category for 'Wounded – Shell Shock'. As this section grew longer it was apparent within days of the start of the Somme battle that, as the paper recorded on 18 July, there was 'an extraordinarily high percentage of cases of shell shock among our casualties'.[23]

Affecting as it did the morale of a fighting unit, the spread of shell shock had the potential to reduce the ability of the British army to maintain its fighting spirit. But as shell shock was seen as contagious, would it merely spread between small groups of men? Or, much more threateningly as it seemed to the army high command, if the situation got out of hand could it conceivably affect entire front-line battalions? If this were allowed to happen the entire fighting spirit of the citizen army, made up as it was of so many volunteers, might be undermined. Commanders would have to take action to prevent this.

6

'No More'

The Pals battalion officially designated as the 11th Battalion The Border Regiment, and recruited from the market towns, mines and agricultural estates of Westmorland and Cumberland by the eccentric Earl of Lonsdale, had begun training in Carlisle, Kendal and Workington, finally coming together to train as a single unit at a racecourse outside Carlisle. Its commanding officer, Lieutenant-Colonel Percy Machell, was a true professional and cared deeply for the welfare of his men. Without an adjutant and with hardly any experienced officers alongside him, he struggled at first, but slowly the situation began to improve. A small group of officers were appointed, including a competent adjutant. Most of the rest were young men from university OTCs. Alongside Machell, only two other officers (out of thirty-one) had any pre-war military experience. An elderly regimental sergeant-major from the Indian army, RSM Cowie, was brought out of retirement and strove to install some marching discipline in the new recruits.

By March 1915 the battalion was at full strength. Khaki uniforms now began to come through and when the first proper rifles were assigned to the battalion, it at last began to look like a military unit. But its training still consisted mostly of route marching, drilling and physical fitness. None of the officers had any experience whatsoever of trench warfare.

On a grey, damp day in May the battalion marched out of Carlisle watched by crowds who lined the roads up to four or five deep. It was a proud moment both for the town and the battalion. Training continued first in Yorkshire and then on Salisbury Plain in Wiltshire. Everywhere, the fit, smart recruits with the nickname of the 'Lonsdale' battalion made a good impression. When they left their Command in Wiltshire they received a message from the commanding officer who said he was 'confident that wherever you go you will sustain the credit of the Western Command ... He will watch your military career with great interest.' On 23 November the battalion sailed from Folkestone to Boulogne. Fourteen months after the first men had volunteered, the Lonsdales finally arrived in France.

The battalion travelled by train and on foot to Albert near the Somme. It was allocated a section of the front recently taken over from the French, and which was at the time very much a quiet sector. The battalion was assigned to the 97th Brigade, led by Brigadier J.B. Jardine, a cavalryman who had been in the 5th Lancers; the brigade formed part of the 32nd Division, a unit made up almost entirely of New Army battalions recruited in the north of England and Scotland, under the command of Major-General Sir William Henry Rycroft.

In December the Lonsdales had their first taste of the trenches. They found them in a dreadful condition. The second-in-command, Major Diggle, noted, 'The trenches we had first to take over were very bad ... In many places there were no duck-boards and in consequence, the mud and water was four or five feet deep.' The men were kept busy rebuilding the parapets and shoring up the sides with sandbags. Machell wrote, 'The men are excellent ... I am quite delighted with them. They are not foolish at all, just sensible, and do their job without the smallest fuss, though the hardships for them are damnable ... I have nothing to complain of at all. I am working day and night.'[1]

As winter turned into spring, the Lonsdales settled into trench routine, rotating with the 2nd Battalion The King's Own Yorkshire Light Infantry (KOYLI), and two Pals battalions of the Highland Light Infantry, the 16th 'Glasgow Boys Brigade' and the 17th 'Glasgow Commercials'. They would spend seven days in the forward trench, seven days in support, another seven days at the front and then seven days in reserve. Although this was a quiet sector it could easily flare up, and any action the Lonsdales took was met by a reaction from the Germans. At one point a night patrol spotted a trench battery being installed in the German lines. The shelling of the location on the following day led to heavy counter-fire from the German artillery. Slowly, the casualties began to grow in number, with young officers forming a high proportion of those lost. Once again, in March, Machell noted that he was 'getting short of officers'. But, as commanding officer, he was always industrious in his duties. Diggle wrote: 'For the first six months there was never a night that the CO did not go around the trenches. Not a casual walk round, but four or five hours out. I took the other part of the night. But he was a man of 53, and he did not sleep in the day ... The CO put system and organisation into everything he came in contact with ... protection first, then rest, and then work ... We had the name of being the best Infantry Battalion in France, among any of those who had anything to do with us.' At the end of May, Machell was mentioned in dispatches – as was the whole battalion – 'for consistent good work', a high accolade.[2]

That same month, the brigade was moved to the Authuille Sector, opposite a German stronghold bristling with machine guns, protruding into the British lines, and known as the Leipzig Redoubt or Salient. The whole brigade must have been aware of growing preparations for the Big Push, although of course they did not know exactly where and when it was to come. With the division wanting more information about an enemy machine gun nest about forty yards behind the front line, known as the Bull's Eye, along with details of the units occupying the German lines, the Lonsdales were ordered to carry out a raid on the German trenches. The call went out for volunteers, and four officers and 82 men were selected from those who came forward. A young officer named Lieutenant Barnes was put in command and for three weeks he trained the men nightly a few miles behind the front, where the layout of the enemy trenches taken from aerial photographs had been exactly replicated. Under the keen eyes of the CO, the volunteers carefully rehearsed every aspect of the raid.

On the night of 5 June, the British artillery laid down a barrage on the salient and the Bull's Eye. The men in the raiding party crawled into No Man's Land, and as the barrage lifted they blew up the remains of the barbed wire with high explosive Bangalore torpedoes before leaping into the German trenches. The men were in the enemy lines for about ten minutes. They captured eleven prisoners from around the Bull's Eye and killed about twenty-five other German defenders. On the call to withdraw, they moved slowly back across No Man's Land but, responding quickly, the German artillery began to fill the area with shell fire. Many men were hit as they withdrew, including Lieutenant Barnes. In total six men were killed and seventeen wounded. Barnes's body was later found just twenty yards from the safety of the British trenches.

The raid was regarded as a success and compliments poured in from brigade and division headquarters. Both Haig and Rawlinson were keen on trench raids like this.

They thought it kept up the aggressive spirit of the men, obtained useful information about enemy dispositions and, most importantly, helped to sustain morale. In fact, at battalion level, such raids were very unpopular. They were thought to be wasteful of life; the Lonsdales' raid on the Bull's Eye had cost them many good men including one of their best young officers.

Nevertheless, in June, trench raids up and down the Somme sector were ordered nightly and during the week-long bombardment at the end of the month the troops carried out several raids each night. Many lost their lives and when unwelcome information came back, like the fact that the shelling had failed to cut the barbed wire or that the Germans were surviving in their deep and extensive dugouts, it was ignored or regarded as an exaggeration. In the case of the Lonsdale raid, it was concluded after interrogation of the German prisoners that they were 'poor specimen Saxons' belonging to the 99th Reserve Regiment. An officer in the 31st Division later wrote that orders 'to carry out raids were most unpopular and were at the same time costly in personnel and besides was not good for the morale of the men'.[3]

As the Lonsdales endured several months of transfers into and out of the front, so they began to suffer from another of the characteristic problems of trench life. Unusually for an MO working with a battalion in a busy regimental aid post, Lieutenant George Notman Kirkwood of the 11th Borders kept scrupulous records of every patient he dealt with. Kirkwood was a Scot who had studied medicine and surgery at Glasgow University, qualifying in 1905. According to the Medical Directory he practised in Penrith in 1907 and 1908, and over the following two years at the Cumberland Infirmary in Carlisle. In 1910 he emigrated to the Cape Colony in South Africa, where he seems to have continued working as a doctor. But in 1915, Kirkwood returned to Britain to serve his country and was commissioned a lieutenant in the RAMC. In October he was appointed MO to the Lonsdales. He seems to have been popular in the battalion, and like many MOs soon became a well-known and respected figure.

The battalion's war diary listed every casualty suffered by the Lonsdales as the battalion got to grips with life on the Western Front. By 6 February 1916, when they had been in the trenches for six weeks, nine men had been wounded and two killed, and it was now that Kirkwood listed his first man as wounded with shell shock. Four days later, after a heavy bombardment along the front, a second victim of shell shock was recorded. Three weeks on, after shelling had blown in a dugout, burying three men, a third man was noted as suffering from shell shock. Over the next few months Kirkwood listed more cases. The numbers were not high, although as a proportion of all wounded they totalled about 17 per cent.[4]

When the seven-day artillery bombardment began at the end of June, the German batteries repeatedly fired back into the British lines. On 25 June, the enemy retaliation was described as being 'very heavy during the afternoon'; one man was wounded and two were listed as suffering from shell shock. The following day, two men were killed in the German shelling and thirty more were wounded; on this day alone nine were diagnosed with shell shock. It's difficult to know how to interpret these numbers. It is possible that such an incidence of battle trauma was typical of all units rotating in and out of the front line, although many MOs did not itemise shell shock cases separately from the other wounded. By comparison, the war diaries of the 6th and 8th Battalions of the Border Regiment recorded no cases of shell shock (although that does not mean they did not have any). The war diary of the 7th Battalion listed cases in some months and not in others, probably depending upon the officer keeping the diary for the month. In December 1915, when the 7th was in Ypres, its War Diary listed eighty-nine officers and men as wounded, six of whom (approximately 7 per cent) were listed as having shell shock.

It is possible that Kirkwood had a particular interest in shell shock and in the emotional traumas suffered by the men for whom he was responsible. It is not clear from the surviving documents whether he was more likely to list a man as having shell shock than any other MO, or whether the Lonsdales did actually suffer a higher incidence than other battalions. The evidence is not conclusive either way. And although the Lonsdales were suffering cases of shell shock, the incidence was not much higher than the average across the rest of the British army in the first six months of 1916.[5]

On 21 June, Machell received his orders for the Big Push. The 32nd Division and the 36th (Ulster) Division to its left, the two front-line divisions of X Corps, faced one of the most formidable sections of the German line. In front of the 32nd was the Leipzig Redoubt, the salient where the Lonsdales had carried out their raid a few weeks before. The German front was not one line of trenches but many, ascending a ridge from the lower ground known as Nab Valley. The westward-facing line of the redoubt was packed with machine gun nests, sited so that each was able to cover a wide trajectory with enfilade fire. They could not only fire across No Man's Land and into the British trenches but behind the lines as well, where a series of small woods offered the only cover available. A little further north, at a spur of the ridge that ran along the whole front, was Thiepval. The village was by now little more than piles of rubble where houses, a church and a chateau had once stood. But the Germans had set up many machine gun emplacements in the cellars of these buildings, often linked by tunnels. From this high position, on the western edge of the ridge, the machine guns could fire north and south. Behind these front lines, on the reverse slope of the ridge, were a further series of strongholds, running from the Schwaben Redoubt to Mouquet Farm in the south. They too were well constructed with impressively strong defences.

On the right flank of the X Corps front, 97th Brigade faced the Leipzig Redoubt along a front of about half a mile. The 17th Highland Light Infantry was to storm the redoubt at 7.30 a.m. The stretch of No Man's Land to the west of the salient was relatively narrow at 200 yards; that to the south and east was much wider at about 600 yards, and was swept by machine guns from the east where on a small incline along the slope of the Nab Valley the Germans had built yet another fortified emplacement called the Nord Werk.

As this stretch of No Man's Land was swept by fire from the salient to the north and enfilade fire from the stronghold to the east it was decided there would be no assault at this point. Having successfully assaulted the Leipzig salient from the west, the plan was for the occupiers to move along the German trenches bombing their dugouts as they progressed into the southern edge of the salient. They would then expel or capture the defenders and consolidate this section of line as well.

Machell and the Lonsdales were to wait in reserve behind the main British front line. Their orders were that at 8.30 they were to move forward, leapfrog across the Highlanders who would have occupied the German front lines, and advance on their second line at Mouquet Farm, a total distance of about a mile and a half. This they were to capture and consolidate, reinforcing it with machine guns that would be sent up from the brigade's heavy machine gun company.

The day before the assault, Machell issued his own orders

to the battalion. They began, 'The GOC [32nd] Division expects us to take Mouquet Farm and to keep it. I told the General that he could rely on the Lonsdales to carry out his orders.' Machell then gave precise information about the deployment of each of his four companies. In his succinct style he wrote, 'All not hit *must* push on. *Must* do our job. If all goes well, I stay proper place.' Battalion commanders had been told to remain in the rear in order to keep in command of events. Machell continued, 'if goes badly, I come up and see it through.' Machell went from company to company, making sure that every officer and NCO knew what he had to do. Just as in the successful raid three weeks before, he wanted everyone to know exactly what was expected of them. Mouquet Farm should be in the hands of the Lonsdales by noon.

The artillery bombardment at this section of the front, as elsewhere, looked impressive but did not deliver what the infantry hoped and needed. None of the principal machine gun emplacements had been hit, and the rubble at Thiepval provided ideal opportunities to hide the machine guns when they were brought out. A battery of two Royal Artillery 9.2-inch howitzers, some of the heaviest guns, were damaged by a 'premature' shell explosion which put both guns entirely out of action. And the bombardment again failed to inflict sufficient damage on the barbed wire, which continued to prove a major obstacle. On the morning of the attack, the gunners had strict instructions to follow a precise time-table, lifting the barrage backwards from the front line to the second line, and then further back still as the day progressed. Their orders were that this could not be changed other than by a senior divisional staff officer. When the barrage got way ahead of the advancing troops, there was no way of bringing it back and concentrating shell fire on the deadly machine gun positions in the first line.

On the evening of 30 June, each man received 220 rounds of ammunition, a waterproof sheet, two sandbags for filling, two full water bottles, his rations for a day and a one-pound tin of meat and biscuits. At 10 p.m., exactly on schedule, the Lonsdales filed into Authuille Wood, where they occupied newly dug assembly trenches about 400 yards behind the front line. They deployed perfectly and despite the barrage and counter-fire raging around them, did not suffer a single casualty. Morale was high and the men were doubtless looking forward to showing the enemy what the Lonsdales could do. The moment they had awaited for a year and a half was fast approaching.

Brigadier Jardine decided to position his assault troops well out into No Man's Land in the minutes before the barrage was to lift at 7.30. As an observer attached to the Japanese army in the Russo-Japanese War, he had noted how close the Japanese pushed their assault troops under the cover of the artillery barrage before assaulting the enemy lines. Elsewhere along the front, officers who decided to push men forward into No Man's Land were advised to position them no more than 100 yards from the enemy line. Jardine decided to move his two battalions of the Highland Light Infantry to within about thirty to forty yards of the German line. When he had suggested this as a tactic to Rawlinson in person his idea had been ignored, but in this instance it proved a brilliant success. At precisely 7.30, as the barrage lifted to the rear German lines, the Pals of the 17th Highlanders charged forward the few yards into the German trenches and, as the *Official History* put it, 'in one well organised rush overran the front of the Leipzig salient'.[6] They captured dozens of prisoners who were still in their deep dugouts, overcoming within just a few minutes one of the strongest points on the German front line.

Without delay, the Highlanders, supported by the men

coming up from the 2nd KOYLI and the 16th Highland Battalion, moved on to cross the 150 yards to the next German line, known as the Hindenburg Trench. But now they were exposed to machine gun fire from both sides and began to suffer heavy losses. Meanwhile the defenders had fully recovered after the lifting of the barrage, and those attackers who tried to bomb their way through to the southern edge of the salient came up against stiff resistance. At this point, Jardine intervened and, against standing orders, instructed the artillery to ignore their prearranged schedule and to pull their fire back to the trenches his men were now trying to assault. As a consequence the battlefield filled with smoke and explosions as the artillery rained its fire on the Hindenburg Trench and the groups of British infantry withdrew to the Leipzig Redoubt.

At exactly 8.30, in accordance with the timetable, the Lonsdales prepared to move out from their trenches in Authuille Wood. In the smoke and dust, Machell was unable to see clearly the situation ahead of him. But, having received no further orders or update from brigade headquarters, he assumed the enemy positions had been captured and all was going according to plan. The Lonsdales now had a complex manoeuvre to achieve. They had to move from the wood to the north until they were behind the lines from which the Highlanders had launched their assault, and then wheel to their right and march east across an area of the front no more than 100 yards wide into the section of the Leipzig salient, which was now occupied. There were no communication trenches for them to use, so they had to move across open land. The men emerged from the cover of the wood in what was called a 'blob' formation, with each half-platoon of about twenty men advancing in columns two wide, slightly to the side of the column in front. The men were in excellent spirits and as they moved out there were reports that they were

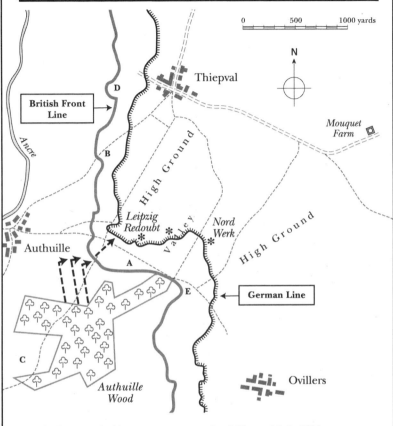

Attack by 11th Borders, The Lonsdales, on 1 July, 1916

0   500   1000 yards

N

British Front Line

Ancre

D

B

Thiepval

Mouquet Farm

High Ground

Leipzig Redoubt

Valley

Nord Werk

High Ground

Authuille

A

E

German Line

C

Authuille Wood

Ovillers

* German machine guns not captured at 8.30 a.m. 1 July, 1916

---▶ Route of 11 Borders

A to **B** – the front to be attacked by 97th Brigade led by two Highland Light Infantry battalions at 7.30 a.m.

C – 97th Brigade Headquarters

D to **E** – the front covered by 32nd Division of X Corps

Line to the north of **D** to be attacked by 36th (Ulster) Division of X Corps

A to **E** – area where there would be no attack because No Man's Land too well defended by enfilade fire

Line to south of **E** to be attacked by 8th Division of III Corps cheering loudly and had begun to sing the hunting song 'John Peel', a known favourite of the Earl of Lonsdale.

What followed was nothing less than a massacre. The German machine-gunners positioned to their east in the Nord Werk at the head of Nab Valley spotted the battalion on the move and opened fire. The machine guns were more than a mile away but were perfectly situated to hit their enemy with enfilade fire, as so many German guns were. The Lonsdales also came under intense fire from the machine guns of the southern edge of the Leipzig salient, which had not yet been captured. The first wave of the battalion, B Company, was almost entirely wiped out. Without flinching, the next wave, C Company, moved out from their trenches in the wood and scores of men were again cut down. A few moments later the third wave prepared to move forward. At least some men now were reaching the old front line from which the Highlanders had advanced. But Machell was growing increasingly concerned. In accordance with his message the day before he decided he had to go forward with his men. He leapt up from the front line to lead the third wave. As he emerged from his trench he was immediately hit in the head by a machine gun bullet. He was probably dead by the time he hit the ground. The shocked adjutant stopped to look at Machell's body and was hit too. The men, however, relentlessly continued to move forward. Some got through from the old front line and joined the Highlanders in the captured positions at the Leipzig Redoubt. But there were very few of them.

Later in the day, some of the survivors reassembled in Authuille Wood. A roll call was held. The battalion had suffered one of the highest casualty rates of that dreadful day, losing 490 men and 25 officers out of a total of about 850. One hundred and eleven were killed; 385 wounded; 19 were missing. Not only the commanding officer of the battalion, but the second in command, the adjutant and every one of the company commanders had been killed or wounded. Only six officers were still alive.

It is, of course, impossible to know what Machell was thinking when he leapt up to lead the third wave, whether he thought he could make a difference or whether he simply wanted to do as he had always done, to lead by example and act as an inspiration to others. Certainly the men had shown extraordinary courage and bravery in their determination to keep moving forward under fire, but their effort had been entirely futile. They had contributed nothing to the day's advance. Nearly all the casualties had been taken in a hail of machine gun bullets in ten to twenty minutes. The husbands, fathers and brothers of families across Westmorland and Cumberland now lay in the mud of Authuille. As the regimental history later recorded, 'Men could do no more.'[7]

There were not many witnesses to tell the story of what had happened. Lance Corporal F. Allan was one of the few and he later recalled the events: 'I was a field clerk with Colonel Machell and the adjutant. The previous day the CO had said "If things go badly, I'll come up and see it through" ... ' On the morning of the attack at 8.30, 'The Colonel was fidgeting and watching the progress of his men and eventually decided to go and lead them on himself but as soon as he left the trench he was shot through the head and killed. Then the adjutant was severely wounded as he leant over the colonel's body. The CO's batman, his bugler and two runners were all killed but I was only knocked over by a shell and stunned.'[8]

The loss of such a popular figure as Lieutenant-Colonel Machell was a bitter blow not only to the battalion but to the whole community from which it had been raised. *The Times* carried a short tribute on 10 July in which Machell was described as a 'fine specimen of an English gentleman

[who] gained the sympathy and respect of all alike'. The *Daily Telegraph* printed another tribute a few days later by a survivor who said Machell was 'shot through the head whilst springing forward with a company of his battalion into one of the most murderous concentrations of cross fire ever seen in this war. He went forward at a slightly earlier stage than he might otherwise have done, because he with one of his companies saw how the triple barrages of machine-gun fire was mowing down the lines of their comrades in front. To all present his gallant death was precisely what each day of his life had been to every one who was privileged to know this unfailing strong man – a vividly compelling inspiration to duty, an undeniable stimulus to effort ... It was the Machell stamp which he placed on every member of that brave band of Border men that has won them honours wherever they have been, in England or in France. He asked no more of any man than he himself gave always.'9

A few days later the *Penrith Observer* carried an account of the attack in colloquial dialogue by an anonymous private recovering in a local hospital, having been wounded in three places during the assault, in his arm, hand and thigh. The man described the starting point of the assault as 'a kind of a bit of a wood'. He was in the third wave, with 'B and C Company being afore us ... But ye'd have wondered to hear how loud our lads were singin' and cheerin' like at a football match.' He recalled seeing the earlier waves 'movin' in the open like past the wood, till the fire caught 'em and they went down like grass'. His story continued, 'I was beside the Colonel in the front trench. I carried bombs, ye see. The Colonel, he was to go wi' the last line after us. But when he sees the second line cut down that way an' our time come "Oh Damn!" says he, just like that, and he ups an' over the parapet. "Come on, me lads" he said, like that, and just at that moment he was hit and kind o' staggered, an' afore I could get till him like, he fell backward into the trench again.'

Despite the loss of their commanding officer, the remaining men of the third wave still advanced: 'We was singing "John Peel" like mad ... an' cheerin' to raise the dead.' As he moved forward the private received the first of his wounds. 'I got a bullet in me arm – here – directly I was on the parapet, an' somehow it made me stumble like an' I fell. But I went on as quick as I could; me havin' the bombs ye see ... It was just past their first line I got this one in me hand. A bit sore like that was, more'n the arm, but not so very bad but what I got on all right till this third one got me here [in the thigh] an' I fell in a shell hole near the second line.' The private had clearly succeeded in reaching the Leipzig Redoubt, where he handed over his bombs to a lance corporal. He remained in the shell hole, bleeding and no doubt in great pain, until the evening when stretcher bearers came out, although the Germans continued to rake the area with machine gun fire. The private crawled into a trench and across a pile of German corpses, finally reaching British lines. 'T'was after dark I got in and the MO at the dressing station he said, "You're all right, lad," he said like that, an' he gave me a cigarette.'

Stretcher bearers took the wounded man back to a field ambulance unit from where he was evacuated. But despite the destruction of his battalion, his final comment to the local paper was one of defiance: 'Our boys is all right. Ye see they're not afeared o' the Boche – not at all.'[10]

For the rest of X Corps, the day proved typical of 1 July 1916. There were some tremendous achievements but they were frittered away during the long and bloody day. For the men of the 36th Division, almost entirely Protestants who had been members of the Ulster Volunteer Force before the war, the advance fell on the anniversary of the Battle of the Boyne, the great victory of William of Orange over the Catholic armies in 1690.[11] They went forward with unbounded optimism and confidence, shouting the old Ulster battle cries 'No surrender' and 'Remember 1690'. Some even wore Orange sashes and ribbons as they advanced, 'with rifles sloped and the sun glistening on their fixed bayonets, keeping their alignment and distance as well as if on ceremonial parade, unfaltering, unwavering'.[12] Despite heavy losses, the 9th and 10th Royal Inniskilling Fusiliers, supported by the Royal Irish Rifles, broke right through the German front line and got into the Schwaben Redoubt on the reverse side of the ridge, in the German second line. Four hundred prisoners were taken. The Inniskillings almost fought their way to the next redoubt but being by now, ironically, ahead of schedule, they were shelled by the British artillery, who did not know they were so far forward. As a consequence the Ulstermen got no further than the Schwaben Redoubt, although it soon proved impossible to reinforce those who were holding the position because of intense and accurate enemy shelling. Once again, groups of attackers who had penetrated the enemy lines found themselves isolated from reinforcements and steadily running out of water and ammunition.

Meanwhile, the 32nd Division had little success beyond the Highlanders' capture of the western edge of the Leipzig Redoubt. The ruins of Thiepval proved impossible to storm. The machine guns hidden in the cellars of the ruins swept the approach up the hill to the spur with deadly fire, causing tremendous losses. The situation was confused when an Allied pilot reported seeing what he thought were khaki uniforms moving about in the village, so the artillery were told to cease their bombardment. The corps and divisional commanders had no reliable information all day as to what was happening as the usual fog of war descended on the battlefield. Accordingly, the reserve division of X Corps, 49th Division, which could have made a real difference at either the Schwaben Redoubt or at the Leipzig salient, was instead broken up, separate battalions being dispatched to different parts of the front where they were too small to have an impact.

Intense fighting continued all day long and by afternoon the Germans were counter-attacking heavily, although their reserves were held up by British artillery fire. Of the Schwaben Redoubt, the German commander announced that it was a 'point of honour for the division to recapture this important point today'.[13] By late that evening they had overwhelmed the remnants of the Inniskilling Fusiliers and the Irish Rifles, who had tried desperately to hold on to the position but were now killed or forced to surrender. The commander of the 9th Battalion Royal Irish Rifles described the scene as a 'field of gore' where 'seven hundred dead and wounded lie around in perhaps a quarter of a mile square'.[14]

By the end of the day British forces had been pushed back everywhere and their only gain was the Leipzig Redoubt, rushed by the Highlanders in the first minutes of the battle. The 32nd Division had lost 3,949 men, including the Lonsdales; 36th Division had lost 5,104 men killed, wounded, missing and taken prisoner. But the glory of the attack on the Schwaben Redoubt would live on in Ulster history.

It took some time for the senior commanders to take stock of what had happened on the first day of the battle. Haig seems to have been the first to grasp that victory had been achieved in the south and that this was the area in which to press forward over the next few days. But once again he was at cross-purposes with Rawlinson who, still clinging to his 'bite and hold' strategy, hesitated for several days waiting for German counter-attacks. Haig failed to press Rawlinson into action and the time lost was critical. The German army had known an offensive was coming, but had been surprised by the scale of the assault and the width of the front under attack. Their losses had been severe. In the seven-day bombardment the Germans had suffered about 7,000 casualties, while about 10–12,000 men had been killed, wounded and taken prisoner on the first day.[15] Although German losses amounted to barely one-third of those sustained by the Allies, this was still serious, and on parts of the front the Germans were reeling. The woods along the southern tip of the Thiepval ridge, at Delville, Trones and Mametz, were almost empty of German troops and a determined attempt to seize them would have captured important parts of the German second line, saving tens of thousands of lives that would be lost trying to take them in the coming weeks.

However, Haig did make some changes at senior level. The commander of the 46th (Midland) Division, Major-General the Hon. Edward Montagu-Stuart-Wortley, had failed to press his attack at the very northern end of the battlefield in the diversionary action at Gommecourt. The other division involved in this action, the 56th (London) Division, having fought well but suffered heavy losses, had been supposed to meet up with the men of the 46th behind Gommecourt Wood, thereby cutting it off. But Montagu-Stuart-Wortley had called off his attacks in the afternoon when he realised they had been unsuccessful, leaving the Londoners of the 56th isolated and exposed. Haig called for a court of enquiry to investigate the failure, but before its conclusion he dismissed Montagu-Stuart-Wortley and sent him home in disgrace for failing to show the appropriate fighting spirit, a procedure known as 'degumming'. Even though, by calling off his attack, the general had saved the lives of many hundreds if not thousands of his men, Haig was making it absolutely clear that he would not allow units or commanders to fail to show the right fighting spirit.[16] Major-General Thomas Pilcher, commander of the 17th (Northern) Division, was also sent home in disgrace a few days later, accused of lacking initiative and drive, even though one of the division's battalions had suffered the highest casualty rate on 1 July. Montagu-Stuart-Wortley and Pilcher were not the last generals to be sent home in disgrace from the Somme, but their examples were there for all to see, just as Haig intended.

The other significant change Haig made was to split Fourth Army. He wanted to promote his protégé General Hubert Gough, whose Reserve Army had stood about during 1 July with nothing to do. In fact Rawlinson had stood down the reserves at lunchtime, just at the point when they could have made a real difference in the south. Haig wanted to bring Gough's aggressive spirit to bear on decision-making. So the two corps to the north of the Albert–Bapaume road were reassigned to Gough and his Reserve Army. The men of 32nd Division, including the Lonsdales, now had a new army commander, although very few of them would have been aware of this, or cared much if they had known. But his appointment would later prove to be critical for them.

For the 250-odd survivors in the Lonsdales, the days after the massacre of 1 July proved particularly gruelling. They were withdrawn from the front and put into the reserve line for a week. But there was not much rest to be had. The survivors were formed into two incomplete companies and placed under the command of two young second lieutenants, Ross and Welsh, who had not taken part in the failed assault. Both men had been in OTCs two years before. Captain Palmer from the 2nd KOYLI was given temporary command of the battalion. But effective leadership of the dazed survivors was now in the hands of a handful of NCOs.

For several days the men had to sort out the kit of those who had been killed and personal effects were sent to their families. Then they were told to carry rations up to the front-line troops. This was a slow, frustrating business, hampered by incessant German shelling of the communication

trenches. Most unpleasantly of all, the survivors had to dig
out the dead bodies of their own pals and those of other
units; according to a later report, they lived for several days
'in the atmosphere of decomposed bodies'.

No descriptions of this gruesome week by members of
the battalion have survived. But Gerald Brenan of the 5th
Gloucesters, who was put on similar duty at exactly the
same time, later recalled how ghastly it had been when he
'was brought face to face and in the most repellent way with
the consequences of the battle'. Brenan described the task
he was given: 'My platoon was detailed for a burying party.
The bodies of our men who had been mashed to pieces in the
assault trenches had been brought up by night on a trench
railway and bundled out onto the ground. Legs had broken
off from trunks, heads came off at a touch, and nauseous
liquids oozed out of the cavities. The stench was overpower-
ing. Our job was to cut off the identity disks and bury these
decomposing corpses in shallow trenches. After a few hours
of this the fear of death had so entered into me that if I had
been ordered to go over the top next morning I should not
have been able to.'[17]

On the evening of Saturday 8 July, the two half-compa-
nies of the Lonsdales were sent back to the front line. They
immediately came under shell fire from German artillery.
What happened next was later recorded in detail.[18] A few
hours after arriving back in the trenches, the MO, Lieutenant
George Kirkwood, diagnosed nine men with Shell Shock W.
On the following day, Sunday 9 July, the temporary battalion commander, Captain Palmer, who had not yet had time
to get to know his men, received an order from Brigadier
Jardine that there was to be a bombing assault that night on
the enemy trenches. The Lonsdales were to cross No Man's
Land and capture about 200 yards of German front line,
bombing the Germans out of their dugouts. This was part of

an attempt to 'straighten the line' in advance of a new offensive in a few days' time. Palmer instructed Second Lieutenant
Ross to organise his troops for an assault.

For the men, whose memories of witnessing the slaughter
of the bulk of the battalion were only a week old, it was the
last straw. At 9 p.m. on Sunday evening, three and a half
hours before the raid was due to take place, several men went
to see Ross and told him they were sick 'as their nerves could
not stand'. They asked to see the MO. Ross said, 'I thought
that if I allowed this all the men of the party would do the
same as their nerves were in the same condition. I therefore
refused the request.' This was reported back to Captain
Palmer, who expressed surprise: the young officers had earlier been confident that they could organise the men for an
attack. At 10.45 p.m., Palmer decided he should send for the
MO, and Lieutenant Kirkwood was dispatched from his aid
post into the forward trenches.

Kirkwood, who had been with the battalion since its
training days in England eight months before, knew the
men well and was a popular MO. On his way up to the
front through the communication trench, several men said
they wanted to see him, but he refused to stop and hurried
forward. When he reached the forward trench the Germans
had started to shell it again and Captain Palmer was
'prostrate', so the temporary adjutant, Second Lieutenant
Lowthian, who had been the battalion machine gun officer
before 1 July, asked Kirkwood to carry out a medical inspection of the men to see if they were fit to fight. Kirkwood
immediately saw what should have been obvious to any
experienced officer. The men were at their nerves' end. The
heavy shelling had no doubt brought fears that even more
death and destruction was to follow the nightmare of the
previous Saturday.

Kirkwood came quickly to his conclusion. He decided

the whole unit was 'unfit'. As it was now only an hour or so before the attack was due to take place, Kirkwood wrote a short report which Lieutenant Ross himself immediately took back to brigade headquarters. It stated: 'In view of the bombing attack to be carried out by 11th Border Regt, I must hereby testify to their unfitness for such an operation as few, if any, are not suffering from some degree of shell shock. 9 July 1916. Signed George H Kirkwood, Lieutenant RAMC.'

At 11.45 p.m., Brigadier Jardine told Ross that he did not believe the MO's report and the attack was to go ahead as planned. Ross pleaded for a delay, but this too was denied. He went back to the front and ordered the men to follow him. He would lead the party and 2nd Lieutenant Twynam, the other infantry officer who had survived the 1 July attack, would bring up the rear. The core of the attacking party would be formed by four experienced sergeants who had also survived the massacre a week before.

The bombing party prepared to head into a sap in No Man's Land, but the attempt to launch the attack was a fiasco. Several men got lost in the trenches, which had been rebuilt after recent shell fire. Others took a wrong turning. As they passed the bomb store where they were to pick up grenades to throw into the enemy lines, many men failed to collect bombs. Others simply refused to go over the top. It became clear to Ross that he could not lead his men forward; as he later said, 'I knew that there was great lack of the offensive spirit in the party.' As he could not get the men to advance, Ross bravely decided to use his own initiative, and he abandoned the assault soon after 1 a.m.

This was clearly a collective act of disobedience. It was not a mutiny, as the men continued to act, or at least pretend to act, in a combat role. But they were evidently opposed to going over the top again, for they had failed to pick up grenades from the bomb store and had become lost in the trenches. Two crucial elements of unit cohesion had collapsed in the 11th Borders. They had lost their *esprit de corps* after the massacre of 1 July and the death of the commanding officer. The morale of the battalion was at rock bottom. And the remaining junior officers had neither sufficient status with the men to motivate them, nor the ability to intervene and protect them from what they thought were bad orders. The duty of care junior officers usually showed towards the welfare of their men was entirely missing.[19]

When Brigadier Jardine heard of the failure of the attack he was furious. He ordered the arrest of the four sergeants on a charge of cowardice. The officer commanding the 32nd Division, General Rycroft, announced on the following morning that a court of enquiry would be held to investigate what had gone wrong. Clearly, the high command was on edge. In the view of senior officers, distant as they were from the men in the front trenches, the incidence of shell shock was getting out of hand. Was this a case of mass malingering, or had shell shock infected all the remaining men of the battalion? Whatever was happening, it had to be stamped on. Someone had to be blamed for the fiasco of the night before. Most importantly for army discipline and morale, an example must be set.

The court of enquiry was quickly convened and took place three days later on 13 July. It was not a court martial but was intended to find out exactly what had happened. But everyone who attended knew how serious this was. First to give evidence was Captain Palmer, the temporary battalion commander. He tried to blame Ross, saying that he should have told him in advance about the condition of the men. Ross then gave his evidence, accepting responsibility for calling off the assault but saying 'the men were not ready' to fight. Clearly he had sympathy with those under his command. When Lieutenant Twynham gave his evidence he said that 'one or two dozen' men had come to see him during the course of the Sunday saying they were suffering from shell shock. He said he had tried to reason with them and told them 'to pull themselves together', advising them to get 'as much rest as possible as they had been carrying up equipment all day'. In his evidence, Lieutenant Lowthian, the temporary adjutant, clearly felt that Palmer bore some responsibility for not knowing how bad the situation was.

Then came the turn of Lieutenant Kirkwood, the MO. Knowing that army courts of enquiry often dismissed the evidence of MOs, he had prepared a certificate outlining in full why he had decided the men were not in a fit state to go over the top. Having already sent this certificate to brigade headquarters, he stood by it during the court proceedings. It makes for fascinating reading.

Kirkwood wrote:

I gave my opinion that the men were unfit, and that opinion was based on the following,

The attack on 1st July when the battalion lost all its officers and more than half of the men had had a most demoralizing effect and the men had not recovered their mental equilibrium.

The few days rest at Contay sorting out deceased comrades kits did not improve their mental state.

Carrying up rations under heavy and intense shell fire.

Digging out the dead in the trenches and carrying them down as well as living in the atmosphere of decomposed bodies.

Exposure in open trenches under continuous shelling and without sleep.

Twenty men that day (9th July) had been sent to the Advanced Dressing Station suffering from shell shock.

Kirkwood had signed and dated the certificate. He might not have realised quite how far he was sticking his neck out.

After Kirkwood, Brigadier Jardine gave his evidence. He reported, 'I had no idea that the Battalion was in such a state nor had I been told so by anyone. I believed the Battalion to be in good spirits.' Looking back, he faithfully recounted that 'Within thirty minutes of zero hour on the first day of the attack (1 July) all the officers became casualties. This was a shock but not many units would have collapsed as this one did.' For him it was absolutely clear what was behind the events. The reason was 'that the late C.O. Lt-Col Machell who was a splendid example as a C.O. kept everything in his own hands and NCOs had not been accustomed to act on their own responsibilities in absence of officers'. In other words, the battalion's morale had disintegrated on the death of Machell. Jardine argued that it was the 'mental disability' of the men that had stopped them fighting. 'And that mental disability was caused by the failure of the NCOs to preserve the right spirit – to encourage the men and to set a good example in the absence of officers.'

Jardine was no Blimp. He was a modern officer who had done well on 1 July by using his own initiative and had achieved one of the few successes that day by ensuring that his Highland battalions reached the Leipzig Redoubt. But he had little time for Kirkwood, who he probably thought was a soft touch. He told the court, 'I don't attach much importance to the MO's ideas. The Battalion has been less under fire than others in the Brigade and I hear of practically no case of shell shock in it.' For him the platoon sergeants, whose arrests he had ordered, were to blame. They had 'failed in their duty'.

The papers of the court of enquiry were then passed up through the chain of command, and at each level the more senior officer could reverse an action or confirm it. The papers went next to the divisional commander, Major-General Rycroft, who came to a harsh conclusion. First, of Jardine, he said, 'It is a pity that this battalion was detailed for the duty. The Brigadier had fever else I am sure he would have known the condition of the Battalion and not detailed it.' He recognised the record of the Lonsdales, writing that 'This Battalion has done most excellent work since coming out [to France] and I regret that some NCOs and men should have tarnished its reputation.' However, he concluded that there was not sufficient evidence to charge the four sergeants and ordered their release. His fury was entirely focused on one man: 'Evidently the MO, Lt Kirkwood RAMC, who has been with the Battalion during the winter showed undue sympathy with the men on this occasion. Sympathy for the sick and wounded men under his treatment is a good attribute but it is not for a MO to inform a CO that his men are not in a fit state to carry out a military operation. The men being in the front line should be proof that they are fit for any duty called for.' Rycroft announced that Kirkwood was to be immediately relieved of his duties and sent home in disgrace.

The papers were passed on to the commander of X Corps, Lieutenant-General Sir Thomas Morland. He commented that 'The Battalion is one of the best in the 32nd Division. It carried out before the present operations (July 1st) a most successful raid and its spirit was very good. On July 1st it lost all the officers present with the Battalion and more than 500 men. It is a pity it was selected for such an enterprise.' He confirmed Kirkwood's punishment and regretted that there was not enough evidence to take disciplinary action against the four sergeants.

Finally, when the papers arrived on the desk of General Hubert Gough, the commander of Reserve Army of which the Lonsdales were now a part, the true bulldog voice of high command made itself heard. Gough was known for his pushy, hands-on approach and was what today would be called a micro-manager.[20] He relished getting involved in the details of the Enquiry and wrote, 'The facts disclose a deplorable state of discipline and an entire absence of courage and of any soldierly qualities amongst the NCOs and men of the battalion.' He blamed the temporary battalion commander, Palmer, for 'Weakness and disinclination to take responsibility'. By asking the MO to see the men, he said, Palmer's action 'was tantamount to questioning the orders he received and was calculated to encourage the spirit of indiscipline and cowardice already shown'.

But Gough's full ire was kept for Kirkwood, of whom he wrote, 'The conduct on the part of Lt Kirkwood RAMC shows him to be totally unfitted to hold a commission in the Army or to exercise any military responsibility.' He went on, 'Immediate steps must be taken to remove Lt Kirkwood RAMC from the service. The certificate which he signed and the reasons given by him in support of it conclusively prove that he has no conception of the duties and responsibilities of a regimental MO and so long as he is allowed to remain in the service he will be a source of danger to it. There can be no doubt that the conduct of the men and the failure of the men are largely attributable to this officer's extraordinary ideas of duty.' It is clear that Gough had found the man he wanted to make an example of. The Medical Corps must be made to understand that it could not encourage 'wastage' by approving large-scale cases of shell shock.

However, this particular fight was not yet over. The RAMC rallied to Kirkwood's defence. The Director of Military Services in the 32nd Division wrote to his commander that 'Kirkwood has performed his duties conscientiously and well. The late C.O. Lt-Col P.W. Machell, had a high opinion of him. The sick rate of the Battalion was never excessive and he did very good work during the recent fighting in attending to the wounded and except for the present regrettable incident he has given complete satisfaction.' The appeal was rejected.

It was only when the news of Kirkwood's dismissal reached Sir Arthur Sloggett, Director of Military Services in France, that he was able to bring some sanity to the case. He wrote that the whole sequence of events was 'deplorable' but that Kirkwood 'appears to have been made the scapegoat'. He pointed out that 'Lieutenant Kirkwood did not volunteer his opinion but was *ordered* to give it and send it direct to the Brigade Headquarters in accordance with instructions from the Adjutant, and this opinion was not acted on, so it can hardly be argued that the conduct of the men was due to his action.' Sloggett continued, 'I do not agree with the opinion of the Commander [Reserve Army] that he is a source of danger to the service if he remains in it. He will still be able to do work at the Base and with the alarming shortage of MOs now, it would be most inadvisable to remove him from the service.' Kirkwood was demoted to the level of an orderly and sent to work at a base hospital. No doubt this was humiliation enough.[21]

The whole court of enquiry had revealed the sorry state of affairs in the army after the collective trauma of 1 July. Junior officers, some only just over twenty years of age, were acting in temporary positions of command far above the level their training and experience had prepared them for. Men still shattered from seeing their pals shot down in front of their eyes were too traumatised to return to the front trenches so soon and go over the top again. Commanders behind their desks felt they needed to stop the 'wastage' and take a stand to prevent shell shock from becoming contagious. However, the worst was yet to come.

The message Gough wanted to send out was aimed not only at the RAMC and MOs up and down the Western Front, but at the men. He wrote of the incident, clearly in a fury, that

The Face of Shell Shock.
Top: one of the first war photographers, Roger Fenton, records shell-shocked and dishevelled Captain Lord Balgonie of the Grenadier Guards, Crimean War, 1855. *Bottom*: frame of film promoting the work of Dr Arthur Hurst shows a shell shock victim. Note the staring eyes.

The Lonsdales, 11th Battalion, Border Regiment.
Top: drilling at Blackhall racecourse before uniforms arrived.
Bottom: marching out of Carlisle, May 1915.
(© Cumbria's Museum of Military Life Carlisle Castle)

The officers when the battalion left for France, November 1915. Second row, third from left is Lieutenant Colonel Percy Machell, next to him (centre) is the Earl of Lonsdale, next to him is Major Diggle, second-in-command. Lieutenant Kirkwood, Medical Officer, was absent. Only six officers survived the 1 July assault. Second Lieutenant Ross, front row, cross-legged second from left, led the failed raid on 9 July. (© Cumbria's Museum of Military Life Carlisle Castle)

The Guns.

Top: eight-inch howitzers firing from the Fricourt-Mametz valley, August 1916.
Bottom: the destruction caused by a single shell on a German machine gun post near Guillemont, September 1916. Men had to live at all times with the prospect of sudden death or mutilation from a shell fired from miles away.

Over the Top.
Top: anxious faces of Lancashire Fusiliers waiting to go over the top in a sunken road near Beaumont Hamel, 1 July 1916. *Middle*: men lined up ready to go forward on the Somme. *Bottom*: a shell shock victim staggers back from the front and needs help to walk. Top and bottom are frames from *The Battle of the Somme* film, August 1916.

(© IWM)

Doctors and Patients.
Top: William Brown, William Halse Rivers (seated) and Grafton Elliot Smith at Maghull Hospital near Liverpool. *Bottom*: Captain Siegfried Sassoon; Charles Samuel Myers, after the war; Lieutenant Wilfred Owen. (© John Rowlands /

Shell Shock Victims.
Top: patient suffering from chronic movements, classed as 'Shell Shock W' and wearing the distinctive wounded uniform of blue suit, white shirt and red tie. *Bottom*: Private Harry Farr; from May 1915 treated for five months with shell shock; on 18 October 1916, executed for cowardice.

Aftermath.
Top: Roehampton Hospital, 1916–17. 240,000 men lost limbs in the war but the physically disabled found it far easier to find work than those who suffered from mental problems. *Below*: a group of long-term shell-shock sufferers pose for the Ex-Services Welfare Society at their home at Eden Manor, Beckenham, 1929. Today known as Combat Stress, it is the leading veterans' mental health charity in the UK. (© Science & Society Picture Library / Getty Images)

'It is inconceivable how men who pledged themselves to fight and uphold the honour of the country could degrade themselves in such a manner and show an utter want of manly spirit and courage which at least is expected of every soldier and every Britisher.' He ordered the public humiliation of the Lonsdales in front of the rest of the brigade. Accordingly, on 17 July, General Rycroft assembled the survivors of the Lonsdale battalion. They were not to bear arms. All the other available units of the brigade were gathered and told to carry their weapons. Rycroft read out a short reprimand to the officers and men of the Lonsdales telling them that the army commander 'considers those who failed in their duty have brought disgrace not only on themselves but also on the battalion to which they belong'.

For the 250 survivors of one of the worst massacres in the history of the British army, this public disgrace in front of their peers must have been extraordinarily hard to take. The battalion that had been raised with such pride and enthusiasm in the autumn of 1914, that had performed its duties in France so well and had been widely praised and mentioned in dispatches, that had suffered so terribly on 1 July, was now the object of vilification from its own commanders. But the senior figures in the British Army had made it absolutely clear. They would not stand for excessive levels of shell shock. The discipline and morale, possibly even the fighting spirit of the entire army was at stake.

7

Attrition

The collective punishment handed out to the Lonsdales in the middle of July 1916 made it clear that the British army would not tolerate mass cases of shell shock. If a whole unit looked as though it was going down with war neuroses, then the fact would have to be covered up somehow. From now on, the story of shell shock would be that of individuals or small groups, and of the many different attempts to treat the problem and get men back into the fighting line.

Private Arthur Hubbard, a clerk in Streatham, south London, before the war, had joined the 14th Battalion The London Regiment, a London Scottish Pals battalion. He had gone over the top with the 56th Division in the diversionary attack at Gommecourt on the morning of 1 July. Five days later his mother and sisters received a letter he had sent them from hospital in Ipswich, where he was recovering from shell shock. He wrote:

Dear Mother and All
    No doubt you have been worrying about me very much but now you can rest assured I am quite all right suffering from slight Shell Shock.
    Went over and took the Huns 4th line of trenches on

Saturday morning at 7.30am and held same until 3.30pm in the afternoon when by that time their artillery had completely wiped our battalion out, and what was left of us had to crawl back to our own trenches but the bounders mowed us down with machine gun fire as we were retiring. I managed to get back safely after a long and weary struggle over 300 yards of rough ground. I got buried over in their second line by a shell but managed to work my way out, my steel helmet saved my life ... I shall be quite myself in a week or two, as you will notice by my writing only my nerves are shook up, severe head-ache now and again when my mind is on the affair ... Have scores of adventures to tell you all when I get home.

So for the present must close with fondest love to all.

I remain

Your Aff[ectionate] Son

Arthur[1]

Arthur Hubbard wrote to his mother or his sisters every few days, and each letter conveyed a little more of the horrors he had witnessed. On 7 July he wrote, 'They have treated me splendid since my admission. My temperature went up pretty high yesterday but has gone done [sic] to normal today. All I am worried with now is weakness in the back and headache at rear of head ... It was a terrible sight that I shall never forget as long as I live ... We had strict orders not to take prisoners, no matter if wounded. My first job was when I had finished cutting some of their wire away, to empty my magazine on 3 Germans that came out of one of their deep dugouts bleeding badly and I put them out of misery. They cried for mercy, but I had my orders, they had no feeling whatever for us poor chaps. Soon after that I was waiting for more excitement when one of their huge shells burst a few yards away smashing my rifle up and at the same time covering me with about a ton of soil. It's a lucky thing

I hadn't got my helmet off at the time of having a blow, or I don't suppose I would have been so lucky. Soon after that one of our Majors came up to me and asked me what was wrong and no sooner had he finished his sentence a sniper caught him clean through the throat and he was dead in less than five minutes.'

Hubbard clearly did not suffer bad physical effects from the shell shock, and by the end of the month he was well enough to be helping on the ward, which had now filled to capacity. One hundred and ten wounded men arrived in one day alone. Hubbard wrote, 'I am busy most of the day helping the Sister and Nurses to dress the patients and of course am kept on going. The Sister said she will be very sorry when I have to go away which will be any day now, so if you write to me and I have been shifted to convalescence she will send the letters on to me, there is no telling where I shall go, and perhaps only be away for a week, then home for ten days leave.' In August, Hubbard was sent to a convalescent camp in Eastbourne. Eager to reassure his mother and sisters that all was well he kept telling them that the camp was excellent, the weather was glorious and he was feeling a lot better.

But it's clear that Hubbard was not recovering, and was still haunted by memories and almost certainly nightmares of being buried alive, of the deaths he had been responsible for and those he had witnessed. 'All I know,' he wrote at the end of August, 'is we had 121 fit men left out of 1,200 after the attack.' In October he left the convalescent camp and visited the widow of the major whose death he had witnessed. She naturally wanted to hear a first-hand account of what had happened to her husband, but evidently telling the story was very upsetting for poor Hubbard.

By November, Hubbard was still not better. He had returned to the London Scottish training camp near Winchester, but it was apparent that he was not capable of returning to active service. He was called to a medical board, which would most likely assign him to non-combatant duties. He wrote, 'This medical board has not arrived here yet so cannot give you any news just yet, am living in hopes of something good in the near future that will suit my requirements as long as this war lasts.'

It's not recorded what happened to Hubbard except that he never returned to the fighting front. Throughout, he had maintained in his letters the cheery attitude of a loving son and brother so as not to distress his mother and sisters. His handwriting was clear and firm. Hubbard was no doubt one of the many thousands of men who, although not physically scarred by the war, lived with terrible memories of what he had seen and done and was never able to return easily to civilian life. Tragically, even though only in his early twenties, Hubbard took his own life shortly after the end of the war. Shell shock was cited as a contributing factor.

At the root of all war neuroses like shell shock was fear. Every soldier felt fear. He was lying if he said he did not. But men did not want to admit their fear or show signs of it to their chums, so they suppressed this entirely natural emotion. William Tyrrell, a MO who treated hundreds of cases of war neurosis, said, '"Shell shock" is born of fear. Its grandparents are self-preservation and the fear of being found afraid. Any emotion which has to be repressed or concealed demands an unrestricted but well-controlled output of nervous energy ... Under its stimulus a man squanders nervous energy recklessly in order to suppress ... and mask or camouflage that which if revealed will call down ignominy upon his head and disgrace him in the eyes of his fellows.'[2] In other words, fear and the fear of showing fear were both causes of the problem. MO Charles Wilson asked, 'Is there anyone who does not feel fear?' He answered that there might be the occasional 'happy soul' who 'never had to make an effort to carry on ... Perhaps he was killed or wounded and was remembered as a man without fear.' But Wilson argued that such men were incredibly rare; no one can in reality get used to the modern battlefield and 'no man can go on for ever, sooner or later all men feel fear'.[3]

Soldiers in the early twentieth century seldom talked about fear, adopting a brusque or even macho style to disguise their feelings. The popular heroes of the age from *Boy's Own Paper*, or from the works of Rudyard Kipling or G.A. Henty, did not show fear. Consequently, the common phrases of a soldier's language often made light of the danger they all knew they were living with. As one soldier wrote, 'if you did ruminate much on the real meaning of the things you do and the things that are done to you, your nerves would crack up in no time.'[4] So various phrases were adopted to neutralise the horrors of trench life. In order to avoid acknowledging directly that a comrade had been killed, soldiers would say he had 'copped a packet' or 'been topped off'. Steel helmets and bayonets were referred to as 'tin hats' and 'tooth picks'.[5] 'Cheer up, cockie, it's your turn next' was a phrase intended to cheer a fellow soldier.[6] It has been argued that ridicule and irony were particularly British traits inherited by the citizen army from Edwardian popular culture.[7] However, it is more likely that all soldiers in all armies have used humour as a strategy to cope with the horrors of war, although it is particularly remembered today among the British soldiers of the Great War.

The black humour of the popular songs sung by British soldiers during the war is a perfect example of this. In order to play down or mock danger, soldiers would add new words to popular ballads or music hall hits. Of the many now well-known wartime soldiers' songs, three examples clearly make the point. When a high-velocity shell was fired, faster than sound, from one of the smaller field artillery pieces, a soldier heard the 'whizz' for only an instant before the 'bang' of the explosion, so there was virtually no warning of an incoming shell. This was the soldiers' version:

Hush! here comes a whizz-bang
Hush! here comes a whizz-bang
Now you soldier boys
Run down those stairs
Down in the dugout and say your prayers.
Hush! here comes a whizz-bang
And it's heading straight for you.
And you'll see all the wonders of No Man's Land
If a whizz-bang hits you.

Another song expressed with a strong dose of fatalism the exhaustion and cynical hopelessness of being under continuous artillery fire:

Bombed last night, and bombed the night before
Gonna get bombed tonight
If we never get bombed any more.
When we're bombed, we're as scared as we can be
Can't stop the bombing sent from higher Germany.
Chorus: *They're over us, they're over us,*
One shell hole for the four of us,
Thank your lucky stars there are no more of us,
'Cos one of us can fill it all alone.

Gassed last night, and gassed the night before . . .
etc.

The traditional army marching song 'The British Grenadiers' was adapted for the following favourite. After four verses asking 'If you want to find the Sergeant', 'the Quarter-bloke', 'the Sergeant-Major' and 'the CO', the song ends with lines that were terribly poignant after the first day of the Somme:

If you want to find the old battalion,
I know where they are, I know where they are, I know where
    they are
If you want to find the old battalion, I know where they are,
They're hanging on the old barbed wire,
I've seen 'em, I've seen 'em, hanging on the old barbed wire.
I've seen 'em, I've seen 'em, hanging on the old barbed wire.

What was different about the level of fear felt in the First World War from that experienced during most other conflicts, before and since, was that it was constant. Not only, in previous centuries, had battles been over in a day or so, but in later conflicts, like the Second World War, soldiers experienced extremes of fear for relatively short periods between long spells of utter boredom. But in the First World War, even behind the lines men were at risk of a stray shell, an attacking aircraft or a freak explosion. Charles Wilson described a man who, having survived a terrible time at the front, was resting in a wood near Poperinghe, miles from the line, enjoying the quiet of a summer evening when out of the blue a shell crashed through the forest and took his head off. In another story, Wilson told of the last of four brothers to survive. It was felt that his family had done its bit and so he was given safe jobs in the battalion that would keep him away from the front. He made himself useful around headquarters and became batman to the transport officer. One morning an individual enemy aircraft came over and dropped a single bomb. It hit the man and blew him to bits. Wilson concluded that the 'wear and tear' of the war was continuous and there was 'no such thing as one moment's complete security'.[8]

The First World War has often been called 'an artillery

war'.[9] The vast majority of wounds came from shell fire, about 67 per cent in the British army and up to 76 per cent in the German.[10] When at or near the front, men had to accept that at any moment they or the person standing next to them might be blown to pieces or terribly mutilated. A shell could maim or horribly disfigure a man. If it killed him, his remains were likely to be scattered over a wide area. There are countless reports from men who found legs, arms or other body parts suspended in trees or hanging from the parapet. And enduring the risk of this went on for days and days. Then, after a battalion had gone through its rotation with a week or ten days' rest, the men had to go back up to the front and face the whole thing all over again. There is much evidence to show that the worst anxieties came on the evening before a battalion was to go back up the line to the front, when anticipation of the horror of the trenches would obviously be at its maximum. William Tyrrell remembered, 'With the men [as against officers] the most fruitful period in the production of "shell shock" was (1) the height of battle, (2) the hour before going over the top (3) the evening before going back to the trenches after a rest period.'[11]

The trenches of course offered protection during an artillery bombardment. This was the reason they had been dug in the first place, to provide a hiding place from which troops could defend a line. But they amplified the psychological effect by preventing any possibility of 'flight or fight'. Men simply had to cower down and endure. The lack of any option to escape from a trench during an artillery bombardment created a sense of powerlessness among front-line soldiers. They felt passive and were unable to evade the constant threat. One soldier wrote in his diary that infantrymen in a trench felt 'caught like rats in a trap by such terrific shelling'.[12] Wilson wrote that 'To sit still under bombardment in the trench was more testing than to fight in the open.'[13] An officer who suffered a breakdown while sheltering from shell fire in a trench told his MO that 'Owing to the small area to which we were confined, there was no opportunity of being able to give vent to the pent-up feelings that were in me, and in consequence my nerves were strung up to such a pitch that I felt that something in me would snap.'[14]

Bernard Hart, a physician and specialist in mental diseases at University College Hospital, London, summed it up thus: 'If I am standing in the road and a motor omnibus appears I immediately step out of the way.' However, for the soldier in a trench, the instinct of self-preservation, to get out of the way of danger, was in conflict with what Hart described as 'a group of forces compounded of self-respect, duty, discipline, patriotism, and so forth' which he summarised simply as 'duty'. The purpose of a soldier's training was to instil in him such a powerful sense of 'duty' that it overcame his instinct for self-preservation. When a man was wounded, he could feel a sense of relief; he had done his duty but would be removed from the scene of danger. When he had to stay in the trench, the pressure that built could create what Hart called the 'psychoneurosis' otherwise known as shell shock.[15]

MOs observed that several episodes were especially likely to bring on a case of shell shock. One was being buried alive until being pulled out by colleagues, an extreme state of powerlessness. Arthur Hubbard had suffered this at Gommecourt. Even the fear of being buried alive was enough to turn some men during a bombardment. Another was the use of gas by the enemy, evoking a primitive fear that even the air one breathed could bring poisoning and death. On many occasions, the anxieties that produced shell shock were compared to a soldier's primeval fear of gas poisoning the air around him. As we have heard, the MO of the 4th Black Watch, a tough and battle-hardened battalion, later recorded,

'The very mention of gas would put the "wind up" the battalion at once . . . Gas was a potent cause of anxiety neurosis.' But again the fear was that men might use gas as an opportunity to malinger. The same MO remembered when coming across gas victims that 'some of the men were undoubtedly suffering from gas poisoning, but there were always a large number turned out that were not'.[16] Many of them were suffering panic attacks. In fact a condition known as gas hysteria became a common feature among men on the Western Front and another contributory factor to shell shock. Both the fear of being buried alive and that of gas came from the sense of powerlessness that was felt to be a new and ghastly feature of modern industrial warfare.

Confronting the death of others was something every First World War soldier had to learn to cope with. There is barely a memoir or a diary that does not include some horror story of coming across a corpse. And of course every dead body was a reminder of one's own mortality, often provoking a feeling of 'there but for the grace of God go I'. Private Norman Gladden was in the 7th Battalion Northumberland Fusiliers, part of 50th Division, on the Somme and later recalled coming across the body of a soldier who had only just been killed by a shell. 'The dead man lay amidst earth and broken timber. It seemed like sacrilege to step over him but there was no evading the issue. Never before had I seen a man who had just been killed. A glance was enough. His face and body were terribly gashed as though some terrific force had pressed him down, and blood flowed from a dozen fearful wounds. The smell of blood mixed with the fumes of the shell filled me with nausea. Only a great effort saved my limbs from giving way beneath me. I could see from the sick grey faces of the file that these feelings were generally shared. A voice seemed to whisper with unchallengeable logic, "Why shouldn't you be the next?"'[17]

One outcome of 1 July, however, was evident to all. As the awesome casualty lists started to come through in the following days, no one could deny the courage of the soldiers of the New Army. Stories began to circulate of individual deeds of heroism, as well as of collective acts of bravery and steadfastness in the face of the enemy. Officers and men might be lacking in tactical knowledge but they clearly had an abundance of determination. This attracted remarks at every level. Sir Henry Rawlinson wrote, 'I cannot speak too highly of the spirit and self-sacrifice of our rank and file. The courage of the New Armies is magnificent, and if they had been able to devote more time to training, they would have been able to hold on to many points of importance which they captured from which they were driven by the enterprising German machine-gunners. We have shown the Boches that we can break their lines on a wide front.'[18] Another regular soldier, Major-General William Furse, the commanding officer of the 9th (Scottish) Division, complimented the junior officers in the New Army by writing at the end of July: 'considering the age of our Army, the marvel to me is that we find amongst those who escape the enemy's shells, as many young fellows as we do who have knowledge, instinct and the character to do the right thing.'[19]

This sense that the citizen army had proved itself in its baptism of fire fundamentally affected thinking about the next major element of the offensive. In the first week of July, the Allies made advances along the southern section of the front at Fricourt, La Boisselle and elsewhere. Haig began to press Rawlinson to attack the German second line along the high ground between Bazentin-le-Petit and Longueval. Rawlinson, Congreve, commander of XIII Corps, who had sensed the possibility of a breakthrough on the afternoon of 1 July, and Horne, commander of XV Corps, came up with a radically different plan of assault. They proposed to attack at night after only a short barrage on a narrow front. Haig was initially opposed, thinking the risks of trying to assemble the men in the middle of the night were too great. But in consultation with the corps commanders he was persuaded it was possible and in accordance with his belief that field commanders should make local decisions he gave approval.

Rawlinson concentrated his artillery on a relatively short three and a half mile stretch of German trenches, and at 3.20 a.m. on 14 July the guns opened fire. After only five minutes the shelling lifted and the infantry from three divisions that had crawled out into No Man's Land rushed forward. They achieved total surprise and by mid-morning had won all their objectives. Large numbers of Germans appeared to surrender willingly. British losses were light. It was one of the most successful assaults in the long Somme battle.

However, like most other assaults, the failure came in the follow-through. Rawlinson had the British and Indian cavalry waiting, but it took so long for them to struggle across the abandoned trenches and the shell-pocked landscape that by the time the 7th Dragoon Guards and the 20th Deccan Horse went forward in the evening the impetus had been lost. However, they still occupied the edge of High Wood and were able to look out over the wide valley behind the German lines towards Bapaume. This was one of the few occasions when cavalry were used successfully as a mobile force on the Western Front.[20] But despite the drama of the advance, it took two months to complete the capture of the wood. Once again the Allies had missed the opportunity to seize a substantial amount of ground that would instead be fought over bitterly for the next few weeks. The great success of 14 July has been called a 'tantalisingly incomplete victory' and a 'false dawn'.[21] But it showed many of the doubters that the New Army could successfully adopt more sophisticated tactics. It also demonstrated that if the artillery were able to concentrate its fire on a limited front, then it really could open the way for the infantry, as the commanders had hoped in the seven days before 1 July.

However, those in command would somehow fail to remember these lessons. The Germans were stunned by the advance of 14 July but rushed in reinforcements. The next, long drawn-out phase of the battle was focused on the struggle to win control of a set of woods: Mametz Wood, High Wood, Trones Wood and Delville Wood. These were thick, tangled woods full mostly of oak and birch trees, with a heavy undergrowth of dense hazel thickets, intersected by grassy rides and scattered with ruined cottages all of which provided good cover. And the Germans defended them brilliantly. Each one became the site of a mini battle in itself. General Horne later concluded that 'woods are very trouble-some places'.[22]

The first to be attacked was Mametz Wood. Horne ordered the 38th (Welsh) Division to capture the wood, but its assaults failed. He ordered further attacks on the nights of 7–8 and 8–9 July but neither attack went ahead. Horne felt that the divisional commander, Major-General Ivor Philips, was failing to push hard enough. Philips was relieved of his command, becoming the third general to be degummed and sent home in disgrace in a week.

Over the next few days the 38th under its new commander succeeded in taking the wood. Visiting soon after its capture, Gerald Brenan described the scene: 'After a little we came to Mametz Wood, which had been the scene of heavy fighting. Its trees were torn and shattered, its leaves had turned brown, and there was a shell hole every 3 yards. This was a place where something unheard of in this war had taken place – hand to hand fighting in the open with bombs and bayonets. What seemed extraordinary was that all the dead bodies there lay just as they had fallen, as though they were being kept as exhibits for a war museum. Germans in the field grey uniforms, British in their khaki, lying side by side, their faces and their hands a pale waxy green, the colour of a rare marble. Some of these figures still sat with their backs against a tree, and two of them stood locked together by their bayonets, which had pierced each other's bodies; they were sustained in that position by the tree trunk against which they had fallen. I felt I was visiting a room in Madame Tussaud's Chamber of Horrors, for I could not imagine any of those corpses having ever been alive.'[23]

The ferocious fighting in these gloomy woods and the prolonged artillery duels they unleashed created the ideal conditions for shell shock. The Germans shelled the wood from three sides, firing up to 400 shells per minute at one point. It was in Delville Wood that Private Archibald Burgoyne watched his mates all around develop forms of shell shock, some severe, some apparently only temporary.[24] On 18 July, Burgoyne and the South African Brigade cleared part of the wood. 'The scream and hiss and whine of the shells was frightful. The reverberating explosions in the wood were deafening. Whiz-bangs seemed to just skim our trenches. Some actually struck the parapet and ricocheted into the bush with an unearthly shriek. I used to wonder at men getting shell shock. I don't now ... Men were going down everywhere. And there were no stretcher bearers left. The wounded had to lie where they fell, as men could not be spared to carry them away. Their cries were terrible – especially those with stomach wounds. Those who were able made the best of their way out of the wood – but very few were successful in reaching shelter ... No one who was not present can possibly have any conception of the intensity of the barrage, or the devastating effect of the exploding shells. It was hellish. No wonder the men called it "Devil's Wood" ... Men ducked one shell and were hit by another. Men were buried by one shell and blown out again by the next ... Another chap got Shell Shock and was quite dumb. In the afternoon the shell fire seemed to become more intense ... Beck came running up and threw himself headlong on top of us ... He frightened the life out of us. We hadn't heard him coming. Of course we both opened out on him, but a look at his face stopped us. He was ashen and trembling like a leaf. He and Mathews were in an Observation Post in the open – outside the wood. They were unable to dig in and had endured all that terrific fire without shelter of any kind.'[25]

Shell shock could have unpredictable effects. Sometimes, rather than encourage a man to run and hide, it prompted the opposite, making him reckless and liable to take unnecessary risks. Burgoyne witnessed this when one of the most unreliable men in his company suddenly appeared. 'Mathews came up as cool as a cucumber. Mathews – whom everyone had put down as a "lead-swinger" a "Wheezer" and whom Major Burges had that very morning denounced as a "shirker" before us all. He strolled up to the trench saying "Give us a match, Arch". He lit a cigarette, corroborated Beck's story quite calmly and with full details and strolled off again as though it was a Sunday afternoon in the Park. Hitherto he had funked everything in which there was the slightest hint of danger. He constantly complained of his heart and tried hard, but vainly, to get his "ticket" [to medical care in England]; and now here he was showing us all the perfect way to do it, in a perfect Hell of a place. There is nothing the matter with his heart. There is nothing the matter with Mathews. He had found himself. I have not seen him since. I hope he is safe.'

According to the *Official History*, the South African Brigade had 'covered themselves with glory at Delville Wood'. They had 'steadfastly endured the ordeal of the German bombardment which seldom slackened and never ceased ... had faced with great courage and resolution repeated counter attacks'. The brigade had marched into the wood on 15 July with 121 officers and 3032 other ranks. When roll call was taken six days later, there were only 29 officers and 751 other ranks present.[26] It was a dreadful price to pay for 150 acres of useless woodland.

Captain Bill was leading C Company of the 15th Battalion Royal Warwickshire Regiment, a Pals battalion also known as the 2nd Birmingham Pals, towards High Wood on the night of 22 July when he had an extraordinary escape. First, he had that 'uncanny intuition which I think most front line troops developed that something unpleasant was coming my way and coming very quickly'. As he manoeuvred his men into a road ready to attack at dawn he heard an incoming shell. 'I dropped to my hands and knees in a flash and as I landed a whizz-bang passed between my arms, underneath my body and burst as it struck the ground between my feet. A few inches higher or lower or to either side and this story had not been written. As it was, the back burst of the shell knocked me out, rolled me up into a ball and deposited me in the trench just in front. There I found that I had got it on the insides of both arms and both legs and one boot was half torn away, and later I counted sixty-one small wounds caused by the burning, but fortunately containing no metal. A lucky escape and as close an acquaintance with a bursting shell as one could have and still come through alive.'

Bill was bandaged up by the MO and sent on to a CCS at Corbie, where he slept for twenty-four hours. It was three months before he rejoined his battalion. He later admitted to suffering from shell shock, but this was combined with a sense of guilt that he had let his men down. When Bill wrote the battalion history fourteen years after the war, he summed up his memory of the event as follows: 'On looking back I have never been particularly proud of my part in that night's work and have always felt that by crawling out of the fight I let my Officers and men down badly. The more senior a soldier's rank, from private upwards, the more he should live up to his responsibilities, but those of my old comrades who know what it is to be half shell-shocked will, I feel, be merciful in their judgement. It is the super men who carry on under such conditions and they deservedly win their VCs.'[27]

Major Frederick St John Steadman was serving as a medical officer a few miles to the north in a field ambulance unit with the 60th Division, running the wards in two wooden huts, intended for forty-eight patients but receiving about fifty men per day.[28] So many shell shock patients had arrived at Steadman's dressing station that he quickly began to recognise the symptoms. He wrote to his wife, 'I have become fairly expert in diagnosing the degree of shell shock a man has, as I have seen so many cases now. I "spot" them at once by the nervous twitching of their faces or hands; some frown when they are talked to, as though to answer the simplest question is too much mental exertion. Some have a curious dazed look about their eyes, quite different from anything else I have seen. Some recover rapidly but others remain in the same state for days.'

The minor cases simply needed rest and were not classed in the official statistics as either wounded or sick. 'I have had several men come in with shell shock, with their faces twitching, and hands and arms shaking constantly, who improve at once when they have been made clean and put into a comfortable bed, and had a good night's rest.' Other cases, which would have been listed in the statistics, were more severe and needed more elaborate treatment. 'I have several very interesting but sad shell shock cases in my ward. One man has gone stone blind in one eye (right). Had he gone blind in both he would probably have recovered, but since only one eye has gone, it probably means detachment of the retina from haemorrhage, and I fear he will not recover the sight of that eye. Another man has lost his voice. He and a friend were in the trenches when two trench mortars burst on each of them. His friend has just disappeared. He himself is unhurt, but has lost his voice and his memory for certain things. He does not remember being brought here, for example, although he was conscious apparently all the time. Another man also lost his friend; he had actually been blown nearly 60 yards out of the trench to the top of another! He was, of course, killed instantly. This man's friend is still in my ward, suffering from the shock.'[29]

If the ward was a distressing place during the daytime, it did not get any easier after dark. Steadman wrote, 'All these shell shock cases dream dreadfully at night. They live through their experiences several times each night; sometimes I have to inject morphia to get them to sleep at all. They suffer very much in this way. So terrible are their dreams that they are afraid to go to sleep, worn out though they are. Poor fellows, I just loathe sending them back again [to the front]. I feel utterly wretched when I have to. Some are much too bad to go back, and these I send down the line to the CCS. When there is much noise at night by the guns, these men get into a rotten state. I have seen some cry and beg to be sent away from "those awful guns". I send all these down the line and they will need many months of care, and absolute quiet, if they are ever to recover their nerve.'

On more than one occasion, Steadman had sent a man back to his unit, only for him to reappear at the dressing station a few days later. He described one such case: 'His unit had foolishly given him sentry duty at night, on the first day he returned. Nothing could have been worse for him. He lost his nerve and his reason for a time, and was sent back to me;

he was in a very bad state when I saw him again yesterday, so I sent him straight down the line to the CCS. I think they will send him further down, as I have written to ask them.'

Almost every medical account records the high incidence of psychiatric casualties that accompanied the Battle of the Somme. In August 1916, at the height of the battle, the 86th Machine Gun Company reported that about 80 per cent of the unit had been admitted to hospital 'owing chiefly to the strain of the previous five weeks'.[30] Leonard Stagg, a nursing orderly with a South Midland field ambulance unit, remembered that on the Somme 'one was always seeing cases of shell shock.'[31] Colonel Soltau told the War Office Committee of Enquiry after the war that there had been 'one or two cases in the fighting line' in 1915, 'but nothing which really attracted attention'. He went on, 'It was not until the Somme that it became an appreciable problem' in the field ambulance unit he was commanding. 'We were flooded,' he said, 'with cases in the later stages of the Somme.'[32]

Throughout July, the long lists of casualties continued to fill every major newspaper in Britain. The Pals battalions had been a great boost to the process of recruitment. But now whole districts where a battalion had been raised were plunged into collective grief. People in areas where a locally raised battalion had gone over the top and been decimated, like the Shankill district of West Belfast, Sheffield or Barnsley, Accrington or Tyneside, drew their curtains or blinds to mark the death of a family member, neighbour or friend. It looked as though whole streets had gone into mourning. No one could escape from the losses. They affected everyone at all levels of society. Before the battle was through, the Prime Minister and the Paymaster-General would each lose a son, and the Cabinet Secretary a younger brother. Dukes, earls, doctors, bankers and factory owners, as well as miners, munitions workers, typists and shopkeepers, experienced the loss of sons, brothers, husbands and fiancés. Barely a community in the nation remained untouched. And as people read the lists of dead and wounded, and looked at maps in newspapers and saw the tiny scale of the advances from one unknown small French village to another, they began to question if it was all worthwhile. It was natural that political pressure to reduce the rate of losses would grow.

By the end of the month some Cabinet members were already describing Haig as a 'butcher'. Robertson, as CIGS, had to explain to the Cabinet's War Committee what was happening on the Somme and found he was caught, as he put it, between 'the God of War and the Mammon of Politics'.[33] The professional army view was that in an industrialised war heavy losses had to be expected and decisive results would not come quickly. The politicians, however, wanted to see more tangible gains and less pain. In passing this political concern back to the commanders in the field, Robertson said they should look to avoid further manpower problems, what was officially described as 'wastage'. At GHQ, Haig realised that he had to take heed of what was being said in Westminster. On 3 August he issued a communiqué to all senior commanders calling for 'the utmost economy of men and material' so that when the 'wearing out' battle had concluded, probably in the latter half of September, the 'last reserves' would still be available.[34] The problem of 'wastage' had to become a subject of concern at every point. The number of men being evacuated to England with shell shock was clearly one of these areas of concern.

According to the *Official Medical History*, 'the severe wastage of manpower which the psycho-neuroses were causing in France made the problem of dealing with them urgent towards the end of 1916.'[35] On 21 August, MOs were told 'that it is not considered desirable to evacuate to the base any cases of shell shock amongst officers and men unless there are definite lesions', in other words unless there had been some sort of 'commotional' damage to the brain or nervous system. Two days later, the chief medical officer of Fourth Army demonstrated his anxiety by giving instructions that 'the number of cases arriving at the Casualty Clearing Stations with a tally marked shell shock must be somehow decreased.'[36]

This was the moment that Charles Samuel Myers had long awaited. For some time, he had proposed the establishment of specialist centres to deal with psychological cases of war neurosis. Fearing that such centres would act like a magnet to shirkers and those with 'insufficient stoutness of heart' who wanted to escape the fighting, the army had opposed this for well over a year. The view had been that such centres 'would open up a flood-gate for wastage from the army which no one would be able to control'.[37] But now Sir Arthur Sloggett, Director General of the Army Medical Services in France, decided to listen. At the end of August, he appointed Myers 'Consulting Psychologist' to the army. It looked as though the British army had finally accepted the need for psychology.

Myers toured the front line, visited aid stations and met with generals and medical chiefs. Many patients who had been evacuated to Britain with shell shock took several months to recover once they were out of a military environment. So Myers presented a case that the successful treatment of shell shock, and the reduction of wastage from it, depended upon 'promptness of action, a suitable environment and psychotherapeutic measures' to be provided in France. Victims of shell shock should be evacuated to a special centre as quickly as possible to prevent 'the contagiousness of the affection within a unit'. The centre should be away from the sound of the guns but not so far as to be out of a military environment; men would thus be able more easily to return to their unit. Appropriate psychotherapeutic treatment would restore the patient's 'memory, self-confidence and self control' through a 'judicious admixture of persuasion, suggestion, explanation and scolding'. The specialist MOs who would provide this 'should possess enthusiasm, confidence, cheerfulness and tact'.[38]

In order to keep shell-shocked men in France and avoid evacuating them to Britain, Sloggett cautiously agreed in November 1916 to open four specialist treatment centres at converted CCSs.[39] The principal figure at the first of these was Dr William Brown, a qualified psychologist who had been a student of Myers before the war. Brown had worked at the Maghull Military Hospital near Liverpool before coming out to France. He brought with him a strong sense that the emotional causes of war neuroses could be discovered, often through hypnosis, and treated. He was never popular with leading military figures but was tolerated because he seemed to have the ability to return paralysed men to their battalions.

However, if this was a sign that the army would be taking a softer line, it was only temporary. Myers' star crashed almost as quickly as it had risen. Senior medical figures in the army had never been fully behind him and his new ideas. A few weeks after opening the first specialist centre, his job was split into two and he was given the junior role, keeping control only over the southern half of the front. Brought in over him was his old rival Dr Gordon Holmes, a hardliner on the treatment of shell shock. Holmes was appointed Consulting Neurologist to the Army. Myers complained bitterly but his protests were ignored.

At the beginning of 1917, Myers was sent on two months' sick leave. He returned to France but not to the senior position. Myers put a brave face on it, writing that he had under 'by no means favourable conditions . . . accomplished all that

I was likely to perform in the direction of improving the treatment and disposal of shell shock cases in France'.[40] But clearly he felt that his moment of influence had passed. Later in 1917, he returned to Britain for good, working until the end of the war with Sir Alfred Keogh in the War Office.

Holmes took a fundamentally different view from Myers and his ideas were far more in line with core army thinking. He believed that, before returning a man to his fighting unit, an army doctor should attempt to cure only the physical symptoms of war neurosis. He was not interested, as was Myers, in the underlying psychological causes. They might be related to a man's emotional state before he joined the army and this was consequently not his concern. His no-nonsense approach put the principal emphasis on giving a man a few nights of good rest and regular meals and then telling him sternly 'that there was nothing wrong and there was no need why the patient should not recover'. After a few days of physical exercises the man would then be sent back to his battalion. He told the War Office Enquiry after the war that it was far better to keep a man in areas under military control, on the grounds that 'The further men got from the line the more difficult it was to get them back.' He was still suspicious that men were trying it on; he told the enquiry that 'during the Battle of the Somme a large number of men deserted from the line on the claim that they had "shell shock" and it was necessary to prevent that and keep them within the Army area where they were still under the discipline of the Army and could be reached by their battalion and sent back easily.'[41] Holmes and his new tougher line would shape the attitude of the army medical authorities to shell shock for the rest of the war.

Throughout the relentless summer battles along the Somme, MOs on the Western Front were not allowed to forget the message sent out by the disgrace and removal of Lieutenant

Kirkwood from the Lonsdales for being too lenient on shell shock. Several senior medical directors sent out notes to MOs, warning them to be aware of shirkers and not to confuse other conditions with shell shock. Typical of these was the message sent from the Medical Director of III Corps on 15 October to all MOs under his jurisdiction. It read: 'Cases are very commonly sent to a M[edical] D[ressing] S[tation] during the heat of battle diagnosed hurriedly as Shell Shock (W). Frequently the W is omitted. During the patient's stay in the MDS or Rest Station later it is possible to form a more deliberate opinion, and when as a result it is decided that the diagnosis of Shell Shock is incorrect it should be cancelled, and the new diagnosis substituted. The doctor in charge at Base should be informed of the change of diagnosis.' This instruction was to be distributed to every MO in the corps. The officer who kept this document in his papers wrote that from the directive 'there emerged, I fancied, a thinly veiled invitation to diagnose "S" in preference to "W" ... When the diagnosis was questionable, as clearly it could be, how often I wonder did the official view err in the patient's favour. I do not wonder, really.'[42]

The cases of genuine Shell Shock 'W' where a man had suffered 'commotional' damage to the brain from proximity to a shell explosion were always in a small minority, variously estimated at between 2.5 per cent and 10 per cent of all cases.[43] The vast majority of cases were of 'emotional' damage to a man's nervous system. Although medical opinion was still divided on the matter, Holmes' view prevailed: sleep, relaxation and a rest from front-line duties could cure most of these men. He and others still argued that most war neuroses were the product of physical and mental exhaustion. This was Shell Shock 'S', or in some cases Neurasthenia. Cases of genuine psychological damage with the accompanying severe physical symptoms were also in need of treatment; sometimes these were listed as 'W' but on other occasions as 'S'.

The term 'shell shock' was an increasingly unhelpful one that covered a variety of very different conditions. William Johnson, a neurologist with the army in France, told the War Office enquiry after the war, '"Shell shock" is a misnomer, and its introduction as an official term was deplorable. Soldiers developed the belief that a bursting shell produced mysterious changes in the nervous system which destroyed their self-control ... So-called "shell shock" consisted of a motley of conditions. Its use was a loose proceeding which both obviated the need for accurate diagnosis and at the same time tended to obscure treatment and prognosis.' He concluded that 5 per cent of cases were down to 'commotional' and 80 per cent to 'emotional' disturbance – the remaining 15 per cent were some sort of combination of the two.[44]

The numbers of shell shock cases peaked during the Battle of the Somme. This much at least was universally accepted by military and medical chiefs. At an address to a meeting of the British Medical Association in April 1919, Sir Frederick Mott said emphatically that 'according to his experience the most serious cases of war neurosis occurred in 1915 and 1916.'[45] The alarmingly high numbers in 1916 continued not only to threaten the 'wastage' of troops when they were desperately needed but also to endanger morale. And as the Battle of the Somme ground on through the summer and into the autumn, it seemed that even the toughest, most battle-hardened units could not escape the horrors of shell shock.

8

Yard by Yard – From Pozières to the Ancre

Britain had not been alone in declaring war on Germany on 4 August 1914. Without consulting the governments of the Dominions, King George V made the declaration in Privy Council by royal prerogative on behalf of the Empire. When the governor-generals in each of the Dominions issued the royal proclamation, vast swathes of the globe suddenly found themselves at war with Germany. The Viceroy of India announced that all 250 million Indians were at war. The white Dominions, as they were then called – Canada, Australia, New Zealand and South Africa – all went to war as well. Not that the King or anyone else in London need have worried about objections. Such were the weighty bonds of empire that India and the Dominions unhesitatingly rallied behind the mother country, even if the cause was one about which they knew little.

By the end of the year Indian troops were shivering on the damp and chilly fields of Flanders. The Australian Imperial Force of one division and a brigade, supported by New Zealand troops, had sailed for Egypt. Canadians were beginning to arrive in England and France. And a white South Africa brigade was training in Cape Town.

The newly formed Australian and New Zealand Corps, the Anzacs, saw their first action when they landed with British troops on the Gallipoli peninsula in April 1915, following the failure of the British and French navies to 'force the Dardanelles' and capture Constantinople (Istanbul), the Ottoman Turkish capital. Lord Kitchener personally appointed the commander of the expedition, General Sir Ian Hamilton, who was given a single small folder of intelligence papers and orders to plan an amphibious operation, and was told to be ready in just a few weeks. Unsurprisingly, the amphibious landings were ill-conceived and poorly executed. The men had not trained for landing on a hostile shore and the Turks fought bitterly to defend even this remote corner of their homeland. Overall Hamilton proved weak and indecisive. For months, a form of trench warfare bogged down tens of thousands of Anzac and British troops in stalemate. With summer came heat, endless flies and endemic dysentery. Losses mounted to horrifying levels.

Additional landings at Suvla Bay in August met little opposition but their commander, Lieutenant-General Sir Frederick Stopford, failed to press his advantage. On the afternoon of the landings, officers were seen having a swim off the beach while Stopford took a nap. By the time they moved forward the Turks had arrived in large numbers and the result was stalemate again. Stopford was sent home.

So intense was the fighting that by the end of the year practically every man leaving the peninsula was found to be suffering from shell shock, 'whether he was supposed to be fit or not'. A physician noted that 'Very few could hold their hands out without shaking.'[1] In December, it was decided the campaign was lost and over a period of weeks the remaining men were evacuated. This was the only successful operation in the entire campaign. Total Allied losses amounted to 132,000, of whom 25,700 were Australians and 7,100 New Zealanders.

The Anzac troops' blood sacrifice nevertheless began to generate a new sense of pride in these young countries at the beginning of their journey towards becoming mature and independent nations. Their bravery was largely defined in reaction to British leadership. In Anzac eyes, the incompetence of the blimpish British generals played a large part in shaping the myth of their 'glorious defeat'. Moreover, the Anzac units were not so class-oriented as their British counterparts and enjoyed less formal military discipline. Officers were not always addressed as 'Sir'. Sometimes men referred to each other by their Christian names.[2] The Australians thought British officers were aloof, stiff and too obsessed with discipline. Conversely British officers never doubted that Australians were good fighters, but were constantly shocked by their uncouth behaviour, sloppy dress and lack of deference. They thought the Australians were rowdy, crude and undisciplined.

The effect in Australia of the news of such losses and setbacks had been to galvanise recruitment. Even with the restrictions imposed by military censorship, the limitations of distance and the spread of rumours, Australians could tell the war was not going well. In the eight months after the Gallipoli landings, more than 120,000 volunteers came forward. When the dynamic William Morris Hughes became Prime Minister, the war effort intensified. A new force was gathered in Egypt to train and to defend the Suez Canal from an expected Turkish assault. In March 1916, the first of five Australian divisions and one from New Zealand sailed for France, where the demand for men was growing weekly. As they arrived in Marseilles, a young Australian chaplain preached to the men, saying, 'We know what we have come for and we know that it is right. We have all read of the things that happened in France. We know that the Germans invaded a peaceful country and brought these horrors into it ... We came of our own free wills – to say that this sort of thing shall not happen in the world as long as we are in it ... With our dear ones behind, and God above, and our friends on each side, and only the enemy in front – what more do we wish than that.'[3] It was a great rallying cry. The Australians were coming.

On 1 July 1916, only one set of troops in Fourth Army to go over the top had not been of Anglo-Irish origin. These were the Newfoundlanders, who sustained one of the day's highest casualty rates.[4] Another unit from the Dominions, the South African Brigade, had 'covered themselves with glory' from 15 to 20 July in the struggle to take Delville Wood.[5] Now it was the turn of the Australians. In April the 1st and 2nd Australian Divisions, veterans from Gallipoli, had been assigned to a quiet section of the front near Armentières where they were involved in extensive trench raiding. From this they gained useful experience of trench fighting in France. In July they were sent south to the Somme sector to await their entry into the battle raging there.

Meanwhile, the newly arrived 5th Australian Division was involved in a disastrous action at Fromelles on 19 July, intended as a diversionary operation to draw German reinforcements from the Somme front. Lieutenant-General Sir Richard Haking, commander of XI Corps, enthusiastically supported a plan to attack across waterlogged Flanders countryside against well-defended German lines. The Germans watched the detailed preparations for the assault from an observation post on the top of nearby Aubers Ridge. After a heavy bombardment, the Australians and British troops from 61st Division went forward during the evening. It was horribly reminiscent of 1 July. The artillery had not done enough damage to the enemy lines, so defensive machine gun and artillery fire poured down upon the advancing troops. As the *Official History* put it, the inability of the artillery to 'reduce the defenders to a state of collapse before the assault' meant that 'the infantry, advancing in broad daylight, paid the price.'[6] In places men reached the German lines and overpowered enemy resistance. But, as on 1 July, they could not hold on to these gains and either withdrew or were killed. On the next morning the assault was cancelled.

The Australians suffered 5,333 casualties in the single night of 19–20 July, equivalent to the total Australian casualties in the Boer War, the Korean War and the war in Vietnam combined. The Australian War Memorial has called it not just the worst 24 hours in Australian military history but 'the worst 24 hours in Australia's entire history'.[7] Fromelles was a ghastly failure, succeeding only in further undermining Australian faith in British generals. The fiasco gained additional poignancy when in 2008 battlefield archaeologists discovered a mass grave dug by the Germans that contained the remains of 250 Australian and British soldiers. About half of the bodies were identified from personal artefacts and DNA evidence, and they were all reburied in the Pheasant Wood Military Cemetery at Fromelles.[8]

At the same time as the Fromelles disaster, in mid-July, the 1st and 2nd Australian Divisions were added to Gough's Reserve Army (later to be called Fifth Army). Gough had taken over from Rawlinson the responsibility for an assault on Pozières. Before the war the village had been a small agricultural community consisting of a few farms and orchards, and it was of little interest except for its position at the highest point of the Thiepval ridge. In July 1916 it was an outpost of the German second defensive line. The Albert–Bapaume road went through the middle of the village. Three hundred yards further up the road lay the ruins of a windmill that stood at the crest of the ridge. This commanding position looked north towards Thiepval, which had not been captured on 1 July and still remained firmly in German hands, and south towards Bazentin-le-Petit and the woods over which the two sides were still fighting bitterly. Control of Pozières would offer the opportunity to advance behind the German lines either to the north or south. By means of four assaults the British line inched closer to Pozières and the artillery pounded the village into a pile of rubble.

Gough, ever impatient to move forward, summoned General Walker, commander of the 1st Australian Division, to his headquarters on 18 July. Walker and his men had only just arrived in the Somme region, but Gough told him, 'I want you to go into the line and attack Pozières tomorrow night!'⁹ Walker pleaded for a delay but ordered his men immediately to begin to march the twelve miles to the front; this itself took a couple of days. The Australians were wide eyed as they clambered across congested trenches still piled high with unburied German and British dead. They came under attack from a new kind of shell that did not explode on landing but gave off a gentle, aromatic, grassy smell. The Australians thought the shells were duds until they realised they contained a new poison gas named phosgene. Ten times more toxic than chlorine gas, which had been in use for more than a year, phosgene did not always have an immediate effect and sometimes it was only after several hours that a victim developed symptoms which started with a burning sensation in the eyes, progressed to vomiting and nausea and led to a slow process of suffocation. It was a terrible weapon to come up against and the use of phosgene marked a deadly escalation in chemical warfare.

The Australians eventually got into position to the south of Pozières. Despite their ghastly march to the front they were supremely optimistic. Lance Corporal Horton later summed up the anxious but confident mood: 'though every hour brought more certainly before us the uncertainty of the future, yet this new realization of the instability of existence once over the top did not lessen our desire to make good or shake our knowledge of the fact that absolute success would be ours. All it conveyed was this: on the morrow when the success had been attained, some of us would not be there. It did not affect our will to do or die. It did not detract one iota from the dash of the charge. It simply gave us knowledge and new thoughts – that was all.'[10]

Inspecting Australian troops earlier, Sir Douglas Haig had picked up on their high morale. He had written, 'The men were looking splendid, fine physique, very hard and determined-looking ... The Australians are mad keen to kill Germans and to start doing it at once!'[11] According to the *Australian Official History* the men waiting to attack were the best Australia had to offer. 'In physique and morale they were not surpassed.'[12] Now they wanted to show everyone, the British just as much as the Germans, what they were capable of.

The Australian assault at Pozières formed the left wing of what was to be the third major offensive of the Somme campaign. Six divisions drew up to attack in a line running south-east from the Australians' position: at Bazentin-le-Petit, at High Wood, which had been reoccupied by the Germans after the cavalry were withdrawn, at Delville Wood, and at Guillemont, near where the British lines adjoined those of the French. It was hoped that the French would join the attack also but they pulled out, saying they were not ready. A makeshift artillery barrage was quickly organised and on the evening of 22 July, before the moon had come up, the guns opened fire along the German front. In the Australian lines, an officer recorded in his diary, 'we saw the skyline simply alive with light. Flashes like summer lightning were quite continuous, making one flickering band of light, but this was away in the east behind Fricourt and Montauban. Clearly the British were doing something there. Every now and then a low lurid red flush, very angry, lit the horizon.'[13] The Australians were new to the great barrages of the Western Front and like everyone who had witnessed such a sight before them, they were suitably impressed.

Soon after midnight, on Sunday 23 July, following a hurricane artillery bombardment of only two minutes, the Australians advanced and soon overpowered the few Germans left in their front line. The second wave went forward and despite the growing German artillery fire now pouring down on them, quickly advanced further to occupy most of what remained of Pozières, to the south of the main road. The Australians then began a process of what they called 'ratting', throwing phosphorus bombs into the German dugouts and killing or capturing the survivors as they came up. They then moved forward to the main German line, just beyond the village at the windmill. Here they met much more stubborn resistance. As dawn came up, however, the Australians had captured most of Pozières, firmly entrenched their position and had brought up Vickers machine guns. The Germans mounted a series of spirited counter-attacks, but they were fought off and suffered heavy losses.

Too hastily organised, the British attack on the Australian right was a failure. Battalion officers had not had time to carry out recces and the artillery had once again been spread too thinly. It seemed that the lessons of the successful assault on 14 July had been forgotten already. British troops failed to take an inch of ground. After the previous success this was a bitter disappointment to their commanders. The battle would continue in a series of piecemeal assaults, to straighten the line or to take out a German strongpoint, and the struggle for the woods that could have been taken in early July carried on, clocking up heavy losses. The British failure on the night of 23–24 July made the Australian capture of Pozières look even more impressive and the commander of the adjoining

British division sent a message to the Australians saying his men were proud to be fighting alongside them.

Within a few days the Australian 1st Division completed its capture of Pozières village, but the main German line running through the windmill remained unattainable. By now the men of the 1st Australian Division were exhausted, having fought day and night for more than seventy-two hours.

At this point a new German commander arrived opposite the Pozières sector. General Max von Boehn and his XI Reserve Corps relieved General von Arnim's IV Corps. Boehn had been at Verdun and his was one of several corps transferred to the Somme. That the Somme was beginning to relieve pressure on the French at Verdun was a sign that at least one of the objectives of the battle had been achieved. After the defeat of the infantry counter-attacks, Boehn decided to change tactics and called for a massive artillery bombardment on Pozières to make the Australian positions impossible to maintain. The battle now entered a new phase. The Australians continued to mount assaults, trying to take advantage of their control of the high ground. But the intense and continuous artillery bombardment slowly began to break their spirit.

At first, the Australians were blasé about the barrage and took a cocky attitude towards enemy shell fire. So as to impress their mates, men carrying food or supplies to the front past their fellow soldiers would not duck or even turn their heads when a shell landed nearby. Stretcher bearers would carry on helping the wounded regardless of incoming shells. If they judged the risk was worth taking, the men would carry on without flinching. 'Give it a go' became their catchphrase, expressing the attitude they wanted to portray.[14] But it was impossible to sustain such an approach for long against one of the heaviest bombardments yet put down by the German artillery. Slowly even the tough and confident Australians started to succumb. A sergeant in the 4th New South Wales Battalion wrote in his diary under a barrage from 5.9-inch howitzers, 'Sitting down under heavy High Explosive shellfire is ... very nerve shattering.'[15]

The first cases of shell shock began to appear. Major Rowlands of the 2nd New South Wales Battalion reported 'eight men with shell shock praying to be paraded before the doctor'. One of the battalion's company commanders went down with a bad case of shell shock, while in the adjoining battalion 'nearly everyone has been buried at least once and we are kept busy digging ourselves out of the blown-down trench.' The German shells continued to rain down, and Captain Harris of the 3rd New South Wales Battalion wrote: 'As fast as one portion of the trench was cleared another was blown in. There were no dugouts in which men on post could take shelter, and the only thing to do was to grin and bear it ... The bombardment lasted all day. And during its worst period four shells a minute were falling in or near the company's sector ... The wounded were so many that the stretcher bearers, who were working like heroes, could not get them away. The men who were not wounded were kept busy digging out men who were buried alive by the explosions caving in the trench sides.'[16] All the conditions that made for a high incidence of shell shock were present. The constant whine of the shells, the temptation to guess what each shell was and speculate as to where it would fall, combined to cause intense strain on the nerves – especially in those who had been buried by a previous shell and pulled out by their mates.

As Pozières marked the only area where, at the end of July, the Allies were gaining ground, the fighting here grew in intensity. General Fritz von Below, a tough Prussian, commander of the German Second Army on the Somme, announced that any officer who surrendered a trench would be court-martialled. Few proud German officers wanted to suffer this ignominy. But attempted counter-attacks failed, with heavy losses, and for the first time the commanding officers of German divisions that had failed to recapture lost ground were sent home in disgrace, as in the British army.

However, the Germans maintained their artillery bombardment. On 25 July it was even heavier than on the day before. An Australian officer reported that 'one shell merely filled up the hole the last shell made', while Colonel Elliott of the 12th South and West Australia and Tasmania Battalion described the shelling as 'the worst we ever suffered.' He would serve with the battalion for the rest of the war, yet as he wrote, 'Later we experienced many hurricane bombardments lasting half an hour or more of far greater intensity, but I do not remember any other so severe for such a long time.'[17]

This was one of the rare occasions when the medical services kept a detailed note of those reported wounded and those who were suffering from shell shock. On 24 July, 29 per cent of all wounded were evacuated because of shell shock; on 25 July it was 22 per cent; on 26 July 24 per cent. These were some of the highest percentages recorded during the Battle of the Somme.[18] The *Australian Official History* stated that in addition to those officially evacuated with shell shock, a 'large number' of the remainder who had come through without seeking medical attention had suffered 'effects which in peacetime would be diagnosed as "nervous breakdown".'[19]

On the night of 26 July, the 1st Australian Division was finally withdrawn from the line having lost more than 5,200 men. An Australian sergeant who saw the men as they filed back through Albert thought even the survivors appeared shell-shocked. He wrote, 'They looked like men who had been in Hell. Almost without exception, each man looked drawn and haggard, and so dazed that they appeared to be walking in a dream, and their eyes looked glassy and starey ... I have never seen men quite so shaken up as these.'[20]

The 2nd Australian Division now replaced the 1st. They had to endure the same intensity of shell fire. Haig told Gough to keep a close eye on these new Australian troops. He was beginning to find some of the Australian command-ers a touch arrogant and wrote in his diary that some of their generals 'are so ignorant and (like many Colonials) so con-ceited, that they cannot be trusted [to work out proper plans of attack]'.[21] However, Major-General Legge, commander of the 2nd Australian Division, was rushed into launching a series of offensives and the division suffered heavy losses for minimal gain. German observers at the windmill still had a clear view of the Australian and British lines and could watch the preparations for every assault as they were made.

Haig called for 'methodical progress' along this stretch of the front, by which he meant a series of relatively small-scale but continuous assaults, advancing from Pozières north to Mouquet Farm in order to seize control of the heights of the ridge, wear down the enemy and draw in his reserves.[22] After one such failed assault on 28 July, parties were sent into No Man's Land at night to dig jumping-off trenches three feet deep in preparation for the next attack, known as saps. Each man in the entrenching party was to dig two yards of trench. It sounded simple enough to a staff officer in brigade head-quarters a couple of miles behind the front. But for men who had spent all day under shell fire, living in an atmosphere that reeked in the heat of long summer days with the foul smell of decaying bodies, these night-time trench-digging parties could be appalling. The Germans often mistook them in the darkness for an actual assault and brought down on them a further barrage of fire.

On the night of 31 July, 200 men of the 23rd Victoria Battalion were ordered to dig a sap in No Man's Land that would be used as a jumping-off point for an assault planned the following night. In the party, leading his platoon, was Lieutenant John Alexander Raws. Aged thirty-three and a well-known sportsman in Australia, Raws was an excellent cricketer and a tennis champion who frequently played for the state of Victoria. He had also been a journalist on the *Melbourne Argus* before the war. He left a vivid account of the effect of being under constant enemy shell fire while trying to carry out their task. 'We do all our fighting and moving at night, and the confusion of passing through a barrage of enemy shells in the dark is pretty appalling ... We went in single file along narrow communication trenches. We were shelled all the way up, but got absolute hell when passing through a particularly heavy curtain of fire which the enemy were playing on the ruined village [Pozières].'

Raws and his group finally joined the digging party in No Man's Land, only to find that 'Our leader was shot and the strain had sent two other officers mad.' Raws and another officer took command and the party began digging the sap. At the approach of dawn he led the men back on another journey through hell. 'I was buried twice and thrown down several times – buried with dead and dying. The ground was covered with bodies in all stages of decay and mutilation and I would, after struggling free from the earth, pick up a body by me to try to lift him out with me, and find him a decayed corpse. I pulled a head off – was covered with blood. The horror was indescribable. In the dim misty light of dawn I collected about 50 men and sent them off, mad with terror, on the right track for home.'

Raws summed up the state of his own strained nerves: 'I have had much luck and kept my nerve so far. The awful difficulty is to keep it. The bravest of all often lose it – courage does not count here. It is all nerve – once that goes one becomes a gibbering maniac. The noise of our own guns, the enemy's shells, and getting lost in the darkness ... Only the men you would have trusted and believed in before proved equal to it. One or two of my friends stood splendidly, like granite rocks round which the seas stormed in vain. They were all junior officers; but many other fine men broke to pieces. Everyone called it shell shock, but shell shock is very rare. What 90% get is justifiable funk, due to the collapse of the helm – of self control.'

Raws continued: 'We are lousy, stinking, ragged, unshaven, sleepless ... I have one puttee, a dead man's helmet, another dead man's gas protector, a dead man's bayonet. My tunic is rotten with other men's blood, and partly spattered with a comrade's brains ... The sad part is that one can see no end of this. If we live tonight, we have to go through tomorrow night, and next week and next month. Poor wounded devils you meet on the stretchers are laughing with glee. One cannot blame them. They are getting out of this.'[23] Raws did survive for a few more nights but was killed in action three weeks later on 23 August.

But his work and that of the other trench-digging parties had not been in vain. At 9.15 p.m. on the night of 4 August, after a three-minute bombardment, the Australians left their jumping-off points about 200 yards from the enemy forward trench. They rushed the German lines and took control before most of the defenders had emerged from their dugouts – in this case decisively winning the 'race for the parapet'. During the night they finally captured the wind-mill and took control of the Pozières heights. They captured 500 prisoners and fought off a German counter-attack at dawn. By mid-morning, from this position the Allies had been fighting for since the beginning of July, the Australians could look down the slope of the ridge right across the

German positions from Courcelette to Mouquet Farm and Thiepval.

As if to congratulate them, the German gunners laid down an even fiercer salvo of fire on the positions they had just captured. The men of the 2nd Division, utterly exhausted after a week of fighting by day and night, were replaced by the 4th Australian Division. During a major counter-attack on 7 August the Australian line buckled. Lieutenant Albert Jacka of the 14th Victoria Battalion led his men behind a party of German troops who had advanced over the trench in which he was sheltering. Rallying a small group around him, Jacka fought a furious encounter using bombs, bayonets and rifles, and eventually overpowered the Germans, all of whom were killed or finally surrendered. Jacka had already won a VC at Gallipoli, and the *Australian Official History* described the action of 7 August as 'the most dramatic and effective act of individual audacity in the history of the Australian Imperial Force.'[24] The Australian line held and there were no further German attempts to recapture Pozières.

The German bombardment continued for day after day. Cases of shell shock continued to pour in to the medical aid posts. The Anzac Corps had taken over the CCS at Vadencourt. In early August, an eyewitness reported that nearly every man who waited patiently for his wounds to be treated there was 'shaking like an aspen leaf', a sure sign that they were also suffering from some sort of shell shock.[25] The commander of Fourth Army, Rawlinson, began to grow seriously concerned about the 'wastage' from shell shock. Casualties in Fourth Army were now calculated to total 125,000 officers and men. Rawlinson's chief of staff, Major-General Sir Archibald Montgomery, issued a questionnaire to his corps, division and some brigade commanders asking what lessons should be learned from the last four weeks of battle. Senior officers wrote back extensively about the need for sufficient preparation time for an assault, the need to secure flanks, the best way to advance in line, the most efficient method to shell a wood, to deploy machine guns, and so on.[26] The army was quickly learning an immense number of lessons, and the notes provided a useful and realistic corrective to the rigid and inadequate Tactical Notes issued by Fourth Army in May.

For the rest of August, the Australians pushed forward down the slope from Pozières ridge towards Mouquet Farm, the objective that the Lonsdales had expected to capture by midday on 1 July, and the German fortifications at the head of Nab Valley, from where the machine guns had fired into their ranks as they assembled that morning. But the farm proved too tough a nut even for the Australians to crack. On 21 August, the 12th South and West Australia and Tasmania Battalion reached the farm, but their numbers were too small to enable them to hold off the inevitable counter-attack and they had to withdraw. They realised that the interlinked cellars of the farm made it into a formidable defensive stronghold.

On the same day, the 4th Gloucestershire Battalion and the 1st Wiltshire Battalion of the 25th Division captured the trenches in the south-eastern face of the Leipzig salient. They consolidated their position, picking up where the 17th Highlanders had left off on 1 July. These forward movements were met every time by German counter-attacks that often proved costly. At the end of August the weather started to change and heavy rain turned the ground into a sea of chalky slime. The Australians continued to push on to Mouquet Farm, but were unable to take and hold it, suffering 6,300 casualties in the attempt.

In early September, after six weeks in which the three Australian divisions of the Anzac Corps had rotated in and out of the line, the Australians were withdrawn to rest and recover, and relieved by the Canadian Corps. The Australians had conducted nineteen separate assaults across a front of about one mile, but none had been as successful as the first on the village of Pozières itself and the capture of the windmill ten days later. They had moved the line forward, a few hundred yards here, half a mile there. But Mouquet Farm was still in German hands. The Australians were exhausted by the toll of battle and shattered by the continuous bombardment. They had suffered a total of 23,000 casualties in forty-five days, nearly as many as the casualties in nine full months of fighting at Gallipoli. (British casualties alongside them had been on a similar scale.) Private Athol Dunlop wrote to his sister, 'Anyway, I'm proud of being an Australian and can say without boasting that as fighters they have no superiors and damned few equals.'[27] Artillery barrages were from now on to be judged by comparison to that of Pozières, and very few matched it in intensity of fire and length of continuous bombardment.

However, from the remnants of the Anzac Corps a new story began to emerge. Pozières on the Somme, like Gallipoli, became sacred ground and an important stage in the building of a sense of national identity. Once again, as at Gallipoli, there was a strong sense of bitterness towards the British commanders, and especially towards Haig, who had kept up his policy of launching small-scale attacks against heavily defended German lines. Lieutenant Raws in his last letter home wrote of the 'murder' of many of his friends 'through the incompetence, callousness and personal vanity of those high in authority'.[28] And Australian troops developed an aversion to serving under Haig, a reaction which would become even more pronounced in the following year. During the Battle of the Somme, Australians had without question fought valiantly and stubbornly. Although Australian commanders had led their men in the field, it was British generals who were blamed for failures. And it was Australian heroes who were credited with victories.

Accompanying the Australian forces was an official war correspondent. Charles Bean was a tall, thin, bespectacled figure never far from the centre of the action, usually with a pencil and notepad in hand. He was, in today's parlance, 'embedded' with the Anzac Corps. Having landed at Gallipoli only hours after the first troops, he had endured the same hardships as those troops, was wounded in the Battle of Sari Bair, and he remained on the peninsula, departing only two days before the final evacuation. At Pozières he had again spent time with the men in the trenches, had endured the constant shell fire, had seen exhausted troops stagger out of the line and newly refreshed men march eagerly forward, and had watched and written about all that had happened. He was very moved by seeing men brought down by shell shock. He saw no shame in the fact that cheery, confident and physically first-rate soldiers were reduced to 'gibbering maniacs' by the effect of shell fire and he reported on this regularly. But he was a fierce patriot and immensely proud of the fighting spirit he witnessed daily among the 'Diggers', the common Australian soldiers.

After the war he was granted access to official documents and started to write the *Australian Official History*, in which he would include the powerful testimony of the men he had lived with.[29] Pozières and Mouquet Farm had shown that even the toughest, most confident troops could suffer from a high incidence of shell shock. No one who served on the Great War battlefield was immune to the strain on their nerves. But the battle still had a long way to run.

Haig was determined to keep up constant pressure on the German army along the Somme throughout the summer. At times this was as clumsy as using a battering ram to smash relentlessly against a fortified castle wall. On other occasions,

when the lessons of 14 July were applied and arti...
was concentrated against a small defensive area, the as...
brought unexpected success. Such was the nature of a w...
of attrition. The casualty figures rarely dropped below 2,500
per day.

But the consequences were not one-sided. The German
army was suffering terribly too. More reinforcements were
thrown into the mashing machine along the Somme. German
accounts stress the horror of trying to live through British
artillery bombardments. Friedrich Steinbrecher, a theology
student in Leipzig before the war, was a young German
officer on the Somme. In a letter he described his journey to
the front. 'During the lorry and train journey we were still
quite cheery ... [Then] we were rushed up through shell
shattered villages and barrage into the turmoil of war. The
enemy was firing with 12-inch guns. There was a perfect
torrent of shells ... Now one's eyes begin to see things. I
want to keep running on – to stand still and look is horrible.
"A wall of dead and wounded." How often have I read that
phrase? Now I know what it means ... Day melts into night.
We are always on the alert ... Somme. The whole history of
the world cannot contain a more ghastly word.'[30]

During August, Haig gave up on the idea of a breakthrough and concentrated on 'straightening the line', a
process that sounds clear and simple but was rarely either.
The purpose of 'straightening the line' was to make artillery
fire against the opposing German line more effective. But
still strongpoints like Beaumont-Hamel, Thiepval, Mouquet
Farm, High Wood and Guillemont remained in enemy
hands. In the south, the French too kept up the pressure,
General Fayolle's Sixth Army taking more ground in early
September. Everywhere, the Allies were advancing, but their
progress was measured in yards or metres, not in miles or
kilometres.

The next phase of the Somme offensive was launched on 15 September. Like that of 1 July, the attack took place on a broad front after an intense artillery bombardment in which nearly one million shells were fired at enemy positions. As on the first day of the Somme, Haig hoped for a breakthrough and the cavalry were standing by to break out, seize Bapaume and roll up the German defences. Likewise, as on 1 July, Rawlinson saw the attack in more limited terms. And as on the first day, the attacks were initially successful in many places but overall they failed to deliver the victory that was hoped for. The German line buckled but did not give way.

The Battle of Flers-Courcelette, as the offensive became known, is best remembered for the first use of tanks, one of the few new weapons of war to emerge between 1914 and 1918. The story of the development of the tank has been told many times.[31] Their first use on the battlefield was highly controversial. There were very few of them available. Their crews lacked training. Tactics for working with the infantry had not been worked out. But most of all they were extremely slow, advancing at about 2 m.p.h., and mechanically very unreliable. They could cross barbed wire and fire into enemy lines, but thick mud and deep shell holes presented an insurmountable obstacle. Only forty-nine tanks were ready for action that day, not enough to make much difference even if they had all performed magnificently. Of these, roughly one-third, seventeen, broke down or failed to reach their starting positions. The remaining thirty-two rumbled slowly forward as best they could. Nine tanks did creditably well and their crews dealt with the obstacles they encountered. Nine more made such slow progress that the infantry soon overtook them. The other fourteen broke down during the advance or were stranded in shell holes or trenches. Many of the tank crews inside their noisy, hot, dangerous machines, nearly suffocating on petrol fumes, suffered from nervous breakdown and shell shock.[32]

It was an inauspicious beginning for the new weapon of war. Haig was blamed for wasting the opportunity by revealing the tanks for the first time when they were still in such short supply.[33] On the other hand, if he had not done so he would no doubt have been blamed for failing to use what some protagonists were claiming was a war-winning weapon during the biggest and bloodiest battle ever fought by the British army. The fact was that with tanks available in growing numbers in France by September 1916 their presence would not have remained a secret for long. There had to be a first time for their use, and this was it.

An early morning mist on 15 September soon cleared into a bright autumn day. The barrage moved back from the German front line at 6.20 a.m., when the infantry went over the top with the tanks. On the right wing of the British offensive a German defensive structure known as the Quadrilateral held up the assault, its occupants firing into the flanks of the attacking troops. The hardened and experienced Guards Division did however succeed in advancing for about a mile into the German third line. On their left, the inexperienced 41st Division, which had only been in France for a few months, also did well and captured the town of Flers. An RFC observer reported seeing a tank entering the town, prompting some excited reporting about 'a Leviathan . . . a Behemoth . . . a Tank . . . rolling majestically and alone down the empty main street of Flers long before the place was ours'.[34]

Further north along the front, the New Zealand Division undertook its first major action in France. The New Zealanders had built up a formidable reputation at Gallipoli and now had a chance to show the Germans what they were worth. They did not disappoint and succeeded in capturing their objective known as the Switch Line, although at times their enthusiasm ran away with them and they advanced too quickly and into the British barrage. On their left, the 47th (London) Division had a major struggle to capture High Wood, where the tanks proved useless among the shattered tree stumps; their commanders said they should never have been deployed. But the 47th finally succeeded in occupying the wood that could have been taken two months before on 14 July. Exhausted, they could go no further. Major-General Barter, their commander, was sent home for not pressing on beyond High Wood. To their left, the 15th (Scottish) Division captured the village of Martinpuich, while the 2nd Canadian Division, attacking up the Albert–Bapaume road, seized Courcelette.

British and imperial success was not matched by the French to the south. They attacked with four corps but failed to make a significant advance. And although the British and imperial forces had done well, they had nowhere achieved all their objectives. The *Official History* concluded that the German Army 'had been dealt a severe blow' and had suffered 'heavy casualties', but that on the Fourth Army front 'the results fell far short of the desired achievement' and there was 'no question of a break-through'.[35]

Ten days later, the infantry in Rawlinson's army were ordered over the top once again. This time the intense artillery barrage proved a success and the German positions under assault were weaker than those attacked earlier in the month. Morval and Lesboeufs were captured on 25 September; Combles on 26 September. That same day, Gough's army attacked further north and achieved some notable successes. General Ivor Maxse's 18th (Eastern) Division at last took Thiepval, the focus of so much bloodshed on 1 July. Two days later, the same division seized the Schwaben Redoubt, which had been temporarily occupied by the Ulstermen on the first day of the Somme battle. Unfortunately the momentum could not be maintained and during October little new ground was taken, although German counter-attacks were repelled with heavy losses.

The pressure on the German lines was intense and had been continuous for several weeks. A diary captured by the New Zealanders on 27 September contained the following incomplete final entry: 'No relief. Feeling of hopelessness, apathetic, everyone sleeps under heaviest fire – due to exhaustion. No rations, no drink. The whole day heavy fire on the left. We got heavy and HE shells. Everything all the same to us. The best thing would be for the British to come. No one worries about us; our relief said to be cancelled. If one wants sleep aeroplanes will not let us rest. In the present conditions, one no longer thinks. Iron rations, bread, biscuit, all eaten ... '[36]

By now the rains of autumn had arrived in earnest. Vast areas of the fighting front became seas of mud, rendering movement of supplies, ammunition, guns and tanks almost impossible. The New Zealanders found twenty horses were needed to haul a single artillery piece. The men in the trenches had to cope with increasingly appalling conditions, sinking up to their knees into several feet of wet, slimy mud. Exhausted stretcher bearers struggled to bring in the wounded. When an Australian brigadier was wounded it took four bearers ten hours to carry him even to the advanced dressing station.

But despite this, the Allies had learned lessons from the weeks of continuous fighting. The artillery had now mastered the art of the creeping barrage, moving the line of shell fire forward in proper coordination with the infantry, who might be only fifty yards behind. During October such tactics almost always proved successful. But slowly the number of assaults were reduced in the face of the weather. In early

November, the French scaled their operations right back. There was, however, one last blow Haig wanted to strike.

Allied commanders were due to meet at the French headquarters at Chantilly in mid-November. Haig wanted the British to be able to announce a success at this summit. So Gough's Fifth Army launched a final offensive in the north along the Ancre river, a tributary of the Somme. The attack was directed against many of the objectives that had been assaulted unsuccessfully on 1 July. Little fighting had taken place in the area since then, so the ground was less heavily cratered than elsewhere, and it was less far to bring supplies. The 51st (Highland) Division finally succeeded in capturing Beaumont-Hamel on 13 November, while the 63rd (Royal Naval) Division, a mixture of marines and conventional army recruits, took Beaucourt. However, Serre, the little village further north, proved impossible to capture. These actions, later described as the Battle of the Ancre Heights, cost Fifth Army 23,274 men killed, wounded and missing, although German losses were estimated to be even greater.[37]

On the night of 17 November, the first snow of winter fell along the Somme front. In the final assault, which took place on the following morning, the rested and re-formed 11th Borders made their return to front-line combat. With new officers in command and the battalion augmented by hundreds of new recruits, the Lonsdales lined up once again with the other battalions of the 97th Brigade alongside whom they had fought at the beginning of July. They assembled overnight and in dreadful conditions went over the top again, with heavy sleet driving at them all the while. The battalion war diary proudly recorded that they 'advanced in perfect order to attack. The spirit of the men being a fine sight to see in spite of the intense cold in which they had to lie and wait.'[38] They stormed a German line called Frankfort Trench, just south of Grandcourt, no more than three miles from where Colonel Machell and the battalion had been cut down on the first day of the battle. The 11th Borders seized the trench but after a protracted struggle had to withdraw. This was the furthest point reached by British troops on this section of the front.

Ironically, with the capture of Beaumont-Hamel and the return of the 11th Borders, the Battle of the Somme in the north ended where it had begun. Further south, however, where the assault had been more successful from day one, the Allies had advanced about seven miles into enemy territory. The weather finally brought close of play to a battle that had lasted for four and a half months. But the weather had not brought an end to Haig's resolution to keep up pressure on the enemy. He was determined to sustain the war of attrition. The commander-in-chief sent orders to Rawlinson at Fourth Army and Gough commanding Fifth Army to 'continue offensive operations to a limited extent as far as resources and weather permitted'.[39] He wanted to harass the enemy throughout the winter by every means possible.

The popular view of the Battle of the Somme is that it was a ghastly failure and a futile tragedy. For half a century the prevailing view was one of disastrous losses, incompetent generals, brave soldiers struggling in appalling conditions and the failure to effectively utilise new technology like that of the tank. Winston Churchill summed up this view in his grand history of the war, *The World Crisis*, when he described British troops as 'Martyrs not less than soldiers'. He went on: 'They fulfilled the high purpose of duty with which they were imbued. The battlefields of the Somme were the graveyards of Kitchener's Army. The flower of that generous manhood which quitted peaceful civilian life in every kind of workaday occupation, which came at the call of Britain . . . was shorn away for ever in 1916.'[40]

More recently a different view has emerged, one that

emphasises the importance of the battle for the British army in learning the tactics that would be needed to win the war two years later. Those arguing this view make the case that while casualties were always going to be high in an industrial war of attrition, the Somme was a battle that had to be fought somewhere at some time. The British armies had displayed courage and moral determination in fighting on. While it is difficult to class the Somme as a 'victory', it was certainly not in military terms a defeat.[41] This argument concludes that the real loser on the Somme was the German army, which suffered somewhere between half a million and 600,000 casualties, including many of its best trained and most experienced NCOs and junior officers.[42] Captain von Hentig of the Guards Reserve Division described the Somme as 'the muddy grave of the German army'. Crown Prince Rupprecht of Bavaria concluded that 'What remained of the old first-class peace-trained German infantry had been expended on the battlefield.'[43] And certainly the authorities in Berlin reached the view that the war could not be won on the Western Front and so made a decision to resort to unrestricted U-boat warfare in the Atlantic to try to starve the Allies into submission. This strategy resulted in the entry of America into the war and began the process that led to the ultimate defeat of the German army on the battlefield in November 1918. In this sense, it can certainly be said that the Somme was a pivotal battle in the war.

The Australian divisions that had fought so intently at Pozières in August were brought back into the battle in November. With them came Charles Bean, who trudged up from Albert, visited Delville Wood and Longueval, took another look at what was left of Pozières and finally reached the Australian trenches. Here the liquid mud came up to his knees and every step required a gigantic physical effort. On 5 November, the Anzac Corps launched an assault near

Guedecourt. The line was pushed forward a few yards here and there but fighting had become almost impossible. Bean later claimed these were the worst conditions ever faced by Australian troops in the First World War.[44]

It was in August, while sheltering in a dugout in Pozières as the shells whistled down, that Bean had reflected how words were not enough to pay tribute to the sacrifices he was witnessing. He decided to collect as many photographs and as much cinema film as he could recording the work of the Australian Imperial Forces. He also started to gather letters, diaries, maps and war records relating to the Australian troops, along with what he increasingly saw as the 'sacred relics' of Australian sacrifice and heroism.[45] Coming up with the idea of a 'Museum of War Relics', he pitched it to General Sir William Birdwood, commander of the Anzac Corps, who enthusiastically recommended it to the Australian government back home. The result of Bean's reflections was the establishment of the Australian War Memorial, which would eventually be built as an archive and museum in that nation's capital, Canberra. Similar concerns and interests in Britain led the War Cabinet in March 1917 to establish what would become the Imperial War Museum in London.[46] These museums and many others would still be making records available and providing a memorial to the 'war to end all wars' one hundred years later.

But even as the Battle of the Somme came to its muddy end in the snow and sleet of winter, the military reaction to the epidemic of shell shock was still playing itself out. Some unlucky victims of war trauma were accused of cowardice or desertion and found they had to face another, even more brutal, military response.

9

Rough Justice

Charles Samuel Myers grappled for some time with trying to understand what was happening to men's minds in the course of nervous breakdowns brought on by the trauma of war. As he struggled with the military authorities to make them realise that shell shock was first, not a sign of weakness, and second, could be treated and cured, he also opposed the view that shell shock victims were mostly shirkers seeking to get out of their military duties, to desert. Even though Myers had been admitted into the military hierarchy as Consulting Psychologist after the start of the Somme offensive in 1916 he still felt like an outsider in the army establishment. He summed up the attitude he had to contend with when he wrote that 'from a military standpoint, a deserter was either "insane" and destined for the "mad house" or responsible and should be shot.'[1] The nervous diseases brought on by the war made this simple distinction far more complex and difficult to manage. But it did mean that the military would always see mental illness in relationship to the whole issue of discipline and the systems created to enforce it.

The purpose of military law was to ensure that discipline was maintained and orders were obeyed under the often extreme pressures of the battlefield. And of course picking out men and punishing them was intended to set an example for all the other members of a unit – *pour encourager les autres*, as the French aptly put it. Military law derives its legitimacy from the British Army Act, renewed annually as part of the process of approving the costs of the army in Parliament. Army Field Regulations established different ways of trying offenders, all of which had set procedures that the prosecutors were required to follow. Relatively simple matters of indiscipline could be handled by a man's commanding officer, usually a company commander, a captain, or a more senior officer. These would include acts of drunkenness, refusing to obey an order, using obscene language to an NCO and minor theft. The officer would collect evidence and had authority to issue a range of punishments, including stopping a man's pay for up to twenty-eight days, fining him up to ten shillings or detaining him in the guard house for a short period of time. As a young subaltern, Robert Graves remembered spending several hours every day adjudicating on these minor offences when his battalion were training in England.[2]

More serious crimes were subject to fixed Field Punishments. Field Punishment No. 1 involved tying a man to an object, sometimes a post but more often a wheel on which the culprit was spreadeagled, a practice known by the men as 'crucifixion'. This could continue for two hours a day, for up to twenty-one days – although never on more than three consecutive days. Carried out in a public place, usually near the entrance to a man's barracks or camp, it was a barbaric way of treating a convicted soldier, dating back to the days when soldiers were regarded as 'scum' who needed brutal treatment to keep them in line. During the course of the First World War, most came to see this type of punishment as totally distasteful in a citizen army made up initially of volunteers and later of conscripts.

For more serious misdemeanours on the battlefield there were various levels of military tribunals, or courts martial. The Regimental Court Martial dealt with minor offences of negligence, absence without leave or more serious acts of drunk and disorderly behaviour. It could impose custodial sentences of up to forty-two days. Next up the ladder was the District Court Martial, which could issue punishments to NCOs that included demoting them to a lower grade or sending them 'back to the ranks'. For serious offences it could impose a custodial sentence of up to two years.

At the top of the military legal hierarchy were the General Courts Martial and the Field General Courts Martial. The General Court Martial was the highest form of military court but it was rarely called in wartime. A judge advocate presided over it, supported by up to thirteen officers. The Field General Court Martial was easier to use, requiring only three officers to act as judges, the most junior of whom had to be at least a captain. It was this form of court that was usually set up in France or in other theatres of war, relatively near to the front where an offence had occurred. The two senior courts martial had the power to impose the death penalty for a series of crimes that included desertion, sleeping at post on duty, cowardice, disobedience and murder. For a death sentence to be passed all three officers had to reach a unanimous decision.

There was no appeal, in the usual sense, to the decision of a court martial. The guilty verdict, however, was passed up the chain of command, sometimes with a recommendation for mercy, and a man's brigadier, divisional and corps commander could add comments. In practice these senior officers rarely knew the men individually, so any comments they made usually related to the general level of morale in the battalion of the man found guilty. Finally, the verdict with any recommendations reached the desk of the commander-in-chief – in France until December 1915 this was Sir John French, Sir Douglas Haig replacing him thereafter. The commander-in-chief had then to make a decision as to whether the death sentence should be applied or leniency shown; in the latter case the man would usually have his sentence commuted to one of penal servitude, often with hard labour. French and his successor Haig literally had the power of life and death over condemned men.

During the war years, British military courts sentenced 3,342 individuals to death. The vast majority of these sentences, about 90 per cent, were commuted. But 438 people were executed. These figures include nearly one hundred civilians who were sentenced during periods of martial law, such as ninety-three Irishmen convicted of rebellion after the Easter Rising of April 1916, and various individuals convicted of spying and espionage under the Defence of the Realm Act in Britain. The total number of soldiers in the British and imperial armies who were executed amounted to 343, out of 3,077 sentenced to death.[3] Most of them were shot by firing squad, usually at dawn. The firing squads were sometimes made up of men from the same battalion as the convicted man, although during the war it was decided this was not the best way to conduct an execution and firing squads were appointed from other units. Executions were not carried out in public, but it was required under Field Regulations that the battalion of a man sentenced to death should be called on parade and news of the execution read out to the whole unit – *pour encourager les autres*, again.

The system appears today to be horribly brutal, although of course capital punishment applied in the criminal courts of Britain as well at the time. For instance, 106 soldiers were convicted of murder, which was subject to a mandatory death sentence in both civilian and military courts. The real problem with military courts martial was that the officer-judges could be very inconsistent in their judgements. For instance, prior to every trial the accused soldier could be offered the assistance of an officer to act as 'the Prisoner's Friend'. This was often his platoon commander, who effectively acted as the defending counsel of the accused, although rarely did these officers have any legal training. But at the beginning of the war it was not a requirement for the accused to accept assistance. In several cases, men chose to defend themselves. Others, from the evidence, were clearly overwhelmed by the situation. An ill-educated, working-class soldier faced with his senior officers, individuals whom he was trained to think of as his 'superiors', acting as both prosecutors and judges, could find the whole process utterly intimidating. Courts martial would also look very badly on an accused soldier who had any previous convictions on his record. Furthermore, a hostile remark or damning comment from a witness or from the man's commanding officer could often sway the verdict.

And although medical officers were often called, their evidence was treated with suspicion by many officers and might be totally ignored. William Brown, a neurologist with Fourth Army during the Battle of the Somme, was often asked to give a medical opinion of a man's mental state at courts martial and he found this 'an extremely difficult and distasteful task'. However, he usually ended up giving evidence in favour of the defendant because he felt 'that his state of mind in the line when he was under heavy shellfire, was not the same as his state of mind when he was at the Base'.[4] The natural sympathy medical officers felt towards shell shock victims made many officer-judges highly suspicious of their evidence. As good and loyal officers they were often more concerned with maintaining the honour of the regiment than with establishing the truth about a man's mental health. Although strict procedures were laid down, they were applied unevenly and some courts martial could be over in only a matter of minutes.[5] It's difficult when reading accounts of these tribunals to avoid the conclusion that many of the courts provided only a quick and arbitrary jurisdiction, that the whole process was stacked against the accused soldier and that many judgements were desperately unjust.

The whole system of military law went into immediate operation in the opening days of the war. The first sentence of death was passed on the day after the first engagement by British troops at the Battle of Mons, when Private Whittle was found guilty of falling asleep at his post. However, his sentence was commuted. The first soldier put to death was nineteen-year-old Private Thomas Highgate of the 1st Royal West Kents, who had been in action at Mons and in the retreat that followed. Highgate had deserted at the beginning of September 1914 and was discovered in civilian clothing hiding in a barn. The court martial was swift, his defence was unassisted, and he was shot by firing squad two days afterwards, on 8 September. The next soldier to be executed, two weeks later, was Private George Ward of the 1st Royal Berkshires. Charged with cowardice, Ward did have an officer 'friend' but it seems he offered no defence and again, he was shot two days after being found guilty.[6]

The lingering question over many of these military executions, both during the war and ever since, is whether, with the summary nature of the justice handed out, men who should have been treated for shell shock or nervous conditions were in fact found guilty of desertion or cowardice and shot. The first of many cases to raise this question was that of Lance Sergeant William Walton, who deserted after his battalion had been involved in heavy fighting at the first battle of Ypres in November 1914. He took refuge in a house in a village near St Omer and was not found until March 1915. At his interrogation he had difficulty in answering even basic questions and claimed to have had a nervous breakdown.

Walton repeated the claim at his trial, but the officer-judges called no medical witnesses to provide an assessment and he was sentenced to death. He was shot a few days later. Over the following months dozens of men charged with cowardice or desertion displayed at their trials the classic symptoms of shell shock, which were either ignored or misunderstood by the officers sitting in judgement. By the end of June 1916, one hundred British soldiers had been sentenced to death by a court martial and executed.

In the first days of the Battle of the Somme, Private Arthur Earp was court-martialled on a joint charge of quitting his post and conduct 'to the prejudice of good order'. He was in the 1/5th Royal Warwickshire Regiment, part of 48th Division which was in the line at the northern end of the Somme front near Hebuterne. Earp's battalion did not go over the top on 1 July but was caught up in the intense German shelling of the British lines that followed the launch of the offensive. After two hours under heavy bombardment, Earp told his sergeant that he could stand it no longer and rushed away to seek refuge in a dugout in the support trenches. A few days later he was arrested. At his court martial it was said that he had displayed signs of distress for some time before making off. On this occasion the officer-judges showed sympathy for Earp's mental condition; although they found him guilty they recommended mercy on the grounds of his previous good service and added that the ferocity of the German bombardment was a further mitigating circumstance.

The court's verdict went up the chain of command, his divisional and corps commanders both agreeing with the recommendation of clemency because of his perilous mental state. As usual, the papers arrived on the desk of General Haig, who overruled the recommendation for mercy and confirmed that the death sentence should be carried out. It was unusual for Haig to write anything on the court martial papers that came before him, other than the single word 'Confirmed'. However, in this case he wrote, 'How can we ever win if this plea is allowed?' Furthermore, he rapped the knuckles of the generals who had agreed to commute the sentence. It has been argued that in writing this Haig accepted that Earp had shell shock, but believed that to commute the sentence would be to legitimise the condition and open the flood gates to thousands of others who would see it as a way of escaping the trenches.[7]

Haig clearly felt it essential to maintain discipline in order to prevent a collapse in morale, and this was one way in which he encouraged his subordinates to take a strong stand against the spread of shell shock. He might also have known that Earp's battalion had a bad reputation. In the middle of July, the battalion commander of the 1/5th Royal Warwickshire Regiment sent a report to his brigade commander, Brigadier Dent, complaining about 'the large percentage of utterly useless men' who seemed incapable of using their rifle and bayonet, and noting that 'This class of man is petrified with fear when he meets a German in the flesh.' He concluded, 'There are about a hundred and thirty of such men in my battalion and I would prefer to be without them.'

Brigadier Dent forwarded the report to Major-General Fanshawe of the 48th Division, who decided that the men should be transferred from the Warwicks to a Labour battalion that was unloading ships in the Channel ports. The Labour battalions were made up of men who were sometimes thought to be unfit for combat. The corps commander, Lieutenant-General Sir Aylmer Hunter-Weston, agreed and wrote a note saying, 'These men are degenerates. They are a source of danger to their comrades, their battalion and the brigade.'[8] Nowhere in this exchange is the term 'shell shock' used, but the men in question are described as having a 'vacant, hang-dog look', typical of men suffering from war neuroses. The readiness with which their commander accepted the transfer of up to one-eighth of the battalion's strength to another unit suggests that shell shock had spread badly among the Warwicks; he wanted to get rid of the shell shock victims and replace them with a new complement of eager, fresh recruits.

Later in the year another case similar to Earp's came up. Eric Skeffington Poole had volunteered in 1914 and the following year was commissioned as an officer. On 7 July 1916, Lieutenant Poole was in the trenches with the 11th West Yorks taking part in an assault on Bailiff Wood, near Contalmaison, when a German shell partially buried him. He was examined by a doctor who said he was shell shocked and should be evacuated. Having been in hospital for a month, he was sent back to his battalion which was in reserve, and placed in command of a platoon. On 5 October, the battalion was ordered up into the front line and took part in a bloody frontal assault on Flers which resulted in the loss of eight officers and 217 men. But Poole complained that he was not well and went missing for two days. When he was found he was court-martialled, although his brigade commander had recommended that he should not be charged due to his nervous state. The court martial adopted a harsh line, finding Poole guilty of desertion and making no recommendation for mercy. His brigadier recommended clemency but when the paperwork came before Haig, despite the clear evidence that Poole was not only suffering from shell shock but had indeed been hospitalised by it, he insisted that the death sentence should be carried out. Haig wrote in his diary, 'After careful consideration, I confirmed the proceedings ... Such a crime is more serious in the case of an officer than of a man, and also it is highly important that all ranks should realise that the law is the same for an officer as a private.'[9] Poole was shot on 10

December 1916, the first officer in the war to be executed. By the end of the war, Haig had personally confirmed the death sentences on 255 other ranks and three officers, all of whom were shot.[10]

Throughout the Somme offensive, as we have seen, it seemed clear to those in command that there was a close connection between morale and shell shock. Nearly all senior officers confirmed this view. In giving evidence to the War Office Committee of Enquiry in 1922, Colonel Rogers, Medical Officer of the 4th Black Watch, claimed that the problems created by shell shock could be 'summed up in one word "morale". If the morale is good in a battalion, you will have less so-called "shell shock" or war neurosis. The better the morale the less the neurosis.'[11] Major Adie of the RAMC claimed that shell shock could arise not only in an individual but also in a body of men. He remembered seeing two battalions side by side at the front: 'In one the morale was good – it had a good colonel and officers and a good medical officer – and they had practically no men going down with "shell shock". The other battalion was sending ten men away at a time.' He decided that maintaining a high level of morale was 'the crux of the matter. Keep up the morale of the troops and you will not have emotional "shell shock", at least you will reduce it tremendously.'[12]

Colonel Fuller, who later became a great champion of armoured warfare, reported, 'If a crowd of men are reduced to a low nervous condition, "shell shock" becomes contagious.' He particularly recalled seeing this during the Battle of the Somme in 1916 when, he said, there was a higher rate of desertion of British soldiers to the enemy than at any other point in the war. He remembered what he called the 'moral stampede' or 'panic' of 'crowd shell shock', although he was convinced that this was a temporary thing and good rest and recuperation could soon reduce its effects.[13] Colonel Stubbs of the 1st Suffolk Regiment confirmed that shell shock 'spread very quickly' and 'as soon as one started to come away the rest followed.' He recalled that his battalion's medical officer 'collected about 20 or 30 [cases of shell shock], and he wanted to send them back up the line'. But Stubbs eventually 'got rid of them to some division who put them into a Labour Company'.[14] Not only did the link between war neuroses, morale and the apparent collapse of the fighting ability of entire units in the front line encourage senior officers to view the men's suffering with a mixture of suspicion and contempt, it meant the whole subject of shell shock during the Battle of the Somme raised fundamentally challenging questions about leadership and discipline.

However, it was not just poorly officered battalions that suffered from indiscipline and the failure to obey orders. Popularly known as the Welbeck Rangers, the 17th Sherwood Foresters was a Pals battalion raised in 1915 from among the men of the counties of Nottinghamshire and Derbyshire. After a period of extensive training in England, the battalion arrived in France in March 1916. They went into the front line on 11 June in a position well north of the Somme battlefield near Festubert. As they took over the line the battalion commander noted that 'The officers are keen', the NCOs and the men were all 'good material' and that 'Discipline is on the whole good.' He particularly commented on the good morale in the battalion, adding that 'the right offensive spirit exists.' When the Battle of the Somme began, all units in this section of the line were required to take part in aggressive trench raids to maintain pressure on the enemy along the entire British front. The first of many raids took place on the night of 3–4 July when the Sherwood Foresters and a battalion of the Rifle Brigade jointly assaulted a strongly defended section of the German line, sustaining many casualties. The following day, Brigadier Oldman sent a message congratulating the

Sherwood Foresters on the raid and again commended the battalion for its 'fighting spirit', saying that the raiders had 'brought credit to the battalion by their gallant conduct'. A few days later, none other than the commander of First Army, General Sir Charles Monro, inspected the men to congratulate them. He said they looked 'much steadier than when he saw them last'.[15] The 17th Sherwood Foresters seemed to be an exemplary battalion.

On 5 July, another raiding party was ordered to go out and retrieve some portable wooden bridges abandoned two nights before within yards of the German line. Private George Lowton was allocated to the party but refused to take part; saying that the mission was suicidal and he had a wife and five children to think of, he remained in the trench. That night there was heavy German shelling of the Sherwood Foresters' positions. Three days later, Private Bert McCubbin refused to go out into No Man's Land to occupy a listening post, a dangerous task that involved spending the night on guard in an isolated position known as an 'island' in front of the British line. The Sherwood Foresters remained in their front-line positions until 14 July, completing a highly unusual 34-day stint in the trenches. Although they had not participated in the Battle of the Somme, they had lost five officers and 125 other ranks, even though their battalion war diary records most days simply as 'Trench Routine. Situation normal.'

When the battalion returned to the rest area a great deal of catching up and administration was needed. Privates Lowton and McCubbin were arrested and charged with cowardice and wilful defiance. At their courts martial both men pleaded that their nerves were in a bad state. Lowton said he had been buried for four hours some weeks before when his dugout had been hit by a shell and collapsed on him. McCubbin claimed that he was so jittery when asked

to go out into the 'island' that he would have put the lives
of his comrades in jeopardy. Both men received sympathetic
trials, and although they were found guilty the verdicts
were forwarded with a recommendation for mercy. This
was endorsed up the chain of command until it reached
General Monro, the First Army commander, who had been
so impressed when he inspected the battalion a week before.
Maybe because of his inspection, he was clearly determined
to make an example of the two men; he wrote on the papers
that soldiers who deliberately chose to avoid danger 'would
not be tolerated' because 'all the qualities which we desire [in
a soldier] will become debased and degraded'.[16] He ordered
that the death sentence should be carried out.

Haig, as commander-in-chief, confirmed the decision, and
the two men were shot at dawn on 30 July. It was extremely
rare for two men from the same battalion to be tried and
executed simultaneously. After the gallantry of the Sherwood
Foresters had received such high praise it was even more
surprising to find this particular battalion being so discred-
ited. Ten days after the executions the divisional commander
inspected the battalion and said it was 'the best turn out
he had seen since taking over' and noted that the battalion
appeared to be 'in a very high state of efficiency'.[17] In this
context, the joint execution indicates yet again senior commanders' determination to make a stand against signs of a
breakdown in unit morale. Claims that a man was suffering
from a poor nervous condition would not be enough to save
him from traditional military justice.

The 1st Hampshire Regiment had been among the battalions that went over the top on 1 July. Their assault, just north
of Beaumont-Hamel, had been pinned down by machine gun
fire and the men did not get beyond No Man's Land. It was
a dreadful and costly failure. The battalion remained in the
thick of the Somme fighting throughout July, but at the end

of the month was withdrawn and transferred to the Ypres salient. The night of 8 August was dark and moonless. At 10.30 p.m. the gas gong sounded the alarm that the Germans were launching a poison gas attack on the trenches occupied by the 1st Hampshires. As the men dragged on their gas masks, the Germans also launched a trench raid. Seven men were killed and forty-six wounded in the gas attack that night. During the panic, Private John Bennett fled to the rear trenches. He was charged with cowardice and a week later appeared before a court martial. His company sergeant major reported to the tribunal that 'as soon as shelling starts, he goes all to pieces and goes practically off his head through sheer terror.' Bennett's commanding officer confirmed this and added that while on the Somme in July he had been sentenced to two years' imprisonment with hard labour after fleeing the trenches during a bombardment. The sentence had been suspended and so the man was still with his battalion. Bennett had no 'Prisoner's Friend' to defend him at his trial.

Despite this, Brigadier Rees, who presided over the court martial, took a lenient line, and while finding Bennett guilty of cowardice recommended mercy. When the court papers reached his corps commander, Lieutenant-General Sir Aylmer Hunter-Weston once again decided that a man's nervous condition could not be used as an excuse for desertion. He wrote, 'Cowards of this sort are a serious danger to the army. The death penalty is instituted to make such men fear running away more than they fear the enemy.'[18] This was one of the clearest statements yet that military punishments were intended to deter soldiers from desertion, regardless of their mental state, and to set an example for others to see. Bennett was shot at dawn on 28 August.

Another classic case was that of Harry Farr. A regular soldier from Kensington, London, Farr had joined the West

Yorks Regiment in 1910 at the age of sixteen, claiming to be three years older. He later said that he was proud to be a soldier and to serve his country. In November 1914, Farr was sent with his battalion to France and was in and out of the trenches for six months. In May he was evacuated from the front suffering from shell shock. From hospital, he wrote to his wife, Gertrude, but he was in such a bad way and shaking so badly she could barely recognise his handwriting.

After five months of treatment, Farr returned to his battalion and served at Ypres before his unit was transferred to the Somme. Again, he suffered from mild attacks of shell shock and needed treatment, but repeatedly returned to his battalion. In mid-September, the 1st West Yorks were sent into the front line to take part in a new assault at Flers. Saying that he felt unwell again, Harry Farr did not go with his battalion to the front. On 17 September, he visited an aid station, but they were so busy they could not see him as he was not physically wounded. A sergeant found Farr in the rear and asked what the matter was. Farr said he 'couldn't stand it'. The sergeant called him a coward and ordered him to join a ration party taking supplies up to the front. Farr refused to go even when the men tried to drag him, saying he was too afraid to go to the front. Doubtless this behaviour did not endear him either to the sergeant or to the men in the ration party. Farr was eventually charged with cowardice and a court martial took place on 2 October. He decided to defend himself. No medical evidence as to Farr's condition was given at the trial. His commanding officer simply reported, 'I cannot say what has destroyed this man's nerves but he has proved himself incapable of keeping his head in action and is likely to cause a panic.' The officer did however add that 'Apart from his behaviour under fire, his conduct and character are very good.'[19] The court martial lasted just twenty minutes. Farr was quickly found guilty. No medical board was asked to examine him after his conviction. He was shot on 18 October.

Farr's widow, Gertrude, initially received a widow's pension, but after six months she went to her local post office to collect the pension and was told that it had been stopped. It was only then that the War Office informed her that her husband had been shot for cowardice. She felt so ashamed at what had happened that she kept it from the rest of the family. Neither her mother nor Harry's ever found out the circumstances of his death. Gertrude had to start her life anew and struggle on without her husband's income or pension.

The War Office was in something of a dilemma over whether to tell families when someone had been executed. Sometimes families received a letter saying their loved one had 'died of wounds' or simply that he had been shot at the front. On other occasions, the next of kin were informed of the disgrace, any medals or decorations were withdrawn and the man's army records were erased.[20] But it was official policy that widow's pensions would not be paid to the spouses of executed men, and so the families of married men discovered the truth before long. This policy of course meant that a man's family would pay the price for his punishment.

The issue of executing soldiers did not pass without public debate during the war. Many senior officers not surprisingly felt that the maintenance of discipline in the army relied on the use of punishment. Brigadier Crozier of the 36th (Ulster) Division summed this view up succinctly when he wrote, 'I should be very sorry to command the finest army in the world on active service without the power behind me which the fear of execution brings.'[21] And many others, not only generals, felt that if a soldier let down his mates and refused to fulfil his duty then he deserved whatever punishment was due to him. However, a small but growing group felt

that such a draconian penalty was a leftover from the days
of floggings and the lash. Not only was it inappropriate in a
citizen army, but it was most definitely wrong when a man
was suffering from mental illness and deserved medical
treatment rather than military punishment. During 1917,
questions were asked in Parliament. In October, Philip
Snowden, a pacifist and leading member of the Independent
Labour Party (and later Chancellor of the Exchequer) asked
the Under-Secretary of State for War about the case of a man
in the Royal Scots Fusiliers who that summer had been diagnosed with shell shock but had still been shot for desertion.
The War Office minister said he was not prepared to challenge the decision of the commander-in-chief, Sir Douglas
Haig, who had reviewed the case and confirmed the death
sentence. On 14 December, another Labour MP, Robert
Outhwaite, asked the Under-Secretary to guarantee that no
soldier who had been invalided with shell shock would ever
be executed. The minister replied that he could not enforce
a proposal of this sort. A Conservative member, a retired
general, then said that it was 'a universal practice for a most
complete and exhaustive report to be called for in every case
after a death sentence has been awarded and that under
these circumstances it is practically impossible for any man
to be executed who has suffered from shell shock'. The minister agreed.[22] Whether the claim was made out of ignorance
or in an attempt to mislead the House and the British public,
it was clearly far from the truth.

In March 1918 Haig issued a statement that was read out in
Parliament, confirming that 'When a man has been sentenced
to death, if at any time any doubt has been raised as to his
responsibility for his actions, or if the suggestion has been
advanced that he has suffered from neurasthenia or shell
shock, orders are issued for him to be examined by a Medical
Board ... The sentence of death is not carried out in the case

of such a man unless the Medical Board expresses the positive opinion that he is to be held responsible for his actions.'[23]

Such a claim was again evidently absurd. Men like William Walton, Arthur Earp, Eric Poole, Harry Farr and many others had already been executed having undergone treatment for shell shock. Many more would be shot in future. And even after he had made his statement to Parliament, Haig continued until the end of the war to confirm the death sentence on men who had at some point been treated for war neuroses.

Denials that soldiers with mental illness had ever been shot continued to sound unconvincing. After the war was over a long, public debate about military executions began, but the army refused to disclose the records of the courts martial. They were kept under lock and key in the Judge Advocate General's files, and when finally handed over to the Public Record Office they remained closed for seventy-five years. In 1919, Lloyd George's government responded to the criticism and asked Sir Charles Darling, a senior judge, to investigate the provisions relating to military tribunals. There were several senior military figures on his committee, so it is not surprising that the majority report concluded that the work of the courts martial had been carried out properly and fairly. However, a minority report questioned the fairness of the army's judicial procedures and recommended that soldiers sentenced to death should have a right of appeal in a UK court, giving them the status of civilian criminals.

In 1922, the year the Darling Report came out, another debate in the House of Lords led to the establishment of a much bigger War Office Committee of Enquiry into the issue of shell shock. Chaired by Lord Southborough, the committee collected evidence and made wide-ranging comments about shell shock and war neuroses.[24] However, its conclusions were absolutely clear in endorsing the army and its systems. It reported, 'As regards expert medical evidence and advice in court martial cases, the system pursued in France in the late war seems to have been a satisfactory one ... when any medical question or doubt arose before or at a trial ... the best possible expert advice was placed at the immediate disposal of the military authorities, either in the form of a board or otherwise.'[25] This claim was flagrantly incorrect. Unable to study the records of the courts martial, which were still closed, the committee members relied on the second-hand testimony of senior officers. If they had been given access to the original papers they would have seen that medical evidence was not called upon in a large number of cases, nor were medical boards consulted after a verdict had been reached.

Despite the committee's conclusions, however, concern over the issue refused to go away. During the late 1920s, the subject came up repeatedly when the Army Act was debated each year. In 1925 an interdepartmental committee made up of senior military men concluded, again, that no miscarriages of justice had occurred in military courts martial. But later that year, a Labour Party motion to abolish the death penalty in the army was only narrowly defeated in the Commons. The leading light in the campaign for justice was now Labour MP Ernest Thurtle. Although son-in-law of the celebrated pacifist and Labour pioneer, George Lansbury, Thurtle was himself no hard-line pacifist. He had volunteered to join a London Pals battalion in 1914 and fought on the Western Front. Commissioned in 1917, he was badly wounded at the Battle of Cambrai in November. Using his inside experience and fired by his passion for social justice, Thurtle became a defender of the rights of discharged soldiers and a staunch opponent of capital punishment in the army, forcing a series of debates on the subject.

In 1928, the War Office agreed to remove the death penalty for certain offences, such as striking a superior officer and falling asleep on duty. When, in the following year, the Labour Party formed a minority government, the case for abolition was finally presented. Tom Shaw, a Lancashire trade unionist and Labour Secretary for War, proposed the end of the death penalty for cowardice, although he admitted that the Army Council disagreed with him and argued it was still necessary; the death sentence would remain, however, for desertion. This was not enough for Thurtle, who argued it should be abolished in all cases, and in a free vote his arguments won the day. Although the Army Act was held up in the Lords, it finally became law in 1930. The only crimes now subject to the military death penalty were treachery and mutiny. Notably, there were only four executions on these grounds in the whole of the Second World War.

However, with the records still closed, the sense remained that those who had faced a firing squad in the First World War were the victims of injustice. In the early 1980s, Judge Anthony Babington was allowed access to the court martial records to write a book, *For the Sake of Example*. As a condition of access, he was told that he could not quote directly from the records or name the accused individuals. But the doubts he expressed about the justice meted out in the military courts revived the issue once again. When in the 1990s the Ministry of Defence released the papers of the courts martial, the topic returned to the headlines. Once more questions were asked about the number of men 'shot at dawn', which became a popular campaigning phrase. The evidence at last made it clear that the courts martial had failed properly to take into account the psychological condition of some men. It also showed that they had made no allowances for a soldier's lack of legal experience or education, or for the difficulty he would have found in expressing himself without legal counsel. It was realised, moreover, that evidence had been accepted without proper questioning.

Harry Farr's case became notorious as his widow Gertrude, still alive at the age of ninety-nine, and his family led a campaign for justice. With more questions being asked in Parliament, Prime Minister John Major refused to issue any retrospective pardons. He argued that it was wrong to impose modern judgements retrospectively on historical cases. Others claimed that civilians who had committed murder would have been sentenced to death (by hanging rather than by firing squad) had they been prosecuted in the criminal courts at the time, and that the same should apply to those found guilty of murder within the military. However, as it became increasingly clear that many soldiers had been executed while suffering from various forms of shell shock, public pressure continued to mount. Andrew Mackinlay, a Labour MP, maintained the pressure in Parliament. And at the National Memorial Arboretum in Staffordshire a special memorial to the men shot at dawn, showing a blindfolded soldier facing a firing squad, was unveiled in 2001.

Finally, in 2006, when the Army Act came up for its annual renewal, the Defence Secretary in Tony Blair's government, Des Browne, a Scottish lawyer who had strong personal views on the subject, announced a posthumous pardon for all 306 British soldiers executed for military crimes. Claiming that it would be invidious within the limitations of the surviving records to go through each case one by one, he decided to pardon them all in a single gesture. The phrase 'As recognition that he was one of many victims of the First World War and that execution was not a fate that he deserved' was to be added to the record of each condemned man. Their families were of course delighted.

Most other armies who fought in the First World War also executed men who had been found guilty of cowardice or desertion. The German army executed forty-eight men and the French army about 600 – roughly double the number in the British army – on similar grounds. The French army on rare occasions adopted a policy of collective punishment, picking men randomly by lots from a unit accused of displaying cowardice. They were court-martialled together and shot as a group. The execution of three men from a battalion accused of cowardice during an assault on an invulnerable German stronghold was in 1935 the subject of a book by Canadian writer Humphrey Cobb called *Paths of Glory*. In 1957 Stanley Kubrick turned the book into a classic Great War movie and a chilling portrait of military injustice.[26]

In the British imperial armies, a small number of Canadians, New Zealanders, South Africans, West Indians, Nigerians, Ghanaians, and a group of Chinese labourers, were court-martialled and executed.[27] The exception was the Australian army, which did not allow soldiers to be shot for cowardice or desertion, and in which the only grounds for military execution were mutiny or treacherous dealings with the enemy. Both in the army and among the Australian people at large there was, as the *Australian Official History* put it, 'an invincible abhorrence of the seeming injustice of shooting a man who had volunteered to fight in a distant land in a quarrel not peculiarly Australian'.[28] The reading out of the news of death sentences to men on parade only strengthened distaste for the policy, and so strong was this feeling that no government would have attempted to flout it. The only punishment allowable for cowardice and desertion in the Australian forces was imprisonment, and this did not change throughout the war.

Despite official denials over the last hundred years, the evidence is absolutely clear that some men who had psychologically broken down under the strains of the fiercest and most deadly war fought to date were subjected to appalling injustice. The military authorities believed they had to do whatever was necessary to prevent outbreaks of mass hysteria and a general collapse of fighting spirit, as they believed had been the case with the 11th Borders, the Lonsdales. But this did not excuse the treatment of men who, instead of receiving sympathy and understanding for the terrible mental injuries they suffered, were put up against a wall and shot. It is a shadow that hangs not only over the British army, but over many of the armies that fought in the terrible, brutalising conditions of the Great War.

10

Laboratory of the Mind

By 1914, hospital administrator and reformer Sydney Holland, Lord Knutsford, had been chairman of the governing body of the London Hospital for nearly twenty years. That November, moved by accounts he was hearing from the fighting front, he launched an appeal in the columns of *The Times* to raise money to open a hospital for the treatment of 'gallant soldiers ... suffering from severe mental and nervous shock' caused by the 'excessive strain and tension' of the war. 'They can be cured', wrote Knutsford, 'if only they can receive proper attention. If not cured they will drift back to the world as miserable wrecks for the rest of their lives.'[1] These were prophetic words. Lord Knutsford was way ahead of his time in realising that men with nervous complaints could be treated successfully, and that if they were not they would live on to haunt the post-war world.

The appeal was a great success and raised enough money to open what was called a 'Special Hospital' (as distinct from a mental hospital or a lunatic asylum) at Palace Green in Kensington. Later fund-raising enabled Knutsford to open three more hospitals. He had clearly hit a popular chord in raising sympathy for soldiers suffering from what would become known as shell shock. And in revealing the need for his 'Special Hospitals' he had highlighted the fact that the military medical authorities were unprepared to cope with the large number of psychiatric casualties that presented themselves. His efforts were given the royal seal of approval when Queen Alexandra visited Palace Green in January 1915.

The army dealt with the first mental casualties of the war either in general hospitals or in D Block of the Royal Victoria Hospital in Netley, a ward intended for army mental patients. But this was far too small to cope with the number of cases and in December 1914, the War Office acquired the Red Cross Hospital at Maghull outside Liverpool. Maghull (later called Moss Side Hospital) had been built before the war as a large, airy and spacious establishment to treat epileptics. Having requisitioned it, the War Office initially provided 300 beds. But this soon proved insufficient and another 500 beds were added in huts around the garden. Maghull was intended for the 'other ranks', although a small number of officers were allocated to Quarry Bank House nearby. The Springfield War Hospital in Wandsworth was also given over to the treatment of shell shock, and wards were made available elsewhere in London at the National Hospital for the Paralysed and Epileptic in Queen Square and the Hospital for Epilepsy and Paralysis in Maida Vale. By 1916, even this was not enough and more beds were allocated to nervous cases at the new Maudsley Hospital at Denmark Hill in south London, at the King George V Hospital in Dublin and at the Royal Victoria Hospital in Edinburgh. Eventually hospitals dedicated to the treatment of nervous patients could accommodate 1,200 officers and 4,500 other ranks. Throughout the war these facilities were in continuous demand.

While the need for specialist centres like these was recognised, most cases of shell shock were thought to be mild. As we have seen, great emphasis was put on quiet rest and relaxation, in hospitals near the front, as the principal cure for the victims with badly disturbed nerves. Throughout the war, this would be the first stage at which attempts were made to cure victims of war neuroses. At its simplest level, the process consisted of giving a man a few days out of the line, allowing him to catch up on sleep – always difficult in the trenches – and then being told to 'pull yourself together.' Dr Gordon Holmes said that in many cases a shell shock victim was merely 'shaken up' and that if these men 'slept for 24 hours after a few nights good rest [they] were requesting to go back to the line'. Even when a man exhibited a physical symptom like losing the ability to speak, after a good period of sleep 'we often found that next morning he had regained his speech.' If the men around him said 'You'll be all right soon' and the MO insisted 'that there was nothing wrong and there was no reason why the patient should not recover', then he usually did recover. There was a great advantage, according to Holmes, in keeping these men near the front and under conventional military discipline. Overall, a shell shock patient 'was in a better mood for returning while he was still in the Army area. The further men got from the line the more difficult it was to get them back.'[2]

If an MO could avoid sending a man 'back down the line' to a CCS or base hospital for specialist treatment, he would do so. Charles Wilson, MO with the 1st Battalion Royal Fusiliers, was in his dugout alone in the spring of 1915 when one of his stretcher bearers staggered in, in a dreadful state. A corporal accompanying him explained that the bearer had been in a party of four 'carrying a man on a stretcher when a shell caught them and literally splashed him with bits of the other three bearers. He himself escaped without hurt. Now he seemed done.' Wilson sent the corporal away and decided to keep the bearer where he was until things were quieter. 'I got him to lie down on the stretcher on which I slept. Almost at once to my great wonder he fell asleep. It occurred to me that there might be an outside chance of saving this fellow the mishap of going to the base [hospital] with shell shock. I dropped a blanket down so that he was hidden and made him some hot stuff to drink. He slept for nearly twenty-four hours. When he awoke he seemed all right. He went out with me next day and never looked back again. Fatigue, loss of sleep and the shock of witnessing the death of the other bearers had for the moment used up his will power.'[3] Will power was repeatedly stressed as being at the centre of the cure for shell shock.

The *Official Medical History* recorded that in about 75 per cent of cases the patient could be classed as 'mildly confused'. To describe such men, MOs used phrases like 'appears dazed', 'looks strange', 'is inclined to behave foolishly', 'is dull and takes no interest in anything'. Often the patients could answer simple questions regarding their name and age but were unable to give a clear account of what had happened to them. Usually they could remember being in the line, but at a certain point amnesia would set in and they could recall nothing that followed.[4] This was clearly the point at which the trauma, perhaps witnessing a horrific incident or being buried under the earth thrown up by an explosion, had occurred. Often this confused state lasted only twelve to twenty-four hours; after a few days of complete rest the patient's memory returned and he appeared to suffer no long-term residual effects. Most men suffering from shell shock also felt a strong sense of shame, of having let their mates down, and so were usually keen to return to their battalion as quickly as possible.

However, certain more severe cases were diagnosed as suffering from some form of hysteria. Such patients often lay down with their head under the blanket, wanting to hide, and were resentful of interruptions. A man so affected would appear to understand an instruction but would not carry it out. He would be unresponsive and his face would be full of contortions. Often the symptoms would become more serious after a day or so and he would start to tremble, become mute or his limbs would start to shake. In this state, a patient would sometimes shriek if disturbed or even burst into tears if prompted to recall the moment of trauma. This state would continue for at least a week or ten days. There was no alternative but to send such victims back down the line to a CCS or base hospital, some of which from late 1916 began to specialise in treating nervous patients.

Before the Somme, if a man was sent to a CCS or a base hospital with a severe case of shell shock, he was almost certainly returned to England and would be out of action for some time. Between April 1915 and April 1916, some 1,300 officers and 10,000 men had been admitted to special hospitals in Britain suffering from shell shock.[5] A major problem that arose with these cases was that often a patient's medical notes would be lost as he was sent further down the line from one hospital to another. Initial descriptions of what had happened, or of a man's physical symptoms or diagnosis, were mislaid in CCSs or base hospitals that were struggling to cope with a huge influx of patients. As a consequence, doctors in Britain complained that they were having to start the process of diagnosing and treating a patient all over again.

By the middle of 1916, the general attitude to treatment for shell shock had changed. It was felt that treating men in an environment in which military discipline was loose, or even non-existent, was not appropriate in terms of returning them to the fighting front. Instead of sending a shell shock victim back to Britain it was thought best to keep him in 'Army areas', as they were called. Military prejudice was never far from the surface, and one doctor spoke of the hospitals in Britain being far too 'soft' and of female nurses showing too much sympathy to the men, who were 'petted and given nothing to do'. In these circumstances, he argued, 'I found they got worse. What they required was to remain under strict discipline and that was the only way to get them well quickly.'[6] Another physician argued that if a man found himself in 'an atmosphere of sympathy, consideration and comfort', his anxieties would not go away but were more likely to become fixed. If friends and family members regarded the illness 'as absolutely equivalent in disabling power to a severe wound' then the patient was more likely to believe it and so would be unlikely to make a recovery.[7]

This strange military logic was widely accepted at the time. Charles Myers took the same view when he became Consulting Psychologist to the Army in August 1916, arguing of shell shock victims that 'the Regimental Medical Officer' in the front line aid post 'may still combat their condition by the aid of moral suasion, and he may thereby successfully induce them to return to duty', whereas if they were sent 'farther down the Line, it may take many weeks or months before they are again fit for duty'.[8] Today, it remains a fundamental principle in the care of traumatised soldiers that treatment is provided as quickly and as near to the combat scene as possible. Labelled PIE – 'Proximity, Immediacy, Expectation', the theory is that psychiatric patients should be dealt with close to the front, as quickly as possible, and should be treated as soldiers not like patients, in order to maximise the expectation of recovery. The ideas laid down by Myers and other First World War neurologists have become the basis for military psychiatry ever since.

Yet however much the army would have liked to return its shell shock victims to the firing line as soon as possible, doctors had to admit that some cases were too severe to treat so close to the front. Some patients were too troublesome for standard hospital wards to deal with. Patients were sometimes so wild and excitable that they needed tying to a bed. They would think they were still in the trenches and would interpret normal hospital sounds as those of artillery or machine guns. Sometimes they would call out to the other patients in the ward using the names of mates in their platoon. They would accuse doctors of being Germans in disguise, out to kill them. They would hallucinate and become fearful or terrified. One 21-year-old patient was sent to a CCS where, having been restless for three days, he started wandering away from the ward. On the fifth day he announced that he was going to see his father, who was outside. The slightest noise would terrify him. On the tenth day he came before a medical tribunal, but 'his expression was staring and anxious. He talked rubbish in answer to questions.' He went back to bed and lay there for hours, muttering to himself. By the fourteenth day he had brief attacks of weeping but would then become quite cheerful and talkative. On the eighteenth day, his doctors noted: 'Complains of headaches; his attention is very poor, his cerebration much slowed and he still exhibits terror, both in appearance and behaviour.' His hands still shook. A few days later he escaped from the CCS and found his way almost back to the front line before he was discovered and evacuated to a specialist hospital at the base.

Another patient, a 23-year-old of 'solid and robust appearance', was brought in presenting a 'dazed, lethargic condition'. He lay in bed staring aimlessly and rarely changed his position. He could be persuaded to open his eyes but appeared to recognise nothing. After five days all he would volunteer was to say 'I feel better', and he was totally passive regarding anything that happened around him. After eleven days he began to wander aimlessly up and down the ward, 'but took no notice of other patients and never spoke to anyone'. He was put on a pure milk diet for some days but made no protest. Taken to a concert in the hope of cheering him up, he exhibited no change. On the seventeenth day the doctors still reported a 'strong frowning expression which is persistent' and slight tremors. He would reply to the simplest of questions only after several seconds and 'no account of his history, recent or remote, has been obtained from him'. His habitual position was to sit with his head 'buried between his hands'. After four weeks he was sent to a base hospital.[9] It is not difficult to imagine the nightmares that the poor man must have been going through. Sadly, there is no record of whether he ever recovered.

As there was still no consensus as to the cause of war neuroses, many different cures were tried. It all added up to a great laboratory of the mind. Hypnosis, a tool of French psychologists since Jean-Martin Charcot in the nineteenth century, was sometimes used. Where a shell shock victim had no idea what had happened to him or even which unit he belonged to, doctors could sometimes extract all the details they wanted under hypnosis. Being interested in the concept of lost memory, Myers was among those who treated patients using hypnosis. When the patient awoke, Myers would immediately discuss his experience with him. He claimed that when patients recovered their memory the physical symptoms, the paralyses and tremors, disappeared automatically. Myers recorded excellent results with this technique and in at least one case reported a full recovery.[10] He wrote in 1916, 'No one who has witnessed the unfeigned delight with which these patients on waking from hypnosis, hail their recovery from such disorders, can have any hesitation as to the impetus thus given towards a final cure.'[11] But Myers did not find hypnosis easy and was never happy using the technique. Moreover, most army doctors not only had no familiarity with hypnosis but indeed, they were deeply suspicious of it. It probably seemed very mysterious and foreign to them. Even fifteen years after the war, it seems, the mere mention of hypnotism could raise 'a jolly masculine laugh in RAMC circles'.[12]

So, while by mid-1916 the vast majority of shell shock cases received treatment in France, many seriously afflicted patients were still evacuated to Britain. Here, as the term 'shell shock' covered a myriad of medical conditions, so a myriad of forms of treatment were on offer. Dr Ronald Rows (pronounced Rowse) took charge of Maghull, the first hospital given over to the treatment of shell shock. As an asylum manager for some years before the war he had taken the conventional view that all mental patients should be kept in their beds unless they became troublesome, in which case they should be given 'bath treatment', in other words locked into a wood-encased bath of cold water to calm them down. But just before the war Rows had discovered the work of Freud and Jung. Transformed, he became a great reformer of mental hospitals and now used Maghull as an opportunity to develop his interest in psychoanalysis. Rows would look for the emotional origins of a soldier's problem. He encouraged a caring approach to the shell shock victims who soon filled the long rows of metal beds in his hospital. Photographs show the patients proudly wearing the smart blue uniform of the wounded soldier, with white lapels and red ties.

Rows encouraged his doctors to talk to patients and to use their dreams (or nightmares) to try to understand what was at the root of their fears. According to Freud's approach, the cause of the physical symptoms of shell shock was likely to be a traumatic incident that had been repressed but could be revealed sometimes in a patient's dreams. The men were therefore offered one-on-one sessions for an hour at a time. But there were lots of barriers to break down. The men, mostly from working-class backgrounds, were not used to discussing their feelings in an open, relaxed fashion. Some grew suspicious that their dreams were being used in some way they did not fully understand to decide whether or not they should be sent back to France. A lot of men simply clammed up.[13] But for many patients, finding the cause of their problem and talking it through helped to make the fear disappear, in a form of psychotherapy. Millais Culpin, an army surgeon who transferred from surgery to psychology, wrote with some amazement on arrival at the hospital that 'a new world opened up, when under the influence of the Maghull teaching I began to treat shell-shocked men by the apparently simple plan of getting them to talk of their experiences.'[14]

One of the most senior figures who went to work at Maghull was Dr William Halse Rivers. He would become probably the most famous of the Great War psychologists. Rivers had studied medicine at St Bartholomew's in London, where he became the youngest graduate in the hospital's history. Having worked as a physician in the National Hospital for the Paralysed and Epileptic in Queen Square, he went on to become a clinician at the Bethlem lunatic asylum and in 1897 helped to establish the new Psychology Department at Cambridge University. Among his students was Charles Myers, and in 1898 the pair took part in the anthropological expedition to the Torres Strait, during which Rivers carried out painstaking research on the kinship patterns of the local tribesmen.

From 1902 Rivers returned to his career at Cambridge while at the same time continuing his pioneering ethnographic work, both in southern India and in Melanesia in the south Pacific. In 1915, when he arrived at Maghull, Rivers must have seemed an unusual figure, bringing an academic feel to his treatment of shell shock victims. He was then aged fifty-one, a bachelor who rarely smoked or drank. He was shy, had a mild stammer, did not mix easily and was still obsessed with his ethnographic studies. Very serious in manner, he did not easily engage with the rank and file soldiers being treated there. But he was familiar with the work of Freud and Jung and slowly became drawn into a community in which the interpretation of dreams and the discussion of topics relating to the mind was an everyday activity. He began to realise that Maghull offered him a unique way of understanding the minds not of distant tribesmen but of his fellow Britons.

Maghull soon attracted a rush of bright young academics from the universities who saw work there as a brilliant opportunity to look into men's minds and to apply the ideas of Dejerine, the great French psychotherapist, and Freud. They included Tom Pear, who went on to become a professor of psychology at Manchester University, and Grafton Elliott Smith, professor of anatomy at the same university. Pear would tell his patients reassuringly, 'You are suffering from an illness. It's called mental illness. You are not mad and you are not a lunatic.'[15]

The work at Maghull achieved some renown and the RAMC began sending doctors on three-month courses there to study psychotherapy, dream analysis and the treatment of shell shock. The establishment was rare among British hospitals in showing real sympathy and understanding for its shell shock patients. The men were treated with respect and offered forms of occupational therapy like playing cards or billiards, or working on the hospital farm. It was a classic case whereby the war created a human laboratory for some of the brightest young psychologists of the day to come and experiment and to help solve the problems thrown up. Maghull became a hotbed of ideas that would shape new British psychology after the war. And, ironically, this was all done at the expense and with the encouragement of the War Office.

The Maudsley Hospital in south London was built to treat civilian patients but was requisitioned by the War Office and opened its doors to the first shell shock victims in January 1916. Lieutenant-Colonel Atwood Thorne, a Territorial medical officer, was put in command, while Frederick Mott set up his laboratory there, his influence determining the hospital's line of treatment. He emphasised the need to create an opportunity for the 'quiet repose' of patients, in a place where 'nourishing, digestible' food was on offer. He did not believe that hypnosis or psychoanalysis were 'necessary or even desirable' when it came to the treatment of 'psychic wounds'. But he did believe in occupational therapy and patients were encouraged to grow vegetables in the hospital gardens and work in the poultry house. He built a workshop where men could practise carpentry and metalwork, and donated a piano around which they could gather and practise choral singing. Mott wanted to create an 'atmosphere of cure' by 'promoting cheerfulness and healthy recreation' in order to generate 'that sense of well-being so essential for mental and bodily recuperation'.[16]

At the other end of the treatment spectrum was a violent physical technique called electric shock therapy. Electricity had been used to treat mentally disturbed patients since the end of the nineteenth century and was politely known as the 'faradic battery treatment'. Most of the armies of the First World War used electric shock therapy and in the German army, neurologist Dr Fritz Kaufmann made his name by the severity of his treatment in a hospital near Mannheim. He insisted on a strict regime, hoping that word would spread about the harshness of the conditions in his hospital and thereby deter soldiers from malingering. Kaufmann believed that if a man had experienced a shock, the best way to treat him was to administer another, physical shock. He would give his patients an electric shock lasting between two and five minutes, while shouting at them that they should be ashamed of themselves and should snap out of their condition. Extraordinarily, in many cases this brutal approach seemed to work. Not only did some men recover but they were enormously grateful for their treatment. Sadly, in a few cases, men died undergoing electric shock treatment. About twenty German victims died during the war, while others committed suicide rather than face the treatment.

Understandably, patients greatly feared electric shock therapy. But that was part of the intention. At the National Hospital for the Paralysed and Epileptic, Lewis Yealland from Toronto, who had worked for a short time in asylums in Canada, took up the use of electric shock therapy with a fervent zeal. He believed that hysterical patients were weak willed but had convinced themselves that the physical symptoms from which they were suffering were permanent; therefore they had to be persuaded by the use of an electric shock that they could get better.

Yealland took on patients suffering from hysteria whose arms or legs were paralysed, or who had lost the power of speech, and who had defied previous treatment. He often performed his treatment with some theatricality. The patient would be taken into a room; the doctor would appear and take charge, forcefully explaining that the patient must listen to his instructions while the electricity was being 'administered'. Yealland saw this as an aspect of the discipline necessary to jolt a man into a cure from hysteria. He would begin by administering small amounts of electricity, applying more powerful charges if a patient resisted. Many of his treatments became a battle of wills, yet again, surprisingly, he had a great deal of success. Yealland described curing six cases of mutism one morning in less than half an hour by using 'electricity mixed with persuasion and encouragement'.[17]

Yealland described in detail his treatment of one young soldier who had fought at Mons, the Marne, Ypres, Neuve Chapelle and Loos. After two years' loyal and brave service the young man had collapsed suddenly and was unable to speak. Various treatments had been tried over a period of nine months without success. As a last attempt at a cure, the patient was sent to Yealland. He was brought into a darkened room; the blinds were drawn, the door was locked and Yealland announced, 'You will not leave this room until you are talking as well as you did.' With the man's mouth kept open by means of a tongue depressor, Yealland started the 'treatment' by applying through an electrode attached to the back of his throat a shock so severe that the jolt threw him backwards and pulled the wires from the generator. Yealland kept up the shock therapy, telling the patient, 'A man who has gone through so many battles should have better control of himself.'

After an hour the patient was able to say 'Ah'. After another half-hour, he could pronounce some vowels. Stronger shocks were applied to his larynx, slowly enabling him to whisper the days of the week. At each stage, Yealland bullied the patient, with the intention of breaking his will. When he seemed almost able to speak again, his left arm began to shake, then his right arm, then both of his legs. Yealland told the poor man, 'It is the same resistive condition only manifested in another part.' Each tremor was stopped by the application of further pulses of electricity. After four hours of continuous treatment the man cried out, 'Doctor, doctor, I am champion,' to which Yealland replied, 'You are a hero.' At the end, the patient asked, 'Why did they not send me to you nine months ago?'[18] Today, however, it seems difficult to see the difference between treatment like this and torture.

During the war, although he carried out no formal follow-ups on his patients, Yealland claimed total success for his electrotherapy. However, a recent analysis of the records of the 196 patients he treated at the Queen Square hospital reveals that in at least 13 per cent of cases his treatment failed and 43 per cent of cases were only listed as 'improved'.[19] Yealland's work was denounced by some during the war and soon after, and has become controversial since.[20] At the time, however, he became famous for his successes; patients were sent to him from all over the country to receive his 'cure'.

Dr Arthur Hurst practised another form of theatrical treatment, first at Netley Hospital and then at Seale Hayne, an old agricultural college on the edge of Dartmoor in Devon. Hurst had used both hypnosis and electric shock treatment but gave them up for an alternative, simpler technique. He believed in creating a highly charged and positive atmosphere in which hysterical patients would see recovery occurring in others around them. Dr Hurst was a great showman and made countless claims as to his ability to cure the symptoms of hysteria.

The expectation that a patient would receive a miracle cure was drummed into him from the moment he arrived at the hospital. Preparation might take several days and the nurses would have a vital role to play in explaining to the patient beforehand how wonderful the effects of the treatment would be. On the day of the treatment, the build-up to meeting the doctor turned the encounter almost into a religious experience. When the patient finally came before Hurst, the treatment was by suggestion. Hurst forcibly commanded him to get better and applied some physiotherapy involving powerful manipulation of the arms or legs until the patient was completely relaxed and the power to perform physical movements had been restored. In this process 'the personality of the medical officer is always of greater importance than the particular method.'[21]

At Seale Hayne, a series of films were made to record the

success of Hurst's techniques. These short clips capture some of the sad and freakish behaviour of shell shock victims, recording tragic scenes of men who cannot walk and who roll about on the floor, who shake uncontrollably, who leap under the bed at the mere mention of the word 'bomb'. The purpose of the films was to show victims before and after their treatment with Hurst. Certainly, the patients on film appear to be cured. After treatment they walk briskly and confidently past the camera, feed chickens or work happily on the hospital farm. However, Hurst's many critics were not convinced that removing the symptoms of hysteria was the same as curing the source of the problem. Stories were told that by the time some patients had returned to London on the train from Devon they had already developed new symptoms and were almost as bad as before.[22]

It was officers who suffered mostly (but not exclusively) from neurasthenia, the other form of shell shock. Neurasthenia was seen as a form of nervous exhaustion, often built up over a long period of time and sometimes leading to a breakdown triggered by the simplest event. For instance, one officer had spent eleven months at the front, enduring every type of physical and mental strain. He had been wounded twice, gassed twice and buried beneath a house that collapsed under shell fire. After each of these incidents he had returned to the trenches. Then he was granted five days' leave. Having left in good health, on his return he collapsed in the train station and became unconscious. He was diagnosed as suffering a severe form of neurasthenia. It took some time to find the real cause of the man's distress. The reason for his collapse, it turned out, was not the fear of returning to the front; in fact he was looking forward to going back. But he knew that with so many officers wounded and killed he would have to take on more responsibility and was fearful that he would not be up to the charge. It was the dread of letting his men down, rather than any fear of physical injury, that provoked his neurasthenic breakdown.[23]

Today, far and away the best-known treatment centre for neurasthenia in the Great War is Craiglockhart War Hospital for Officers at Slateford, on the outskirts of Edinburgh and just a tram ride from the centre of the city. Craiglockhart was an old Victorian hydro spa, requisitioned by the War Office in 1916 as a war hospital dedicated to the treatment of neurasthenic patients. By day it was the officers' equivalent of Maghull, humane with a friendly atmosphere; patients could play cricket, tennis, bowls, croquet or use the hydro-pool. They were encouraged to walk in the gardens, to develop their own hobbies or to take on duties such as teaching the local Boys' Training Club. There was even a small farm where patients could grow vegetables and keep chickens. But by night, the mood changed completely. The corridors echoed to the anguished howls of the patients as they relived in their dreams the terrible experiences they had been through.

In October 1916, Dr William Halse Rivers was commissioned a captain in the RAMC and sent from Maghull to Craiglockhart. There, he resumed his study of Freud and spent time analysing his own dreams as well as those of his patients. His persistent, conversational approach was better suited to the officers of Craiglockhart than it had been to the other ranks at Maghull, and Rivers soon acquired a reputation as something of a miracle worker in being able to talk men through their fears, making their memories tolerable and helping them recover. But as time passed Rivers grew increasingly uncomfortable about his role as a military doctor whose principal duty was to send men back to the front and to the horrors that had caused their neuroses in the first place.

Lieutenant James Butlin arrived at Craiglockhart in May 1917. He had been on active service on the Western Front for more than two years. His battalion, the 6th Dorsets, was badly mauled during the battle of Arras in April 1917, with many of its officers killed. Butlin began to complain of being a 'bit nervy'; a few weeks later he was diagnosed with neurasthenia and sent to Craiglockhart, a classic case of a slow build-up of nervous exhaustion. Butlin kept up a frank and entertaining correspondence with an old school chum named Basil who worked in the Foreign Office in London, and his letters have preserved a wonderful profile of life for an officer-patient at Craiglockhart. He described the place as 'a magnificent hydro standing in palatial grounds fitted with all the comforts that man's ingenuity can contrive ... provided one is in by six o'clock and conforms to a few simple rules life is a complete and glorious loaf.' His only complaint was of boredom: 'I am sending for my tennis things as I can see I shall go mad here with nothing to do. I haven't had a drink for a fortnight.' Before long Butlin was seen by Rivers, and he described the encounter to his friend: 'he is a clever man, a bit of a philosopher, an eminent nerve specialist and somewhat of a crank. He extracts from you your life history with such questions as: Is there any nervous trouble in your family? Have you been ill as a boy? Where were you at school? Do you smoke much? etc etc The great idea, as I had been previously warned, is to get you to take up a hobby.' Butlin was determined to avoid taking on anything that seemed like extra work, but he did admit to Rivers that he liked literature. 'The latter was rather a false step as he then asked me to join the staff of the "Hydra" a fortnightly magazine published by the officers here. However I have so far escaped fairly lightly.'

After a while, Butlin's boredom increased and he began mocking the lifestyle at the hospital. 'Can you imagine me, my dear Basil, getting up and taking a swim before breakfast? Doing a little gardening and poultry farming after

breakfast? Fretwork and photography after lunch? Viewing
natural scenery after tea? Reading and writing after dinner
and then to bed?' Butlin eventually found something to
interest him in the form of a beautiful, 'blue eyed and fair
haired', twenty-year-old local girl named May whom he
ardently pursued. They went on several day trips, visiting
local beauty spots, and one evening Butlin brought her back
to Craiglockhart. In a secluded corner of the grounds they sat
down together. 'We were, I admit, perhaps sitting closer than
the warmth of the evening necessitated and in the passion
of love' when they were discovered by Rivers and the commanding officer of the hospital, Major Bryce. Furious at the
breach of hospital rules, Bryce called Butlin to his office the
following morning and told him the rule that he had broken
was to have a visitor on the premises after visiting time was
over at 5 p.m.

Perhaps because of this incident, a week later Butlin was
sent away from Craiglockhart. But his two months' respite at
the Scottish hospital had not cured him. He returned to his
battalion on home duties, but in March 1918 he was classed
as unfit for military service and was retired from the army
on health grounds.[24]

A month after Butlin left Craiglockhart, in August 1917,
another officer arrived, and there started one of the most written about doctor–soldier relationships of the war. Siegfried
Sassoon had been a brave soldier with the 3rd Battalion Royal
Welch Fusiliers and had won an MC in 1916. He achieved
notoriety in singlehandedly capturing an enemy trench on
the Somme in early July, inspiring his men to nickname him
'Mad Jack'. But his view of the war gradually changed. While
recovering from wounds in London in 1917 he came under
the influence of several pacifist friends and decided to issue
what he called a 'Soldier's Declaration' denouncing the war,
making his statement 'as an act of wilful defiance of military

authority, because I believe that the War is being deliberately prolonged by those who have the power to end it.' He went on, 'I am a soldier ... I have seen and endured the sufferings of the troops, and I can no longer be a party to prolong these sufferings for ends which I believe to be evil and unjust.'[25] He refused to return to his battalion and managed to have the declaration read in the House of Commons.

In failing to return to his unit, Sassoon could have been prosecuted for desertion. But influential friends intervened and, instead of a court martial, arranged for him to be sent to Craiglockhart, supposedly suffering from shell shock. Whether or not Sassoon really was suffering from a nervous breakdown was never clear but he certainly suffered from terrible nightmares in which he saw wounded men from his battalion crawling towards his bed.

Rivers met Sassoon and began a long series of conversations with him. In one of their first meetings Sassoon asked Rivers if he thought he *was* suffering from shell shock. 'Certainly not,' replied the doctor. When Sassoon asked him what he was suffering from, Rivers replied, 'An anti-war complex.' Sassoon became fascinated by Rivers and was genuinely grateful to him for tolerating his unusual behaviour, for not lecturing him on his soldierly duties and for providing real companionship. Rivers had suppressed his homosexual tendencies, while Sassoon was becoming increasingly open about his own, and the two men soon became friends. Sassoon described Rivers as a 'father-confessor' figure – his own father had died when he was seven.

Sassoon realised the unique nature of the work Rivers and his colleagues were doing at Craiglockhart. The local medical director to whom the hospital staff reported was highly suspicious of what was going on at the hospital; the consultants often seemed, in his view, to be too friendly with the patients and the place was far too lax in military discipline. At one point the medical director told Rivers that he 'never had and never would recognise the existence of such a thing as shell shock'. Sassoon concluded that 'in the eyes of the War Office a man was either wounded or well unless he had some officially authorised disease. Damage inflicted on the mind did not count as illness. If "war neuroses" were indiscriminately encouraged, half the expeditionary force might go sick with a touch of neurasthenia.'[26]

Although still anguished by the war, Sassoon slowly came around to thinking that his real place was back in the trenches with his battalion rather than in this unusual hospital, 'surrounded by the wreckage and defeat of those who had once been brave'. After three months of 'treatment' from Rivers, he decided that it was his 'mission' to return to the battlefield. He was sent at first to Palestine but eventually returned to France, where he was finally invalided out of the army after being wounded again in July 1918. Both Sassoon and Rivers wrote about their relationship, which became the core of Pat Barker's award-winning 1990s *Regeneration* trilogy of novels, the first of which was later turned into a film.[27]

It is possible that in their relationship, Sassoon had a greater effect on Rivers than the doctor had on the patient. But in any event, soon after Sassoon's departure, Rivers decided to leave Craiglockhart and instead became a psychologist at the Royal Flying Corps hospital at Hampstead in London. The incidence of 'Aviators' Neurasthenia' was high in the RFC, where in the later stages of the war it affected 50 per cent of all pilot officers, although roughly half were successfully treated and returned to full flying duties.[28]

Sassoon had already acquired a reputation as a soldier-poet by the time he was sent to Craiglockhart, but another poet who arrived at the Scottish spa that autumn was more obviously suffering from shell shock. Wilfred Owen, a sensitive young officer in the 5th Battalion Manchester Regiment, had gone through some horrific experiences at the front. Soon after the Battle of the Somme he had been sent with his platoon to a tiny flooded dugout in No Man's Land where he spent more than two days under continuous shelling. Later he fell into a cellar and was trapped there for three days. On another occasion he was blown into the air by the blast of a trench mortar shell and covered with earth and debris. Later still he spent some time lying in No Man's Land alongside the dead body of a fellow officer. Noticing how shaky he had become, the other officers in the battalion sent him to the regimental MO, who diagnosed him with neurasthenia. He was bad enough to be sent back to Britain and to Craiglockhart, suffering from terrible nightmares, what he called his 'barrag'd nights', in which he repeatedly saw the accusing faces of the men he had witnessed being blinded or gassed in front of his eyes.

Depressed, anxious, with a strong sense of guilt and sleeping badly, Owen became the patient at Craiglockhart not of Rivers but of another doctor. Captain Arthur Brock believed that every patient had it in him to cure himself, all he needed to do was to work at it. So he set Owen tasks, like lecturing to the Craiglockhart Field Club, editing the house magazine, *The Hydra*, and most importantly, trying to work through his intense feelings by expressing them in poetry.

Owen was already writing some poetry but had not yet found a style he was happy with. He introduced himself to Sassoon, whose work he greatly admired. Already famous, Sassoon became a source of inspiration to Owen and helped him find his voice in his poems. Sassoon later wrote that he did very little for Owen apart from loan him a couple of books, but the combination of Brock's treatment and Sassoon's friendship changed Owen completely. Instead of having nightmares about the faces of his scarred and mutilated men, he began to confront his dreadful experiences in poetry. He left Craiglockhart towards the end of 1917 a different man, more secure in himself and more confident in his writing.

For several months Owen wrote some of the finest anti-war poems in the English language. These included 'Dulce et Decorum Est', in which he was haunted by the face of a man who failed to put on his gas mask in time, 'Anthem for Doomed Youth', 'Futility' and 'Strange Meeting'. In a draft preface to his poems, he concluded 'My subject is War, and the pity of War', by which he meant that he was not writing about glory, honour or courage, but wanted to be 'truthful' about the utter waste and futility of the war. But Owen was no pacifist. His sense of duty was strong, so he returned to the front in September 1918 and won an MC for bravery. On the early morning of 4 November 1918, in one of the final advances of the war, he was leading his men across the Sambre-Oise canal when he was shot and killed. He was twenty-five years old and his parents received the news of his death one week later as the church bells rang out to proclaim the Armistice. Hardly any of Owen's poems had been published at the time of his death and he remained something of a minor figure for many decades. It was not until his work was republished in the 1960s that his life and poetry came to epitomise the story of the innocent generation that had been sacrificed in the Great War.[29] But it was the treatment for shell shock at Craiglockhart that had helped to transform Wilfred Owen from a shattered and nervous soldier into a great war poet.

Craiglockhart has become famous thanks to its war poet patients. But officers were sent to rest and convalesce in dozens of other smaller hospitals and country houses around Britain. The proportion of officers who suffered from war neuroses was higher than among the other ranks. The ratio of officers to men at the front was approximately 1:30, while that of officers to men among the wounded was slightly higher at 1:24. Among those admitted to special hospitals in England suffering from shell shock in the year from May 1916 to April 1917 the ratio was as high as 1:6.[30]

The treatment of many of these officers was dominated by what has been called an obsession with a 'rural idyll'.[31] From 1916, a Country Hosts Scheme was established in which the owners of country houses could open their doors to convalescing officers. There was a belief that the countryside offered a morally wholesome environment which would be an aid to recovery. In addition, it was widely held that plenty of fresh air and healthy outdoor activities were ideal for both officers and men recovering from shell shock. Sir John Collie managed what were called Homes of Recovery, in which recovering shell shock patients were encouraged to carry out light gardening work. Allied to this was a belief that agricultural labour was a great help to men recovering from war neuroses.

Of course, one simple way of keeping down the numbers officially suffering from shell shock was to stop using the term altogether and make it harder for MOs to diagnose. Within days of the end of the Somme battle, Gordon Holmes and the army medical authorities came up with a new classification system which all front-line MOs were required to adopt. The army still felt that MOs were too sympathetic to the men, that they were too close to them and their diagnoses were not to be trusted in such a controversial area and at a time when 'wastage' had to be strictly limited. So, on 21 November 1916, only three days after the last Somme offensive had ground to a halt in the snow and sleet, the Director General of Medical Services announced that 'the expression shell shock' should no longer be used. Any case displaying nervous symptoms of any sort was simply to be classed as 'Nervous' and 'under no circumstances [to] be recorded as a battle casualty'.[32]

Moreover, the directive introduced a new term, 'NYDN – Not Yet Diagnosed Nervous'. MOs were no longer to diagnose possible cases of shell shock but were to send them back to the specialist centres that had been set up by this time. Only here could a man receive an accurate diagnosis. The centre then sent a further form, W3436, not to a man's MO but to his commanding officer. As if the officers in the front line did not already have enough to do, they now had to fill out a form verifying if a man had been near an exploding shell or had shown any other symptoms of mental disturbance. Predictably, this led to long delays. Officers filled out the forms as and when they could. Meanwhile, potentially serious victims of war neurosis had to wait for days in hospital wards before being officially diagnosed, let alone treated. After all the form filling had been completed, in periods of normal activity approximately 40 per cent of those classified NYDN were eventually diagnosed as Shell Shock 'W' and 60 per cent were diagnosed with the lesser condition of Shell Shock 'S'. This proportion went up to roughly 50-50 during major battles.[33]

Without doubt this new categorisation prevented many genuine victims of war neuroses from being counted as such. It certainly meant that the official statistics looked far more acceptable. Holmes reported that during the four months of the Third Battle of Ypres, from July to October 1917, the titanic struggle that became known as the battle of Passchendaele, Fifth Army counted only 5,346 cases of diagnosed shell shock.[34] In an army of roughly half a million men enduring the mud and horror of Passchendaele, this approximately amounted to a mere 1 per cent of the total force, a figure that defies all belief. Even the uncritical *Official Medical History* concluded, 'Considering the nature of the conditions in this battle area and the nerve-racking character of the struggle, this must be regarded as a very low figure.'[35]

This is a dramatic understatement. During the last year of the war, only 3000 further cases were diagnosed. Although this again seems extraordinarily low it is more believable in relative terms, as the battles of 1918 became more mobile and fluid, and in these conditions the incidence of shell shock was always likely to be lower. The term Shell Shock 'W' had finally outlasted its time; in the final months of the war, its usage was abolished altogether.[36] Outwardly, the army could congratulate itself that the crisis of shell shock had been solved. In reality, it simply refused to count such cases any longer.

It must be asked how effective were the different forms of treatment for shell shock and what was the recovery level of victims? Again, the records are not always complete. Of those diagnosed with shell shock during the Battle of the Somme it is impossible to calculate exactly how many men recovered. According to some records, a figure as high as 87 per cent of those reported to be suffering from shell shock were back on front-line duty within a month. Other figures suggest it was 79 per cent.[37] This would have included all those men who were given a few days' sleep and rest in a dressing station, as well as those diagnosed either with Shell Shock 'S' or 'W'. Between August and October 1917, at the height of the Third Battle of Ypres, detailed records were kept of the far smaller number of official cases than in the previous year. Sixteen per cent of patients were evacuated to base hospitals. Of the rest who were kept in Army Areas, 55 per cent returned direct to their battalions for duty and the remaining 29 per cent were directed to take part in one of the schemes in which recovering patients went to various farms for a month of agricultural labour. After this they automatically returned to their units.[38] The percentages for the remaining thirteen months of the war were similar but with a larger number being sent to base hospitals.

When it comes to the proportion of relapses, the numbers are again difficult to calculate on a reliable basis. All figures relating to the wounded were kept by Army groups, so if a man was sent back to his division which was then transferred from, say, Fourth Army to Second Army, it was impossible to track what had happened to him. If he had a relapse, he would be recorded as a new statistic. However, on the basis of the numbers that can be tallied, a surprisingly low figure of only 10 per cent of men sent back to the firing line had to be readmitted to hospital due to the recurrence of war neurosis. Just 3 per cent were readmitted twice or more. Those sent back down the line by this point were mostly serious cases of neurasthenia; only rarely did this occur with cases of hysteria, when it produced the severest physical symptoms.

All these figures have to be treated with suspicion. By 1917 the army was doing all it could to keep down the numbers classed with any form of nervous condition by using the new NYDN category. However, the figures enabled the *Official Medical History* to conclude that by the end of the war it was far better, in most cases of neurosis, not to place a man in a 'sick atmosphere', in other words in hospital, as this tended only to fix his condition. It was noted that the 'majority of patients ... rapidly improved' when given rest and recuperation as near the front as possible. But at last it was also recognised that, serious, nervous conditions should be treated in special hospitals by specialist doctors as part of a programme properly co-ordinated by a 'consulting neurologist'. This at least was progress of a sort.[39]

The United States of America was the last major power to enter the Great War in April 1917. By then the debate about the causes, symptoms and treatment of shell shock had been well publicised. Determined to benefit from the lessons painfully learned in the European armies, a month after the declaration of war a senior American neurologist, Dr Thomas Salmon, visited the British and French armies to carry out a scientific investigation into the treatment of war neuroses. As a result of his investigation, a neuropsychiatric team accompanied the American Expeditionary Force when it began to build up in France from the spring of 1918. After Salmon's report, the US army decided to follow exactly the procedures developed by that year in the British army, with the vast majority of shell shock cases being treated in dressing stations near the front and only a third being sent back down the line to neurological hospitals, which were specialist wards within the equivalent of Casualty Clearing Stations. One US Army base hospital, known as Hospital 117, located in the small village of La Fauche in the picturesque foothills of the Vosges mountains, acted as a specialist neuropsychiatric centre. Only the most severe 15 per cent of cases ever reached Hospital 117. The guiding principle was to treat men as fast and as near the front as possible in order to keep what was called a 'return to duty attitude'.[40]

The US Army was also good at keeping statistics, particularly from September 1918 when it began to operate as an independent force on the Western Front rather than as an adjunct to the British or French armies. Initially, in the spring of 1918, 20 per cent of all casualties reaching the base hospitals were shell shock victims and war neurosis was regarded as a 'dangerous military menace', as it had been in the British army on the Somme.[41] But as the army grew dramatically in size over the latter three months of the war from 270,000 to 1,450,000 men, and as the conflict became more mobile, the level dropped to half of what it had been in the spring. By the last months of the war, the majority of men suffering from war neuroses were treated effectively near the front. The 'wastage' level of victims who had to be evacuated to the United States was only 1 per cent.[42] These figures show the real improvement of treatment levels in the US Army; as the American model was built on the British and French experience, they also indicate how recovery levels had similarly improved in the Allied armies by the end of the war.

Although the primary task of military doctors was to get a man fit and reliable enough to return him to his battalion in the trenches, that was not all. There was a secondary responsibility, one that became more apparent as the war advanced and as tens of thousands of men were classed as not fit enough to return to duty. That was to advise the post-war pension system on whether or not a man was suitable for state support after his military service was over. The challenges presented by shell shock did not end with the Armistice in November 1918. The response of the medical establishment in the post-war world to the challenges of coping with war trauma would shape the experience of a generation.

11

The Ghosts of War

Charles Wilson was one of literally hundreds of thousands
to have a near escape during the Battle of the Somme.
During a barrage the shelling suddenly intensified, and
Wilson and his colleagues 'got down to the bottom of the
trench, waiting, listening'. Then the situation grew even
worse. 'We heard a shell that seemed by its rising shriek to
be coming near. Then there was a shattering noise, in our
ears it seemed, a cloud of fumes and a great shower of earth
and blood and human remains. As the fumes drifted away I
had just time to notice that the man on my right had disappeared and that the trench where he stood was now only a
mound of freshly turned earth, when another angry shriek
ended in another rending explosion, and more fumes that
enveloped us. Our bit of the trench was isolated now and
as the shells burst all around us with gathering violence it
seemed that the whole Boche artillery was watching this
little island and was intent on its destruction.' Wilson found
that he could not think or act for himself. 'My mind became
a complete blank ... Perhaps I should have got up and run
if my limbs had seemed to belong to me.' Eventually, the
shelling ceased 'and there was peace again and a strange
quietness and the old queer feeling of satisfaction after a bad

time as if something had been achieved, then utter weariness, a desire to sleep, a numb feeling.'

Wilson never forgot this vivid experience, the worst he ever endured as a MO on the Western Front. He had come within a few inches of death. For the next year 'every shell that fell near the trench seemed to be the beginning of a new cataclysm.' Wilson wrote that he did not remember being frightened during the incident, just 'too stunned to think'. But it took its toll later. 'I was to go through it many times in my sleep ... Even when the war had begun to fade out of men's minds I used to hear all at once without warning the sound of a shell coming. Perhaps it was only the wind in the trees to remind me that war had exacted its tribute and that my little capital was less than it had been.'[1]

Wilson lived a prominent and successful life after the war. He became a physician at St Mary's teaching hospital in London, a Harley Street consultant and in the 1940s, as President of the Royal College of Physicians, was one of the principal architects of the new National Health Service. From 1940 he became Winston Churchill's personal doctor, meeting with the Prime Minister every few weeks and regularly travelling with him on his gruelling trips abroad. Wilson, who became Lord Moran in 1943, never suffered from any serious form of shell shock or war neurosis. But still this incident under shell fire on the Somme would come back to him regularly, prompted by the tiniest thing. If the memory of being under shell fire remained with a medical man like Wilson who could understand and rationalise his emotions, it is easy to imagine how it must have haunted the lives of many thousands of others.

Men suffering from the after-effects of shell shock could be irrational and unpredictable, and frequently it was wives and children who suffered most. Tranquil, kind, loving and attentive one minute, a man might suddenly turn for no apparent reason and become brutal, violent and abusive. All sorts of things could trigger such violent mood swings. It might be simply the sound of the wind in the trees, reminding a man of the shriek of a shell (as with Wilson), or a military band playing on the radio. One man, every time he heard the *phut-phut* of a passing motorbike, thought he was hearing machine-gun fire; he would go into paroxysms of fear and had to find a corner to hide in. Other men continued to suffer from occasional shakes or tremors and would become furious if a wife or child noticed or commented on this. Many wives had to put up with their husbands' violent nightmares, the men waking up at night screaming and recalling the terrible events they had experienced. Sometimes the nightmares went on for years, even decades, after the war's end.

Very few ex-soldiers would talk about their wartime experiences. The attitude of the time was to draw a veil over memories of the war and to move forward. Men who had seen terrible sights and had witnessed friends being killed or blown to pieces alongside them were told, 'Put it out of your mind, old fellow, and do not think about it; imagine that you're in your garden at home.'[2] Families knew not to ask husbands and fathers about what had happened to them. The ignorance of what lay at the root of a loved one's anguish must have made living with those haunted by wartime ghosts even more dreadful to bear.

The fragments of surviving evidence only hint at the agony that thousands of families must have endured from the after-effects of shell shock. The wife of a private in the Lancashire Fusiliers reported two years after the war's end, 'He is always complaining of shooting pains in the head. He sometimes sits staring vacantly for hours and at times has not spoken for days, then suddenly gets up, goes out and gets drunk.' Another soldier from Lancashire who suffered

from shell shock was finally discharged from the Maudsley
Hospital in July 1919; on returning home he tried to strangle
his wife in bed. Donald Laing, who served with the Cycle
Corps from 1914 and returned home suffering from shell
shock, was able to get a job as a commercial artist and apparently settle back into normal family life. Four years after the
end of the war he became increasingly unsettled, complaining that his workmates were persecuting him. Like others,
he seemed to see Germans everywhere. Certain that he was
being followed, he dragged his wife and baby out of bed
one night and made them walk across Wimbledon Common
in the pouring rain to avoid the pursuers. Sudden bursts of
unmanly tears, bouts of intense depression, a sense of being
surrounded and pursued by the enemy were all characteristic of the inner demons of these poor men.[3]

Most families did all they could to put up with a strange
and alien father or husband back at home after a long absence
at the front. But sometimes, in extreme cases, it was just too
much. George Munston was at home for Christmas 1916.
Then he went away to fight in Mesopotamia and was unable
to come back on leave. In the Middle East he suffered from a
severe form of war neurosis. In the spring of 1919 he finally
returned home to south London but, alarmingly, he arrived
under escort from the Notts War Hospital. His wife Beatrice
was no doubt delighted to see her husband, who also met for
the first time his eighteen-month-old daughter, conceived
when he was last at home. But Munston was not the same
loving husband he had been. He made wild threats to thrash
his wife and to murder his hospital doctor. Then he said he
would drown himself. After only two weeks, Beatrice had to
contact the authorities and beg them to take him back into
hospital.[4]

From the spring of 1915, the government had accepted
that they had a responsibility to provide welfare support for

disabled veterans who needed help re-integrating into civilian life and finding suitable employment. After the terrible casualties during the Battle of the Somme there was a change of political leadership in Britain. Lloyd George became Prime Minister in December 1916, and created five new ministries to beef up Britain's war effort. One of these new departments, the Ministry of Pensions, assumed the responsibility for the support of disabled soldiers in 1917 and took over the management of 900,000 pensions (including all pensions and gratuities to disabled men, widows and dependents). New pensions were being awarded at the rate of 14,000 per week.

The flat rate for a weekly disabled war pension was 27s 6d, a sum increased to 33s in November 1918 (27s 6d is roughly equivalent to £75 in 2016 value; 33s is roughly equivalent to £90. So the payments were by no means generous.[5]). But the calculation of payments involved a complicated structure that depended upon the scale of a man's disability. The loss of two or more limbs entitled a man to a 100 per cent pension. On the other hand, the percentage payable for the amputation of a leg depended upon whether it was above the knee (60 per cent) or below (50 per cent). Payment for the loss of a thumb or four fingers depended on whether they were from the right hand (40 per cent) or the left (30 per cent). Moreover, payment was increased proportionately as a consequence of the claimant's final rank and number of dependents.

The Ministry of Pensions and the four other new ministries created by Lloyd George have been described as the beginnings of a form of 'war socialism'.[6] But it can rarely have felt like that at the time. The government did accept that mental or nervous disability could be included in the list of injuries that merited a pension, but the details were always going to be more difficult to determine than with the loss of limbs. A doctor had to examine every ex-serviceman to decide whether his shell shock was wholly the consequence

of his military service (in which case it was classed as 'attributed') or whether it derived from an existing condition made
worse by wartime service (in which case it was called 'aggravated'). Attributed pensions could be paid for life; aggravated
pensions were usually paid only for a short period until it
was decided that the shell shock had passed.[7]

From the start the Treasury was horrified by the thought
of the funds that it might need to spend on disabled ex-
servicemen. As a consequence the state bureaucracy was
slow, inefficient and overwhelmingly mean in its allocation of
pensions. The processing and calculation of pension requests
took time. Complex medical opinions had to be sought. And
those administering the payouts seemed to show neither a
sense of haste nor much sympathy to those making claims.
Many victims of war neuroses were made to feel that they
were somehow failed soldiers. No doubt officials were fearful
that unless they minimised the number of payments due, the
floodgates would open and post-war governments would be
crippled by vast legacies of payments that would have to be
made for decades to come.

Even at the front, while the war was raging, some people
grew suspicious that changes were being introduced into the
diagnosis of shell shock victims with a view to minimising
post-war costs. Lieutenant Gameson was a young doctor who
served as a MO with the 45th Field Ambulance during the
Battle of the Somme, treating wounded men as they were
taken from the front-line aid posts to the greater care available in the CCSs. He was very critical of the distinction that
was drawn between Shell Shock 'W' and 'S'. A man diagnosed with Shell Shock 'W' had suffered as a consequence
of enemy action and would potentially be due a pension. A
man diagnosed 'S' was suffering a temporary condition from
which he was supposed to recover. Gameson wrote in his
diary, 'We all knew that shell-shock was highly debatable.'

But he was suspicious about what lay behind the distinction. 'There can be no reasonable doubt that the motive concerned the subsequent status of a man. It concerned the distant questions of the employers' liabilities: PENSIONS [Gameson's capitals].'

In Gameson's view, the distinction between the two forms of shell shock did not stem from a concern to provide men with the best treatment, but was a long-term plan to avoid the payment of war pensions to those who might already have been suffering from a nervous malady before joining the army and to keep down the numbers who would qualify for care having suffered war neuroses. He wrote: 'All this "W" versus "S" stuff seemed a shade tendentious, and it did not only apply to the admittedly difficult Shell Shock cases. Once a man had officially been labelled "W" – and here is the point – he was in a much better bargaining position [in obtaining a war pension] than one marked "S".'[8] Gameson's fears were certainly realised when it came to calculating pension rights after the war.

Most of those who suffered from some form of shell shock and were deemed suitable for a pension were officially classed as having had 'neurasthenia'. Having been applied largely to officers during the war, afterwards this became the standard word to describe the condition of all soldiers who had suffered from war trauma. But other categories were also added, including 'anxiety neurosis' (a term preferred by William Rivers), 'debility' and 'nervous debility'.[9] This indicates yet again the continuing confusion over the diagnosis of shell shock.

However, out of nearly 556,000 war pensions awarded to officers and men invalided out of the army and navy during the war, a total of 34,471 (about 6 per cent) had been given for a disability arising from 'nervous diseases'.[10] By February 1921, the figure had grown considerably; 65,000 men were drawing pensions for disability due to neurasthenia and allied conditions. Of these, an extraordinary 14,771 were still in hospital or attending a clinic. One reason why the overall number had risen so much was that nervous disability was the one form of injury that could emerge *after* the war was over. Of the men still in hospital two and a half years after the war ended, 1,367 had developed symptoms after their discharge from the army. These included many soldiers who had been rewarded for their bravery in the war and had returned to employment, but who had suffered a nervous breakdown after apparently settling back into civilian life. The vast majority had suffered the onset of their disease within six months of leaving the army. Very probably many soldiers had been hesitant about presenting with a nervous disease when still in the army and had only come forward after returning to civilian life.

Reflecting on these figures, the *Official Medical History* noted, 'it is remarkable that after three years of peace so great a number should remain disabled. It is to be feared that a large proportion of them will never recover their full mental capacity.' After a clinical analysis of the figures, the authors concluded that the numbers still suffering so long after the war 'alone would be sufficient evidence, if any were required, that this disease is a real and very serious consequence of war, and further that it is one of the most prolonged and difficult to cure'.[11] These figures also raise the question as to when the war really came to an end. The guns fell silent on 11 November 1918 but the suffering went on. For some, it had barely begun.

However, the number actually receiving pensions after the war was without doubt only the tip of the iceberg. Thousands suffering from shell shock had been refused pensions or denied further treatment and care. There was still a suspicion among officials of malingering, that men were trying to obtain a state pension when they were not eligible for one. In 1919, the provision of military pensions had become a bureaucratic muddle involving three different departments: the War Office, Lloyd George's wartime Pensions Ministry and the Ministry of Labour. It was brought together in that year under the Labour Ministry in order to allow the distribution of pensions through local Labour Exchanges. However, this totally overwhelmed the system. There were long queues outside the exchanges as ex-servicemen waited in line in the hope of finding new jobs and registering for pension payments. Those suffering from mental conditions had to join the queues and wait their turn, and doubtless this added to their distress. But unsympathetic bureaucrats trying to save the state money were not exclusively responsible for such distress. Everyone drawing a pension for an aggravated nervous condition had to attend a medical board at regular intervals to maintain their entitlement. It was often the doctors on these boards who decided whether the pension was payable or not.

As in the war, medical boards could be notoriously unpredictable. Some were filled with ex-RAMC doctors who had considerable sympathy for men suffering from the consequences of shell shock. Others could be made up of doctors who had little or no experience of shell shock and whose instinct was to assume that it was all a case of swinging the lead and trying it on. There was a widespread belief that physical wounds, the loss of a limb, were a sign of bravery and a badge of courage. A man who had lost an arm or a leg had clearly been in combat and had faced up to his duty. Mental conditions were more ambiguous.

Moreover, the medical questions were themselves difficult to answer fairly. How was it possible to tell for sure if a man had picked up his mental illness entirely as a consequence of the war, or if he had a pre-existing nervous condition that had been aggravated by the war? According to the dominant medical opinion, many men who suffered from shell shock had some family background of nervous or neurotic conditions. In which case, to what extent was a prevailing condition responsible for the mental strains brought on by the war? The boards had a difficult task on their hands and although there was a right of appeal against their decisions, it was a time-consuming and complex process.

A few clinics around the country provided treatment for the psychological casualties, but they always had to struggle against financial cutbacks. For instance, in November 1920, the government shut the Maudsley Hospital, which still had a waiting list of ex-servicemen queuing for treatment. Men suffering from shell shock or neurasthenia had to attend medical boards every three months, and as their pensions could be taken away from them as a consequence of the judgement of these boards, the whole process must also have added considerably to the anxiety of those drawing pensions.

The prevailing wisdom was still that lunacy was hereditary. In an attempt to ascertain whether a man's condition was pre-existing or inherited, or had come about because of military service, the War Office wrote to the families of those who had been diagnosed with some form of nervous disease asking if there was a history of mental troubles in the family, 'including uncles and aunts'. Most people seem to have been honest in their replies. Mrs Bertram, in Cheshire, wrote back that concerning her husband, a clerk in the army in France who was hospitalised with shell shock, 'there is no "nervous" or "mental" trouble in any way connected with his family and he has never been like it before and never had fits or touched spirits and very seldom beer and was very moderate and clean in his morals.' However, when she was told that he was in the Lord Derby War Hospital at Warrington, Mrs Bertram knew that he might well be in a seriously disturbed state. Reflecting on the problem of his homecoming, she wrote, 'I could not have him home unless he was well and could go to work as I am not strong enough myself to work and keep him. He was earning good money before joining the Army.' It seems that this wife's love of her husband was somewhat conditional.[12]

Lieutenant James Butlin was one of tens of thousands who felt hard done by. Six months after leaving Craiglockhart, he had a nervous breakdown. As he recovered, Butlin described how he felt in a letter to his pal Basil. 'I still am rather feeble, can't walk far and liable to "come over queer" at the slightest exertion.' In March 1918 he went before a special army board consisting of a major and two colonels who declared that he was 'permanently unfit for military service'. He was now twenty-one years old and had given up university at Oxford to spend three years in the army. Butlin complained to his chum, 'the Army have taken all the best out of me and now wish to turn me out with an inadequate pension ... I am just as likely to break down in civil life where I shall have to work harder than I do now.' Four weeks later he went before a medical board of civilian doctors who assessed him for his pension. Clearly the sum they settled on was not enough for a young man like Butlin, who was without independent means. Again Butlin wrote to his friend that he had been discharged and was 'of course out of uniform. Now what the hell am I to do for a living? Can you tell me the answer to that question? Seriously though, I must get work soon or I shall be broke.'[13] Butlin became another statistic as the war neared its end and thousands of men with shattered minds tried to return to a civilian existence.

Robert Dent, a tough Northumberland miner before the war, had fought on the Somme where he had been hospitalised with shell shock. The neurosis appeared to be mild and after five days he returned to duty. He finally left the army suffering from trench foot and returned to work as a hewer at the local pit. In the summer of 1924 he began to show signs of intense emotional disturbance. His wife, Hannah, testified that he had been 'strong and healthy before enlistment' but was now 'a total wreck'. Dent was taken into Morpeth Mental Hospital, where the doctors put in a claim that he was suffering from a recurrence of the shell shock he had suffered eight years previously. But the Ministry of Pensions refused to countenance this, arguing that there was 'no evidence to connect the shell shock with his present disability, which is of purely constitutional origin and unconnected with war service'. Dent's local vicar, Rev. Fogg, an ex-serviceman who tried to help war veterans, took up the case, writing to the Ministry, 'I am convinced we have a MOST CLEAR CASE [capitals in original]. By Dent's conduct and ravings we have sufficient evidence that he is suffering from shell shock.' Rev. Fogg appealed to the Ministry 'on behalf of people who are suffering acutely as the direct result of the War'. The good vicar's appeal finally carried the day and the Ministry relented, granting Dent a pension.[14] The story reveals not only how difficult it was to crowbar a pension out of the Ministry but also the difficulty of assessing cases of emotional trauma that manifested nearly a decade after the original occurrence.

There was a very blurred distinction between shell shock or neurasthenia, and madness. Some soldiers had been classed as insane during the war and had been passed into the asylum system. This was clearly inappropriate for those who had suffered from shell shock. Montagu Lomax, a retired GP too old to enlist in the military, went into the asylum service to do his bit after war was declared. He was appalled at what he found. He described a twenty-year-old inmate who had suffered from shell shock. The young man was 'intensely confused and had the greatest difficulty in getting the words out that he wanted to say. He was besides thoroughly frightened and in consequence "resistive". He seemed to imagine that everyone around him was a German and an enemy ... and probably took the place for a German prison.' The man sometimes refused to eat, dress properly or obey orders, so he was often kept in solitary confinement in a darkened cell where it was thought he could do no harm.

Lomax reflected, 'Had he been an officer he would have been sent to one of the many luxurious mental homes instituted for the treatment of such cases. Being only a private, he had, like hundreds of others, been simply drafted into a pauper lunatic asylum, where he may become hopelessly insane.' However, the young lad was often visited by his two devoted sisters, whose presence seemed to cheer him up. As Lomax wrote, 'The boy wanted mothering; not dragooning into obedience' by the impersonal, degrading and regimented life of an asylum. Lomax concluded, 'In a country as wealthy as England is, even after all her war losses, it is scandalous that those who have given their all in her defence should be so scurvily treated.'[15]

After the war, the numbers of ex-soldiers in asylums grew from 2,500 at the beginning of 1919 to more than 6,400 by October 1921.[16] With public opinion generally sympathetic to the victims of war neuroses, most people felt that it was inappropriate for ex-servicemen to be assigned to asylums as 'pauper lunatics'. So the Ministry of Pensions gave each ex-serviceman a suit of civilian clothes and 2s 6d per week to assist him. It is doubtful that this did much to ease the men's lot. Some of those sent to asylums were suffering from what was categorised as 'general paralysis of the insane'. This rare condition was a consequence of syphilis, which had been widespread among soldiers during the war years.[17]

But many other ex-soldiers also ended up in asylums, either because as single men there appeared to be nowhere else to send them, or in some cases because their families had found them so difficult to live with after the war that they had certified them. Rifleman Albert Styles had been a personal valet in a gentleman's club in Piccadilly before the war; smart, lively and totally reliable. Having joined up in September 1914 he spent three years in the 13th Battalion Rifle Brigade before losing his arm and suffering from shell shock. In September 1917 he returned to his parents' home at Tooting Bec in south London. He had been granted a pension of 27s 6d for nine weeks which was then to be reduced by one-half. But he was depressed and morose. He sat around vacantly for hours; he had spells imagining everyone around him was a German; finally he barricaded himself in his bedroom and refused to come out or take food. His father called in the medical authorities, who bundled him off to Long Grove Asylum in Epsom. Having survived three years in the trenches he lasted, tragically, only fifteen months in the asylum, dying there of dysentery in January 1919.[18]

The asylum system had been badly run down during the war years. Several institutions had been closed to civilian patients and reopened as military hospitals. Staff had departed in large numbers to join up. Conditions were wretched and the newspapers were full of stories of officers and men who had fought for their country mouldering in cold, insanitary asylum dormitories, akin to the old Victorian workhouses.[19] A charity was established in London in 1919 with the principal aim of keeping ex-servicemen out of the lunatic asylum system. Called the Ex-Services Welfare Society (ESWS), it was founded by a group of well-meaning upper-middle-class women, although its management soon became more professional and was dominated by ex-servicemen. The only charity exclusively dedicated to helping those wounded psychologically after the war, the ESWS set up its own 'recuperative home' at Chartfield on Putney Hill in 1921, opening another at Eden Manor in Beckenham in 1924. But for private charities to work effectively they needed to be hand-in-glove with government departments. In the early 1920s the ESWS fell out with the Ministry of Pensions, who thought it was too political, and it lost its royal patronage and support from the British Legion. Nevertheless, it continued to assist shell shock victims and their families by supplementing the official welfare programme.[20]

However, the neglect of ex-servicemen in the years following the war as the country fell into economic depression went from bad to worse. The sight of destitute veterans begging became common in most cities in the 1920s. Some were legless or armless, many were blind, others bore their scars internally. In London's fashionable West End one particular beggar became a familiar figure as he went up and down the lines of theatregoers. He wore a cardboard placard around his neck on which was written, 'I served through the whole of the war till I was shell shocked at Delville Wood. Now I have a small pension and I also have a wife and child.'[21] Clearly, for this man, it was worth labelling himself as having had shell shock. It must have brought from caring Londoners not only sympathy but also donations of cash.

Pension arrangements after the war were handled in such a way as to provoke a vast number of complaints and no doubt an even greater amount of grumbling. Field Marshal Haig, in evidence to the House of Commons Select Committee on Pensions in July 1919, said he was 'appalled' at the bureaucratic muddle and red tape that led to delays in the provision of adequate pensions. He further criticised the medical boards, accusing them of 'lacking in all sympathy and generosity ... There is no uniformity in their decisions and some treat every wretched individual who appears before them as a malingerer.' Claiming that pensions were so low that many families were forced to live in 'abject poverty', he called especially for a 'more generous and sympathetic treatment to all who suffer from gas poisoning, shell shock and neurasthenia'. Having asserted angrily that 'No man should suffer because he has served his country', he ended his evidence with an appeal to the members of the committee: 'You surely do not want to pauperise any man who has risked his life on the field of battle. You want to be generous.'[22] The former commander-in-chief was rapidly distancing himself from his wartime reputation as 'butcher Haig' and reinventing himself as the veterans' champion.[23]

However, pensions were never intended to provide for all the needs of a veteran and his family. The state was prepared to recognise a level of responsibility for the care and resettlement of disabled ex-soldiers. But the claimants had their responsibilities too. Apart from the very small number who were so tragically disabled that they would never be able to cater for themselves, soldiers returning from the battlefield were expected to look after and provide for their families in the traditional patriarchal way. This involved finding appropriate training or retraining, and then searching out their own employment so they could continue to be head of their household. The pages of the fortnightly magazine *Recalled to Life*, issued by the government and devoted to the welfare of soldiers, sailors and airmen, were not filled with sermons from care workers or state officials but featured articles written by ex-servicemen to address the needs and concerns of other ex-servicemen. For one issue Sergeant J.A. Bennet at Queen Mary's Workshop in Brighton wrote a piece recognising that wartime pensions were never going to be generous and summing up the government's attitude perfectly: 'Your pension is not meant to live on; it is a pension for services rendered, not a retiring pension. To live on your pension is out of the question, it would be a mere existence . . . Do you want to be a respectable self-supporting citizen or a lazy good-for-nothing, depending on charity? Do you want to live comfortably, to have, and to save, money, or lead a miserable, grovelling existence?'[24] No minister could have expressed it more succinctly and colloquially.

The problem facing shell shock victims was that those with mental conditions were the most likely to experience discrimination. Not only were there all the many stigmas associated with mental disease, but when it came to employment those with nervous disorders were traditionally seen as unpredictable, volatile and ultimately unreliable. During the war, shell shock victims had been a group apart. As Private Edwin Bigwood recalled, 'We were all afraid of shell shock. We'd rather lose a leg, be wounded than to have shell shock. We didn't mind being wounded, it was the dread of being shell shocked.'[25] Similar prejudices appeared among employers after the war. The Secretary of the Ex-Services Employment Department explained to a reporter just before the end of the war that many employers were willing to take on physically disabled men but were more reluctant to consider the mentally wounded. He was quoted as saying, 'The men we find employers fight shy of most are "nerve" cases – shell shock, etc. It's easier to fix up a one-legged man.'[26]

The issue of shell shock and the sense that a great injustice had been done during the war never went away; in fact it only grew stronger as a consequence of the complaints about war pensions in the years after the war. During a debate in the House of Lords on 28 April 1920 Lord Southborough said, 'The subject of shell shock cannot be referred to with any pleasure. All would desire to forget it – to forget ... the roll of insanity, suicide and death; to bury our recollections of the horrible disorder ... But we cannot do this, because a great number of cases of those who suffer from shell shock and its allied disorders are still upon our hands and they deserve our sympathy and care.'[27] Southborough suggested setting up a committee of enquiry, and this was duly established by the War Office under his chairmanship with the remit of investigating the different types of 'hysteria and traumatic neurosis, commonly called "shell shock"', to try to establish 'the ascertained facts as to its origin, nature and remedial treatment' and to advise on actions that could be taken in a future war to reduce its incidence.[28] The committee began its hearings in September 1920 and heard fifty-nine expert witnesses including senior military figures, officers with combat experience (including three winners of the VC), several MOs and military physicians. Myers, still smarting from his treatment by the army, was the only significant figure who refused to give evidence. The committee published its findings two years later.

Despite the extensive wartime debate, by 1922 there was still no consensus as to what exactly shell shock was and what caused it. The varied conclusions of the enquiry reflect this. Some parts are quite progressive. The enquiry concluded that 'any type of individual might suffer from one or other form of neurosis if exposed for a sufficient length of time to the conditions of modern warfare.'[29] In other words, war neurosis was not a problem confined to the 'weak', the 'feeble minded' or those naturally inclined to mental collapse. On the other hand, the enquiry also continued to link war neuroses with victims who displayed 'wilful cowardice' and 'contributory negligence' of their military duties, and concluded that the process of court-martialling men found guilty of cowardice during the war had operated 'in a thoroughly satisfactory manner'.[30] The military authorities were found to be not guilty of executing men who should have been excused because of their mental state. The authors of the report thought that shell shock was a totally unsuitable term, 'a gross and costly misnomer, and that the term should be eliminated from our nomenclature'.[31] Although they accepted that it was the term most commonly used to describe a range of nervous conditions and war neuroses, they resented having to use it and consequently put it in inverted commas throughout.

The War Office enquiry reached a series of conclusions without taking the situation forward. First, they concluded that the term shell shock should not be used in future. They concluded that war neurosis or mental breakdown was usually a temporary phenomenon and a man suffering it should not be classed as a battle casualty, any more than one suffering from sickness or disease. They decided that unit morale played a vital role – high morale meant less neurosis. Senior officers should take all measures to ensure that tours of duty at the front were short, that the welfare of men received attention and that men showing signs of neurosis should be taken out of the line and given rest and care. The enquiry praised the models of treatment developed in the army by 1917 – that most men should be treated in forward areas, that only severe cases should be sent to neurological centres, which should be as near the front as possible, and that only in exceptional circumstances should a patient be evacuated to Britain. On the one hand they sanctioned the use of psychotherapy as a form of treatment; on the other, they also supported the use of electric shock therapy. They recommended against the use of psychoanalysis. And finally, they said that in a future war, efforts should be made during the recruitment process to ascertain the mental condition of candidates, and any who showed incipient signs of nervous disorder should be weeded out.[32] The enquiry had aired the subject of shell shock once again in a very public way. But its conservative conclusions looked to many like a cover-up and failed to halt the swelling sense that men had suffered injustice during the war and that this was continuing throughout the pensions shambles in the post-war years.

Numerous clinics set up by the War Office after 1918 to try to treat the psychological victims of war were closed in government cutbacks brought on by the severe economic downturn of the 1920s. And there was pressure on officials to claim as the years passed that shell shock victims had recovered from their problems and no longer needed the pensions they had been drawing. However, by 1937, official figures showed that there were still 35,000 ex-servicemen receiving war disability pensions for neurasthenia and mental conditions.[33] In the 1920s there had been a reduction of the number of ex-officers and an increase in the proportion of rank and file ex-soldiers drawing welfare. But overall, despite attempts to reduce the number of those on benefits, the total remained large throughout the inter-war period.

Shell shock had taught the medical community a great deal about the working of the human mind. Hundreds if not thousands of young doctors had gained experience of treating mental conditions for the first time in their professional lives. A small library of books had been published in the attempt to explain the causes of shell shock, proffering many different approaches to treatment. Psychologists like Grafton Elliot Smith and Tom Pear argued that mental illness was not the reserved territory of degenerates and weaklings, as the parlance of the day had it, but was part of the human condition; anyone could experience it.

All this gave a great boost to psychology in Britain. Lunatic asylums were renamed 'mental hospitals' and those treating them were no longer called 'alienists' but were renamed 'psychiatrists'. The Tavistock Clinic was opened in north London in 1920 to provide therapy for ordinary people who could not afford the high fees charged by Harley Street neurologists. Its founder, Hugh Crichton-Miller, had worked with shell-shocked soldiers during the war. But from the beginning it was open to children and adults alike, and it became a magnet for young, training psychiatrists from across the country who went there to carry out research while at the same time acting as the clinical staff. The Maudsley Hospital, which had treated 12,400 shell-shocked servicemen between 1915 and 1919, reopened its doors in 1923 to all Londoners suffering from mental illness. It adopted several of the therapeutic treatments developed during the war.

The First World War had unwittingly provided a huge laboratory in which psychiatrists could peer into the workings of the human mind, and had brought into the open much of the debate about the various forms of therapy. Shell shock had helped to push back the door against the Victorian and Edwardian shibboleths that surrounded mental health. The study of the human psyche was at last on a large-scale and very public map.

Shell shock cast a deep shadow across the literature of the post-war era. It has been described as the *'mal de siècle'* of the post-war years, influencing everyday life and culture.[34] Rebecca West's *The Return of the Soldier* (1918) was the first of the 'shell shock novels'. It tells the story of Christopher Baldry, an officer who has been shell shocked, through the effect it has on his married life with Kitty. Christopher is in hospital suffering from amnesia and has lost all memory of the recent years of his life and of his marriage. The only relationship he can recall is a summer fling with a woman called Margaret fifteen years before. Margaret, not his wife, is the one notified by the War Office of his shell shock, but she is dismissed when she visits Kitty, who is horrified to imagine that her husband used to love this woman and now has no recall of their marriage. When he returns home from hospital, Christopher is locked in the world he inhabited fifteen years earlier when he was a young man infatuated with Margaret. Kitty eventually decides she has no alternative but to ask Margaret to join them. She meets Christopher, who understands on one level that the relationship is over but still cannot reconcile himself to his current life. Kitty calls in a doctor, a psychoanalyst, who decides to confront Christopher by getting Margaret to bring him his dead child's toys and clothes. This unlocks his repressed memories and he is cured. Margaret leaves, and Kitty and Christopher can resume their life together.

This poignant story attracted many female readers. The book is overlaid with issues of class; Christopher and Kitty are upper middle class, Margaret is lower middle class and depicted as rather drab. But its focus is on how the disabling effect of war on the male can destroy relationships. This is not the soldier's tale of shell shock but the story of its impact on the lives of wives and families.[35]

A.P. Herbert's *The Secret Battle* (1919) takes a different approach and is very much a soldier's tale. Narrated by an anonymous fellow officer, it is the story of the long, gradual breakdown of Henry Penrose. Joining his battalion just before it leaves for Gallipoli, Penrose is full of doubts about his ability to be a good officer and while others fall by the wayside under the pressure of combat, he is determined to carry on and prove himself. When the battalion transfers to the Western Front, Penrose is picked on by the new commanding officer, a regular officer who wants everything done by the book. He repeatedly orders Penrose to lead night relief parties which always come under enemy shellfire at the same spot.

Herbert depicts a classic case of neurasthenia: Penrose is slowly worn down until his nerves are totally gone and he has recurrent nightmares of being under German artillery fire, unable to get away. He is wounded and although offered a desk job at the War Office, decides it is his duty to return to his battalion. There, still being picked on and given the worst jobs, Penrose and a relief party come under fire and he orders the men to withdraw. They are spotted rushing towards the British lines and Penrose is put on a charge of running away under fire. He is court-martialled and in order to defend the honour of the regiment is found guilty of cowardice and shot at dawn. The book ends with these words from the narrator: 'That is the gist of it; that my friend Harry was shot for cowardice – and he was one of the bravest men I ever knew.'

A.P. Herbert was a lawyer with a passion for reform and the novel played on the widespread feeling that many men had been unjustly executed by the military during the war years. He subsequently wrote several volumes of *Misleading Cases*, satirical stories of miscarriages of justice some of which were much later televised by the BBC with Alastair Sim as the judge. Injustice is also at the heart of *The Secret Battle*, along with a realistic account of life in the trenches and a moving description of a slow mental breakdown.

In Virginia Woolf's *Mrs Dalloway* (1925), Septimus Smith is a shell-shocked soldier who has completely lost his identity after the war's end in a form of deferred traumatic disorder. In his wife's words he is 'not Septimus now'. Septimus's mental state has not been properly understood and the doctors are so poor in their treatment of him that in order to avoid further confinement he takes his own life by jumping out of a window. Mrs Dalloway hears of Septimus's death at a party she hosts the same evening and although she has never met him, she comes to admire him for his act. The story is particularly touching and revealing in that Woolf suffered from bipolar disorder and herself tried once to jump out of a window. Sixteen years after publishing *Mrs Dalloway* she committed suicide by drowning.

A very different approach came from Dorothy Sayers, who created a shell-shocked central character who not only survived the war but carried on a successful post-war career and was something of a hero. Lord Peter Wimsey is the archetypal amateur detective. He works alongside the police and uses his aristocratic name and connections without shame. He is a model British lord, a scholar, an athlete, an avid book collector and somewhat eccentric. But it emerges in the stories that he suffered badly from shell shock in France in 1918, and he has recurrences of the problem in several of the books.

Lord Wimsey first appeared in *Whose Body?*, published in 1923; in this book his mind wanders late at night as he sleepily tries to piece together the elements of the crime he is solving and he hallucinates that he is back in the trenches and is deafened by the noise of the German guns. This, apparently, is his first attack in nine months. Lord Peter's valet, simply referred to as Bunter, turns out to have been his sergeant in the Rifle Brigade in 1918 and knows how to deal with the problem. Their relationship reverts to that of officer and servant, and Bunter looks after him and gets him into bed. 'Thought we'd had the last of these attacks,' Bunter says, referring to the night time panic attack. We are told that Wimsey was 'dreadfully bad in 1918' and 'we can't expect to forget all about a great war in a year or two'.[36]

Similar attacks occur in many of the later books, both to Lord Wimsey and to other central characters. The delayed after-effects of shell shock never seem to prevent Wimsey from successfully tracking down criminals, but Sayers brings it in as an aspect of her hero's character, most probably as a reminder that men of his age – Wimsey is in his mid-thirties when the series of books begin – had to learn to live with scars from the war no matter how outwardly glamorous, calm and collected they appeared to be.

Many wartime memoirs were published after the Armistice and they often drew out the heroism and courage of those in battle. But ten years after the war had ended a new wave of anti-war memoirs became fashionable, not only emphasising the horror of the trenches but also the comradeship shared by men at the front while usually pointing at the utter futility of the war. Such a view soon proved to be the dominant vision of the Great War years. In Britain, Robert Graves led the new publishing boom with *Goodbye to All That* (1929). Siegfried Sassoon, already known for his poetry, produced a trilogy of autobiographical works, *Memoirs of a Fox-Hunting Man* (1928), *Memoirs of an Infantry Officer* (1930) and *Sherston's Progress* (1936). Edmund Blunden's account *Undertones of War* (1928) was part memoir and part poetry anthology. Most of these works were evidently autobiographical, others were novels but largely based on actual wartime experiences, like Frederic Manning's *Her Privates We* (published anonymously in 1930) and Richard Aldington's *Death of a Hero* (1929) and *Roads to Glory* (1930). In Germany, war veteran Erich Maria Remarque's *Im Westen nichts Neues* was first published in serial form in 1928 and was soon translated into English as *All Quiet on the Western Front* (1929). Within a year the novel had sold 2.5 million copies in twenty languages, including a million copies in Germany and one-third of a million in the English language. Hollywood soon came calling and the book was turned into a feature film, one of the early 'talkies', directed by Lewis Milestone in 1930.

Many of these wartime memoirs cover the Somme and nearly all speak openly in places about war neuroses of one sort or another. Most include painful descriptions of men who have succumbed to nervous breakdowns. In many of the memoirs and novels, particularly in those written by veterans who had served on the Somme like Graves, Sassoon and Manning, battle trauma is described as pretty much a standard feature among men who had been long at the front. Soldiers are described as being 'played out', or 'done in' or of having 'lost his head'. Graves recounts how after six months of continuous front line duty officers 'began gradually to decline in usefulness as neurasthenia developed' and those who had been at the front for more than fifteen months were 'often worse than useless' and even a danger to the rest of their company.[37] Within a little more than a decade shell shock had become an accepted fact of trench life in the literature of the war.[38]

A fundamental shift of values had come about during the four and a half years of war. Not only had two million men willingly given up their peacetime lives and volunteered to fight for King, Empire and Country in a citizen army, but three million more had been conscripted by the state to leave home and fight. Of these, 723,000 British soldiers, sailors and airmen were killed between August 1914 and November 1918. Two million more were wounded in some way. Approximately 16 per cent of males aged between eighteen and forty-nine, or nearly 1 in 6 of the adult male population, were therefore killed or wounded in the war. And the total losses suffered by Commonwealth soldiers amounted to another 200,000 dead. The war had been called a 'War for Civilisation'. After this, it seemed absurd that a man could volunteer and risk his life fighting to defend British values and the British political system but could not vote in an election when he returned home. The right to participate in political society was no longer seen to derive solely from the ownership of property but was more broadly seen as belonging to every civilian. The popular slogan was 'Fit to fight; fight to vote'. At the end of the war, the Representation of the People Act in 1918 recognised this fact. Universal suffrage for all men over the age of twenty-one was introduced. Before the war seven million men had the vote. In the first General Election after the war, thirteen million men voted.

The same Act is remembered for revolutionising the electoral status of women. Before the war the suffragettes had loudly demanded 'Votes for Women' but many men and women were deeply opposed to this. However, during the war, two million women had done their bit by volunteering for military and medical organisations and by working in munitions factories. In addition, women took on almost every job that had previously been seen exclusively as 'man's work'. The 1918 Representation of the People Act therefore also gave women the vote for the first time. By this time, even those who had opposed women's suffrage before the war now approved. Inequality still existed: only women over the age of thirty were allowed to vote. But in that first General Election after the war eight and a half million women voted for the first time and the first women were elected as MPs. In 1928 women attained the vote from the age of twenty-one. Ten years after the end of the First World War, universal adult suffrage had finally been achieved.

The post-war treatment of shell shock victims and the disabled was another aspect of this social revolution. Out of warfare had come welfare. The state had accepted a far greater responsibility than ever before for looking after those physically disabled in war while fighting for their country. The cost of pension provision for veterans was a considerable charge on the national economy. In the financial year 1913–14, the government welfare budget had amounted to £22.5 million. By 1921–2 it had risen to £179.5 million and would stay at the same or a slightly higher level for most of the inter-war period.[39] Furthermore, by 1922, the majority of those unemployed (600,000 out of one million) were ex-servicemen. However, when it came to shell shock victims and the tens of thousands of personal tragedies of men unable to escape from wartime ghosts, there was a collective failure to address the issue properly. While recognising the sacrifices made by so many during the war, the state badly let down the victims of war trauma.

It's impossible not to be critical about the wartime

approach to shell shock. The army had in the main failed to see the problem as one of individuals who under the pressure of a modern war needed understanding and treatment. It imagined shell shock to be a collective threat to military morale and discipline. Just as many generals saw the regular pre-war army as well disciplined and utterly reliable, so they mistrusted a citizen army, fearing it would prove to be weak and unpredictable under fire. Senior figures often ordered a brutal and inhumane response to anything or anyone they perceived as being too sympathetic to psychiatric casualties. Moreover, many other men suffering from trauma caused by the war were not properly identified or treated during the war years. Some who should have been cared for and treated for mental distress were subject to a harsh and summary military justice system. Others suffering from shell shock were simply omitted from the lists of casualties in an attempt to massage the figures so as to claim the problem had been solved. After the war, many failed to receive the pensions they deserved. Handouts, when they were made, were miserable and insufficient. They were distributed unevenly and unpredictably and the process of handing them out considerably increased the stress of those to whom they were due. Charitable organisations helped but could never do all that was needed. It was a shameful response to those who had willingly done their bit in war and were now in distress. Ironically, it was Sir Douglas Haig, whose command had contributed to the suffering of millions in the first place, who summed up the post-war situation in his evidence to the Parliamentary Select Committee by claiming it was 'a disgrace to a civilised state.'[40] These were strong words for such an established figure to use about the pensions system. But they were entirely justified.

Epilogue

In May 1980, the members of the American Psychiatric Association gathered for their annual meeting in San Francisco. That year's was a special meeting, at which the members were to review their Diagnostic and Statistical Manual of Mental Disorders. The Association is the principal organisation representing professional psychiatrists in the United States, and has worldwide influence. Its manual is highly respected and is used internationally to define mental disorders, a sort of global psychiatrists' bible.

When they gathered in San Francisco in 1980, the members of the association had many issues to review, but one stood out. During the Vietnam War, from 1961 to 1975, the levels of combat trauma had been particularly low. Psychiatric casualties were reported as being ten times lower than in the Second World War and three times lower than in the Korean War.[1] However, in the years following the end of the war veterans had reported what was called an 'epidemic' of delayed mental problems. It was described as a 'time bomb' for the future.

There appeared to be several reasons for this. The war had been immensely controversial and deeply unpopular among the American people. Society in much of the western world during the 1960s and 70s had gone through major changes and had become broadly hostile to military culture and values. Vietnam veterans appeared to suffer from a lack of respect, feeling they had been rejected by society and even blamed for the war, and consequently many experienced difficulties in readjusting to civilian life. The use of drugs and alcohol had become widespread. The stereotype of the Vietnam 'vet' was the sinister, troubled, often violent outsider, epitomised by the psychotic Travis Bickle, an ex-Marine, portrayed by Robert de Niro in Martin Scorsese's *Taxi Driver* (1976). Observers and journalists summed up the phenomenon by speaking of a 'post-Vietnam syndrome'.

A set of activists had formed working groups to study the syndrome in the years preceding the review of the *Diagnostic and Statistical Manual*. Many of them had been strongly opposed to the Vietnam War, and they lobbied hard at the association's meeting to include a new definition of the delayed effects of trauma. What followed in 1980 was formal recognition of a new mental disorder that was given the name post traumatic stress disorder (PTSD). This was something quite different from the condition categorised as 'shell shock' sixty years before. There were none of the immediate physical symptoms that came from hysteria – the shakes, the deafness and blindness, the paralysis that had plagued the poor victims of shell shock. PTSD was a disorder that came on after the sufferer had experienced a traumatic event, sometimes within six months, sometimes later. A key feature was the re-experiencing of the trauma, either through flashbacks or dreams of the event, or through a feeling that it was recurring. The condition was not limited to ex-servicemen. It was clear that anyone who had been through an exceptional form of trauma, and this could include being in a road traffic accident or observing some horrific occurrence, or having been raped or endured child abuse, could experience it.[2]

Large-scale analyses followed the classification of PTSD, including the federally funded National Vietnam Veterans Readjustment Study. This massive survey demonstrated that while the majority of veterans had settled successfully back into civilian life, an extraordinary minority of 30.6 per cent of male Vietnam veterans (over 960,000 men) and 26.9 per cent of female veterans (1,900 women) had experienced some form of PTSD.[3] In defining PTSD and including it in its new manual, the American Psychiatric Association had effectively created a new mental disease and given it a form of legitimacy. US federal resources were now allocated to the counselling of veterans suffering from PTSD. And it has since become the most common term used to describe combat stress.

The British army was, of course, not involved in the Vietnam War (although the Australian army was, and its veterans also suffered from high levels of PTSD and difficulties in settling back into society). The next conflict involving British troops was the Falklands War of 1982. The Falklands campaign was short, lasting only twenty-five days from the landings at San Carlos Water to the recapture of Port Stanley, and the troops who took part were considered to be in the elite battalions of the British army, with a high state of morale. There were very few reported cases of 'battle shock' during the war. But despite the flag waving and the patriotic revival prompted by the war, in the years that followed more and more cases of PTSD among veterans were diagnosed, attracting considerable media attention. This had the effect of putting the Ministry of Defence itself on the defensive, arguing that such media interest would undermine the fighting spirit of the armed forces and that a man's mental state after he returned to civilian life was his own business and a private matter. The MoD was fearful that the obsession with legal rights which became apparent in the 1980s would open the floodgates to endless claims for compensation.

The short Gulf War of February 1991 created its own 'Gulf War syndrome'. At first this was thought to be linked to the handling of depleted uranium shells by the Allied forces, along with the cocktail of vaccines given to service-men in advance of the campaign to protect them from the possible use of chemical and biological weapons by Saddam Hussein's forces. In the years following the war, many veterans reported they were suffering from headaches, feelings of listlessness and an inability to concentrate. Some suffered from chronic pain, while there was a higher than usual proportion of birth defects among their children. In Britain the King's Centre for Military Health Research was established at King's College, London to investigate the syndrome and explore whether it was the consequence of the toxins in use during the war or another manifestation of PTSD. Once again, as in 1919, officials feared that ex-ser-vicemen would pretend to have the syndrome in order to obtain benefits, although there was no hard evidence that this was happening.

In the US many surveys were conducted, including, in 2001, a study of 15,000 US Gulf War veterans and 15,000 control veterans. Some of these surveys have been accepted as valid and some challenged in that their sampling did not meet epidemiological models. The general conclusion reached in 2006 by the US Institute of Medicine was that because veterans exhibited such a range of different symp-toms there was nothing that could uniquely be described as a 'Gulf War syndrome'. This has been broadly accepted in Britain, but the Kings Centre still insists that service in the Gulf War 'did adversely affect the health of some personnel'. The subject remains one of dispute and controversy.[4]

Since then, the British military has been involved in several full-scale engagements, including the conflicts in Bosnia in the late 1990s, in Iraq from 2003 to 2011 and in Afghanistan from 2001 to 2015. These have involved some of the most intense bouts of combat since the Second World War. In fierce fire-fights in Iraq and Afghanistan, British troops have fired off the same number of rounds per unit as their fathers did in the bitterest battles in the Western Desert or in Normandy. At times the army came near to running out of ammunition. The potential for combat-related trauma was high.

Although society today regards itself as far more under-standing and tolerant of mental health issues than one hundred years ago, the problems facing ex-servicemen as they return from a period of wartime service can be as trou-bling today as they were for some of those returning home in 1919. In July 2012, a report revealed that one in ten pris-oners serving time in prisons in England and Wales were ex-servicemen, many imprisoned on charges of violence. This was three times higher than the number claimed by the government.[5] It has often been said that the military devotes a lot of time and money to training men and women to become killers, but none to de-training them and helping them to settle back into civilian life. Just as in 1919, limbless ex-soldiers today are treated with great sympathy by a gen-erally supportive public. They are given therapy and some of the best treatment in the world at rehabilitation centres like Headley Court in Surrey and the Queen Elizabeth Hospital in Birmingham. That is clearly a very good thing. But those whose minds have been damaged or who find it difficult to cope with 'civvy street' are once again often left to struggle on and face their own demons.

In February 2014 Lord Ashcroft, appointed by the Prime Minister to act as his Special Representative on Veterans' Transition, published a review of the situation. In this he rec-ognised that in the second decade of the twenty-first century,

91 per cent of the British public believed that 'it was common for those leaving the Forces to have been physically, mentally or emotionally damaged by their Service career.'[6] While this view was less disastrous than the stereotype of the angry, moody, drugged-up Vietnam 'vet' was in the United States, it clearly created an image of the British ex-squaddie that harmed the prospects of many ex-servicemen and women in finding work. The stigma surrounding the 'service leaver' made employers wary. The Ministry of Defence claims that 85 per cent of those leaving the forces find employment within six months and re-assimilate into civilian life without difficulty. But it is hard to believe that the situation is quite so rosy. Ashcroft called for new industry initiatives to help men and women trained with specific skills to find work in a marketplace that was often calling out for people with exactly those skill-sets. He wanted service leavers with only four years' service (and this would include many of those who fought in Iraq and Afghanistan) to have the same support as those with longer service records who were given more help in the past. All service leavers who had completed basic training, he argued, should receive a full resettlement package.

But the problems have not gone away. Christopher Grayling, the Justice Secretary, reiterated in December 2014 that the state owed a 'duty of care' towards anyone who had served in the military: 'These are people who served our country, in many difficult and stressful situations. The least we can do is try and ensure that we look after them and make sure that we help them get their lives back together again.'[7] This could have been said by a government minister one hundred years ago. But the reality is still far removed from the assertions of official concern.

Combat Stress is the leading veterans' mental health charity in the UK. In 2015, it helped more than 5,900 veterans suffering from anxiety, depression or PTSD to 'get their lives back'.[8] Its foundation in 1919 as the Ex-Services Welfare Society provides a direct link from today to the troubles of those suffering from shell shock after the First World War. Emphasising this continuity between the present and the past, Dr Walter Bussitil, the Medical Director of Combat Stress, who runs a 34-bed residential treatment centre in Leatherhead, Surrey, sees himself as running 'today's version of Craighlockhart'.[9] But there are no veterans to be seen quietly convalescing in bath chairs in a modern Combat Stress treatment centre. In a manner that fits the twenty-first century, the help offered today includes the teaching of basic domestic skills such as how to cook and how to use a washing machine, skills which men who have been in the institutionalised world of the military for up to twenty years may have entirely missed out on.

Hundreds of charities have been set up over recent years to help veterans returning from Britain's recent combats. Due to the financial cutbacks following the end of the war in Afghanistan, their services will be in much demand as about 20,000 servicemen and women leave the armed services. Millions of pounds are raised every year from a sympathetic public who want to help the returning 'heroes'. Combat Stress is still treating thousands of veterans from previous conflicts, of whom those who served in the 'Troubles' of Northern Ireland provide the largest number, although the charity still receives requests for help from veterans from the Falklands War and the first Gulf War. Research indicates that about 4 per cent of veterans from the recent wars in Iraq and Afghanistan (one in twenty-five) are suffering from PTSD, although the proportion is higher (6.9 per cent) among those who experienced front-line combat. Veterans from the earlier conflicts who present themselves do so on average fourteen years after their discharge from the military. Veterans of Iraq and Afghanistan present about two years after leaving the military. Despite the current awareness of the difficulties faced by ex-servicemen, and the high public profile of groups like Help for Heroes, it seems that servicemen and women are still reluctant to seek help for mental health problems while they are serving in the military. The macho image still prevails, and many servicemen or women, especially officers, think that admitting to nervous conditions will stigmatise them and damage their career prospects. Many of those who present themselves in the years after leaving the armed forces have a range of other conditions that are sadly typical of war veterans; there is a high incidence of alcohol disorders, depression, unemployment, periods of homelessness, behavioural problems manifested by outbursts of anger and violence, and spells in prison or in the criminal justice system. It is a gloomy modern litany of the consequences of damage to the mind caused by the stress of combat.

Trauma is a difficult issue to define. Everyone suffers from the stresses and strains of life: the death of friends or relatives, the loss of jobs, the break-up of relationships. Almost everyone gets depressed at some point in their lives. This is all part of being human and what we would call 'normal'. But some people respond to distress in a particular way, experiencing a strong sense of inadequacy, delusions of guilt, or a complete loss of hope. In some circumstances the depression that follows is so severe that sufferers may self-harm or attempt to take their own lives. That is abnormal behaviour. But where is the line between the two? When does a normal response become abnormal? In the case of ex-servicemen and women, the line is even more difficult to define because, added to the universal complexities of everyday life, they are presented with the challenge of reintegrating into civilian society when a conflict is over or when many years of service come to an end.

Soldiers are trained not only to survive under the extreme pressures of the battlefield, when the fear of death or mutilation is commonplace, when they might witness friends being dreadfully wounded or killed, but to continue to function and to maintain the killer instinct in these circumstances. Such instincts are utterly alien to most civilian life. The individual values that prevail in most civil societies are replaced by the group spirit and group loyalty that underlies most military organisations, usually summarised as *esprit de corps*. That is what a period of 'basic training', as it is called in most armies, is designed to instil. Weeks of drilling, parades, inspections and tough physical training separates a soldier from a civilian by equipping him or her with the psychological mechanisms to carry on operating when tired, hungry, cold and under fire. The values that are inculcated are obedience to authority, aggression, loyalty, and intense pride in the military unit in order to give the protection of colleagues a higher priority than mere self-protection, to build a 'band of brothers'.[10] On returning to civilian life these qualities are no longer required and can be massively destructive, while at the same time ex-soldiers find they have lost the strong camaraderie and sense of purpose that comes with being in the military.

Forty per cent of the £15 million annual funding for Combat Stress is provided by the state, through the Ministry of Defence and the National Health Service. The remaining 60 per cent comes from private charitable donations. Headley Court with its state-of-the-art rehabilitation facilities was funded by Help for Heroes. It seems extraordinary, one hundred years on from the intense public debate about shell shock and the difficulties encountered by veterans attempting to settle back into civilian life after the Great War, that the state should be so reliant upon private charity in the form of Combat Stress, Help for Heroes and the many other organisations that help ex-servicemen and women reintegrate into society. Perhaps it is a sign that modern traumatic disorders are largely delayed and so are reported after a veteran has left the military. Maybe it suggests that those who are trained by society to kill on its behalf will always struggle to reintegrate into normal, peaceful civilian life. Or perhaps it simply makes one ask if society has learned anything in this regard in the last one hundred years?

There is a clearly observable cycle in military psychiatry since the First World War. A great deal of expertise in treating the trauma suffered by soldiers is built up during a war, and this overflows into the rest of psychiatry, improving the treatment of all nervous cases and trauma victims. But, in the cutbacks of expenditure that follow most wars, this knowledge is put aside and forgotten, and consequently has to be learned anew in the next conflict. Most of the lessons learned during and after the First World War were lost in the 1920s and 30s; as a result, they had to be learned again during the early years of the Second World War. The progress made by 1945 was again forgotten over the next few decades and had to be rediscovered after the Vietnam War. With the wars in Iraq and Afghanistan now hopefully over, we are once again at the end point of the learning cycle. A great deal of expertise has been built up and real progress has been made in understanding the psychiatric injuries of combat and trauma. Will all this be forgotten again in the decades to come? This will be one of the challenges of future decades.

However, one hundred years ago, the First World War left British society deeply scarred by the experience of war. Five million men had fought in the army. Two million women had either volunteered for the armed services, to join nursing organisations or to work in wartime factories. One in six adult males had been killed or wounded by the war. The survivors tried to adjust to civilian life some without limbs, many blinded, others haunted by traumatic memories they could not cast off. Those who had fought for King and Empire ended up filling the dole queues after the war. Even a high proportion of those who had survived without serious physical or mental wounds suffered an ongoing sense of guilt, that they had survived while others alongside them had not. Harold Macmillan, a future Prime Minister, never got over the feeling that the best of his generation had been lost on the Somme and elsewhere on the Western Front and only the second-raters had survived to inherit the post-war world.[11] Very few adults who lived through the years from 1914 to 1918 were unaffected by the experience of war. Historians have written about the changes that deluged British society.[12] But within the tsunami of suffering that engulfed all European societies, the story of those who had suffered from mental trauma stands out. It was not understood at the time. It was often misdiagnosed. The sufferers were frequently blamed for their problems, either as degenerates or as malingerers. In the worst cases they were shot as cowards. This is not a war record to be proud of. Nor is it a story one can be dispassionate about.

The debate about the treatment of shell shock and the development of military psychiatry in the First World War did, however, have two immensely significant outcomes. First, it showed that mental health difficulties were not exclusively the problems of the weak, the feeble and those genetically geared to insanity. Anyone could face such problems. Even the fittest and most highly motivated soldier could suffer from battle neuroses. Second, it was clear that Victorian attitudes were entirely wrong, that mental diseases could be treated and that 'lunacy', as it was called, in its different forms was not incurable. The learning process now extends back one hundred years to the first cases of men attending front-line aid posts with mysterious shakes and curious paralyses that left doctors puzzled. From this early incomprehension a great deal of important work was done and a huge shift in understanding mental health followed. The lasting consequences of the shell shock debate were a recognition that anyone could suffer from mental ill-health and that it was possible to be cured of mental disease; the traditional locking away of lunatics as 'incurables' was no longer acceptable. Out of the immense suffering of the war-time years came at least some progress.

APPENDIX 1

Numbers

'Unfortunately we have been unable to obtain any reliable statistics covering cases of "shell shock".'[1] So wrote the
authors of the *Report of the War Office Committee of Enquiry
into 'Shell Shock'* in 1922. The 'absence of statistics' caused
much concern to the members of the committee, who greatly
regretted that they had 'failed to obtain' the information they
thought was essential to assess the true scale of the problem.
If this was the case in 1922, it is no less true today that, one
hundred years after the events this book deals with, it is not
easy to calculate precise figures for the numbers of psychiatric casualties during the Battle of the Somme.

What is not in contention is that from day one of the battle
there was a massive increase in the incidence of shell shock.
Every source without exception confirms this. But precisely
assessing from the available evidence the numbers of those
affected is immensely difficult. Most lists of the wounded
make no differentiation between types of wounds – head
wounds, abdominal injuries, bullet or shrapnel wounds,
or war neuroses. Furthermore, the different categories into
which shell shock victims were assigned, Shell Shock 'W',

Shell Shock 'S', Neurasthenic and later NYDN (Not Yet Diagnosed Nervous), makes analysing the total number of those suffering from psychosomatic injuries even more difficult. The *Official Medical History* records that there were 16,138 battle casualties in France from shell shock in the months July to December 1916. This was over four times more than in the previous six months, when there had been 3,951 casualties; and more than twelve times greater than in the six months July to December 1915, when there had been 1,246.[2] If this gives an indication of the rate of increase in the incidence of shell shock, it still does not convey anything like the real number of cases; it only includes Shell Shock 'W' and not Shell Shock 'S', nor does it include all of those diagnosed with Neurasthenia. According to the *Official Medical History* the total number of cases would have been at least double this, while Ben Shephard claims that numbers 'probably need to be multiplied by at least three to give a real sense of the scale of the problem'.[3] Most historians would agree with the eminent psychiatrist who wrote that 'the true proportion which neurosis bore to the total medical casualties of the War was vastly underestimated in official statistics.'[4] Whatever the exact number, shell shock had been transformed from a disease into an epidemic almost overnight.

There are, however, other ways of trying to calculate the numbers involved. At the end of July 1916, the 2nd Division was sent down from the quiet sector at Vimy to join the fighting on the Somme. On 26 July it relieved the 3rd Division and took over its role in the struggle for Delville Wood, which it finally succeeded in capturing a few days later. On 8 August, the 2nd Division attacked again to the south of the wood towards Guillemont. New to the Somme fighting, the divisional medical authorities recorded precisely the type of casualties incurred in the two-week period from 26 July to 11 August. The total number of wounded was 2,945. Of these, the number of shell shock cases was 501.[5] Shell shock victims therefore amounted to 17 per cent of the total number of wounded.

The Australian forces recorded the number of shell shock victims in the 1st Australian Division over a five-day period from 22 to 26 July. Of a total of 2,200 recorded as wounded, 376 were suffering from shell shock. Fascinatingly, this averages out at exactly the same proportion, 17 per cent, although on one day of severe shelling, the figure was as high as 29 per cent.[6] The figure of 17 per cent was also the percentage of shell shock cases recorded in the 11th Border Regiment, the Lonsdales, in the months before going over the top on 1 July.[7]

At 17 per cent of the wounded, the number of shell shock cases during the whole of the Battle of the Somme would have totalled the colossal figure of more than 53,700.[8] And yet we can still not be certain that these numbers, where they do exist, include all of those diagnosed as Shell Shock 'S' and all officers diagnosed with Neurasthenia. In innumerable cases, if a man was taken out of the line for a few days' rest and reassurance and then returned to his battalion, he would not have been classed in any of the official categories as a battle casualty. It is likely, therefore, that the total number of cases suffering from the variety of nervous disorders that came loosely under the label of 'shell shock' was much higher.

Professor Edgar Jones of the King's Centre for Military Health Research, co-author of the principal textbook on the subject, *Shell Shock to PTSD*, has also tried hard to calculate the total numbers involved. By studying 3,580 shell shock cases admitted to 4 Stationary Hospital between January and November 1917 he has been able to track the rise and fall of the incidence of shell shock. This, not surprisingly, correlates closely with the incidence of general wounds, as the army was involved in several major battles during those months.[9] Furthermore, he has looked at the proportion of psychiatric casualties in later wars when numbers were more accurately reported during high-intensity battles. He calculates, for instance, that during the heavy fighting of the battle for Normandy in June–July 1944, the percentage of psychiatric casualties was expected to be between 10 and 30 per cent. In fact the three British army divisions in VIII Corps recorded rates of 21 per cent, 11.6 per cent and 14.7 per cent (an average of 15.8 per cent) in the first part of the battle and an average of 18 per cent during the final stages of the breakout, when the fighting was at its most severe. Data collected from the experience of the US Army in the Mediterranean and in the south-west Pacific theatres in October–November 1943 is also in line with these percentages.[10] Jones concludes that in the heaviest fighting of the First World War, like that during the battle of the Somme, it is fair to estimate that 20 per cent of those wounded were suffering from psychosomatic disorders. This happens to coincide exactly with the figure reported in the US Army in the spring of 1918 before that army fully organised its neuropsychiatric care.[11]

It seems likely therefore that the total number of men on the Somme suffering from war neuroses was slightly higher than 17 per cent. We can consequently estimate the total number of psychiatric casualties to be somewhere between 53,700 and 63,200 (20 per cent of all casualties). This huge number equated to the loss of three whole divisions from shell shock in one six-month period. The official figure for July to December 1916 was four times as great as over the previous six-month period, and if this rate of contagion of shell shock was to increase at only half that level during the next year, the British army could have been looking at the loss of perhaps the equivalent of nine divisions (180,000 men) from shell shock during 1917.

There is no evidence that anyone calculated such exact figures at the time, or that numerical predictions of shell shock losses were on this scale. However, they did not need to be. It was clear to all senior figures in the army that from July to November 1916 the incidence of shell shock had reached epidemic proportions and was totally unacceptable. This loss of men was openly referred to as 'wastage'. The *Official Medical History* admits, 'the severe wastage of man-power which the psycho neuroses were causing in France made the problem of dealing with them urgent towards the end of 1916.' War neuroses, it said, opened up 'a flood-gate for wastage from the army which no one would be able to control'.[12]

This is one of the reasons why the term 'shell shock' became so unpopular with military medical authorities after the Somme and its use was officially banned in 1918. It also explains why the new delineation of NYDN (Not Yet Diagnosed Nervous) came into use at the end of the battle and why the 'official' incidence of shell shock dropped so extraordinarily during 1917.[13] The easiest way to reduce the numbers suffering from shell shock was simply not to record many of the thousands of cases that presented themselves.

In 1931, revised casualty numbers were published in a further volume of the *Official Medical History*. These indicated that during the period August 1914 to November 1918, 143,903 British soldiers were treated for 'functional diseases of the nervous system (including neurasthenia and shell shock)'. But other categories almost certainly included psychiatric casualties, including 'mental diseases', 'debility' and 'functional diseases of the heart'; if added in, these total a figure of 325,312. This amounts to 5.7 per cent of all Britons who served in the army during the war years, by comparison to 4.6 per cent of those in the German army.[14]

Shell shock was of course inextricably bound up with the

general morale of the troops. As became clear in the evidence given to the War Office Committee of Enquiry in 1922, a battalion with poor morale was more likely to suffer from high levels of nervous disorder. Battalions with high morale might suffer from very little shell shock. So the haemorrhaging of large numbers of men had to be prevented. It is the actions taken by the army to try to do this during the battle of the Somme that are at the core of this book.

APPENDIX 2

War Trauma Before the First World War

During the First World War the epidemic of nervous diseases among soldiers was widely regarded as a completely new phenomenon, a side effect of the horrors of modern, industrial warfare. This led the War Office Committee of Enquiry in 1922 to note that 'we have no evidence of "shell shock" in previous campaigns', and to conclude that this was not extraordinary 'when it is borne in mind that the use of high explosives, of the violence and intensity developed in the recent War, was wholly unknown in the conflicts of the past'.[1]

In fact there is evidence that soldiers have suffered various sorts of mental disturbances throughout the history of warfare. Historians have found descriptions of what could be classed as war trauma in Herodotus's account of the battle of Marathon in 490 BC, in Homer's *Iliad* and in the work of Roman writer Lucretius. Shakespeare describes symptoms that would have been familiar to many First World War MOs in *Henry IV Part 1* when Lady Percy asks her husband, Hotspur:

Why dost thou bend thine eyes upon the earth
And start so often when thou sit'st alone?
Why hast thou lost the fresh blood in thy cheeks;
And given my treasures and my rights of thee
To thick eyed musing and curs'd melancholy?
In thy faint slumbers I by thee have watch'd
And heard thee murmur tales of iron wars.[2]

The problem with all reported cases of mental disorders among soldiers at war until the mid-nineteenth century is that writers could describe symptoms in very different ways. So a wide variety of accounts *might* have described those suffering from war trauma but there is no way of proving it. From the seventeenth century soldiers were sometimes described as suffering from 'nostalgia' – a type of melancholy thought to be produced by a longing to return home, which in some cases could easily have been a form of trauma brought on by the stress of warfare. A Swiss physician, Johannes Hofer, published a detailed study of this mysterious disease in 1678 and proposed various treatments in the form of purges to improve digestion and release a man's vital spirits. Another term for a malady identified within military ranks was 'soldier's heart' or 'irritable heart', of which the symptoms were exhaustion and breathlessness, a high pulse rate, sweating, a parched tongue and attacks of giddiness. Again this may have been a manifestation of war trauma. On the other hand, during the Napoleonic Wars a large number of soldiers in the French army who were perhaps suffering from trauma were simply classed as insane and were discharged with no real attempt to identify the cause of their insanity.

The intensity of the fighting during the Crimean War from 1854 to 1856 produced more cases that baffled the doctors. One officer described joining the survivors of his unit two days after the Battle of Inkerman: 'Every general and staff officer in our division was killed or wounded. The people who are left appear dazed and stupefied and unable to give us any idea of our position or chances.'[3] At the time, doctors again put this down not to nervous exhaustion but to what they called 'disordered action of the heart'. Roger Fenton took the first photograph of a victim clearly suffering from war trauma in 1855 in the Crimea. This extraordinary photo is of Captain Alexander Leslie-Melville, Lord Balgonie, of the Grenadier Guards, who had endured several Russian bombardments during the siege of Sebastopol. Only twenty-three years of age, Lord Balgonie is not in uniform as elite army officers usually were when photographed after battle. Instead, dishevelled, he looks out beyond the photographer with classic staring eyes. Balgonie was sent home from the Crimea but died only two years later.

During the American Civil War from 1861 to 1865, it was recognised that soldiers could suffer injury to their nervous systems without any signs of a physical wound. There was no agreement as to what caused this nervous disorder and a variety of explanations were put forward. Some maladies were put down to a phenomenon called 'windage', where it was thought that a man had been affected by the close passing of a shell or bullet. It is possible that the term 'windy', referring to someone who lacks courage, derives from this. Another doctor came close to describing what would later be called shell shock when he gave an account of injuries produced by the explosion of a shell near a man, causing 'compression of the brain' and leading to physical symptoms like blindness, deafness or paralysis.[4]

Throughout the rest of the nineteenth century military doctors sought explanations for strange behaviour of soldiers at war that did not appear to have physical origins. In the British army a debate about 'disordered action of the heart' came to focus on whether the traditional soldier's belt, pack and knapsack straps were too tight, and on long route marches or in the hot climates of India and Africa acted to constrict the heart. As a result of this debate adaptations were made to the traditional uniform of the British infantryman.

By the end of the century, a condition popularly called 'railway spine' had been identified in civilians who suffered from trauma as a consequence of having been in a railway accident. This was put down to the violent shock caused by the accident, which led to inflammation of the spinal cord producing a disturbance of the central nervous system. Sometimes a victim was unaware at first of having been affected, feeling perhaps merely a little giddy, but within a couple of days he or she might be physically incapacitated and unable to carry out basic tasks. This became a major issue in late Victorian society as lawyers sought to blame the railway companies for the trauma suffered by accident victims. On the other hand, lawyers working for the railway companies produced medical opinions that put the symptoms down to pre-existing conditions in those claiming compensation.

The new concept of 'neurasthenia' was moreover introduced from America in the last decades of the century. The term described a disease of the nervous system without physical origins but which could nevertheless substantially weaken or exhaust an individual with varying degrees of severity. Nervous exhaustion was thought to generate a range of physical symptoms, including paralysis of the limbs. This was believed to be a function of modern, urban, stressful living. A small number of men were diagnosed with neurasthenia during the Boer War of 1899–1902. But overall that war did not alert the newly formed Royal Army Medical Corps to the problem of nervous diseases. More than 6,000 files have survived relating to pensions awarded by the Royal Hospital at Chelsea to Boer War veterans. Less than 1 per cent of them relate to cases of psychosis, depression or psychological disorders.[5]

In the Russo-Japanese War from 1904 to 1905, many cases of psychiatric casualties were recorded in the Russian army, and in a revolutionary step the Russians set up a forward hospital for the treatment of such cases. More than 3,000 cases were counted. Observers from France, Britain and Germany noted these casualties and warned of their likely existence in future wars. But in Britain this did not act as a wake-up call. Only one medical observer, Captain R.L. Richards, tried to sound the alarm. In the army medical journal *Military Surgeon*, he wrote: 'A future war will call at least equally large numbers of men into action. The tremendous endurance, bodily and mental, required for the days of fighting over increasingly large areas and the mysterious and widely destructive effects of modern artillery fire will test men as they have never been tested before. We can surely count then on a much larger percentage of mental diseases requiring our attention in a future war.'[6] They were prophetic words. But no one seemed to hear them.

APPENDIX 3

Shell Shock in Other
First World War Armies

All the armies fighting during the First World War experienced a high incidence of war neuroses. The various conditions were given several different names. The Germans used words including *Nervenschock, Kriegshysterie* (war hysteria), *Granaterschütterung* (shell disorder) and *Granatexplosionslähmung* (shell explosion paralysis); the French used terms like *Traumatisme dû au bombardment* (trauma from a bombardment), *syndrome commotionnel* (commotional disturbance), *choc traumatique* (traumatic shock) or *psychose traumatique*. Both the French and German armies took a harsh line towards their psychiatric casualties.

In the decades before the Great War, the acknowledged leading experts on hysteria, hypnosis and psychotherapy were French. In the late nineteenth century, Professor Jean-Martin Charcot became known as the father of modern neurology and helped to define many mental disorders including epilepsy, stroke and hysteria. His successor at the Salpetrière Hospital in Paris, Jules-Joseph Dejerine (see Chapter 3), was a pioneer in psychotherapy. But despite their international influence the neurologists of the Salpetrière Hospital held little sway over the French army.

In France, as in Britain, the military medical authorities, led by Prof. André Léri at the Army Neurological Centre, decided initially to separate victims into two groups: first, those suffering from 'commotional' and physical damage to the brain and nervous system caused by proximity to a shell explosion; second, those suffering from an 'emotional' disorder, where the physical paralyses were seen as a manifestation of hysteria. In 1915, the French army was the first to set up forward treatment centres near the front in order to treat patients within a military environment. Georges Guillan, a senior military neurologist, argued that psychiatric disorders 'are perfectly curable at the onset ... such patients must not be evacuated behind the lines, they must be kept in the militarised zone.'[1] The French consequently led the way that the British and other armies would follow.

But it would be wrong to think that the French army took a soft line towards its psychiatric casualties. Far from it. French doctors were obsessed with weeding out cases of malingering and, following the approach of Joseph Babinski, adopted a tough, brusque attitude to soldiers suffering from nervous disorders. Often the treatment went little further than giving a soldier a few days' rest and then forcefully telling him that he had recovered and must follow his duty and return to his battalion, that he was 'either a loyal, self-sacrificing wounded *poilu* or a cowardly, self-serving, simulating *embusque* [shirker], a victim or a villain'.[2]

Dr Clovis Vincent at a hospital in Tours was known for his harsh techniques, which combined electric shock therapy with a vigorous verbal assault, telling his patients they must pull themselves together and face up to their soldierly duties. Vincent achieved notoriety when in 1916, gleefully holding out two electrodes, he approached a new patient who rather than succumb to painful electrotherapy punched him five times in the face. The man was put on a charge of assaulting a senior officer. At the military trial, scientific opinion rallied behind Vincent but public opinion was largely behind the soldier, and although he was found guilty he was given only a suspended sentence.[3]

Optimism in the first years of the war that the French medical authorities had the problem under control declined later as the general morale in the French army deteriorated sharply during 1917. More and more soldiers were apparently developing hysterical symptoms in areas behind the line during their treatment for physical wounds and were unwilling to return to their units. There are no complete sets of figures for psychiatric casualties in the French army between 1914 and 1918, but in an army of that size there is no question that it would have run into many hundreds of thousands.

By contrast, the official medical history of the German army, the *Sanitätsbericht*, is very precise and lists the total number of cases treated for war neuroses between August 1914 and July 1918 as 613,047, or 4.6 per cent of all the men who passed through the army during the war.[4] This figure is probably of a similar order to that in the armies of all the major protagonists.

In Germany, psychiatry was more highly respected before the war than in Britain, but there was still disagreement between psychiatrists as to how to interpret the many hysterical symptoms that seemed to appear in soldiers at the front. Hermann Oppenheim argued, just as many British neurologists did at the start of the war, that war neuroses were the result of physical damage, tiny lesions in the brain and the nervous system that caused the many strange forms of paralysis. However, by 1916, the prevailing opinion in Germany was that these neuroses were of emotional or psychological origin. Max Nonne, probably the most famous German military doctor, treated more than 1,600 patients during the war and acquired the reputation as a *Zauberrheiler*, or magic healer, although his technique was the relatively familiar one of hypnosis. Nonne, who had studied in France before the war, initially believed that no German soldier would ever suffer from hysteria, but soon had to reassess this view as hundreds of soldier patients came before him displaying classic symptoms.

Max Kaufmann, based in a hospital near Mannheim, adopted a more radical approach. He was another who saw treatment as a battle of wills; he would apply strong doses of electricity for several minutes at a time while shouting orders at his patient (see Chapter 10). Although he had many successes, about twenty patients died while undergoing his electric shock therapy and at one point there was a revolt of patients awaiting treatment. Even the provincial German assemblies, and finally members of the Reichstag, began to question the validity of this form of treatment.[5]

The Americans came into the war late and were determined to learn the lessons picked up by the Allied armies in the first three years of war (see Chapter 10). They treated most shell shock victims near the front, and only transferred the most serious cases to a specialist neuropsychiatric centre known as Hospital 117 in the calming and beautiful setting of the Vosges mountains. By the last months of the war this enabled the American authorities to claim a high recovery rate among their shell shock victims. Of the recorded 7,500 psychiatric cases during the battle of St Mihiel in September 1918 (approximately 5.5 per cent of those who took part in the battle), 65 per cent returned to duty after a few hours or a couple of days of rest at the front; 20 per cent after up to two weeks' treatment at one of the neurological hospitals; and 14 per cent after treatment at Hospital 117. The 'wastage' level of victims, those who were evacuated to the United States, was only 1 per cent.[6]

One figure who might have been expected to be active in the intense debate about the causes, symptoms and cures of psychosomatic disorders was Sigmund Freud. However, he remained completely remote from the conflict. Not only was he terribly disillusioned by the outbreak of war, seeing it as a failure of civilisation to subdue man's primitive instincts for violence, but he was also bewildered by the use of science to generate ever more dreadful forms of killing. Freud remained in Vienna, treating his dwindling number of private patients and lecturing at the university, but he contributed nothing to the treatment of psychiatric casualties in the Austro-Hungarian army. He wrote a paper on the physical manifestations of hysteria but did not publish it. He seems to have preferred to maintain a sort of scientific neutrality with respect to the war effort. The Great War had torn to shreds the pre-1914 world of science where ideas and scientists could cross borders so easily. But Freud chose to stand apart and hope that in the future, science would once again be a unifying force in world affairs.

APPENDIX 4

The Somme Battlefield Today

The site of the Somme battlefield today is an area of beautiful, rolling countryside with few visible scars of the intense Great War fighting. In the 1920s the French government encouraged farmers to return to the devastated, crater-pocked landscape, still littered with the detritus of war, to begin the massive task of reclaiming the land for agriculture. After nine decades of intensive farming most reminders of the conflict have vanished and it requires an immense effort of the imagination to recall the horrors of battle. But a good battlefield guide can bring alive the stories that were once acted out there.

The most visible signs that this is the location of one of the longest and bitterest battles in history are the cemeteries and memorials scattered everywhere. There are French and German cemeteries, but far and away the most numerous are the 242 cemeteries maintained by the Commonwealth War Graves Commission on land given in perpetuity by the French nation. They contain 153,040 Commonwealth graves, of which approximately two-thirds bear the names of those buried. The other one-third contain the remains of bodies of soldiers who could not be identified.

The bodies of men recovered during the course of the war were hastily interred by their pals where they fell in dozens of tiny burial grounds, or in more formal cemeteries alongside hospitals and Casualty Clearing Stations. However, it was impossible to recover many of the bodies during the battle as the fighting raged on. When the Germans withdrew to the heavily fortified Hindenburg Line in February 1917, many bodies that had lain out in No Man's Land or elsewhere throughout the winter were brought in and buried in hundreds of small cemeteries by the men of V Corps, who then occupied this stretch of the line. But, of course, by this point many of the corpses being recovered were unidentifiable.

After the Armistice the whole area was swept at least six further times for bodies and the cemeteries created in 1917 were concentrated into a smaller number of sites laid out by what was then called the Imperial War Graves Commission. The leading figure in this operation was Fabian Ware, an educationalist who had become commander of a mobile ambulance unit during the war. He took on responsibility for the Directorate of Graves Registration and Enquiries and began the task of listing and photographing all existing burial sites. After the war, Ware forcefully argued that all the dead should be properly buried, officers and men together, as near to where they had fallen as possible. He argued that the headstones should not be crosses (as in the French war cemeteries) as they represented the deaths of members of an imperial army that included Jews, Muslims, Hindus and Chinese as well as Christians.

A fierce debate ensued, but in 1919 the Secretary of War, Winston Churchill, backed Ware, arguing that the cemeteries should be sites of national remembrance befitting a democratic age in which everyone should be remembered equally. Every soldier, regardless of race, creed or status, was given a uniform headstone and the graves were laid out in straight lines. Rudyard Kipling was commissioned to come up with some of the phrases that adorn each cemetery, such as 'Their Name Liveth for Evermore' (Ecclesiasticus 44.14) and, on the headstones of the unidentified bodies, 'A Soldier of the Great War – Known unto God'. Max Gill created a new typeface to standardise the lettering on every headstone. Some of the best-known architects of the day, including Sir Edwin Lutyens, Sir Reginald Blomfield and Sir Herbert Baker, designed features like the Stone of Remembrance and the Cross of Sacrifice, made of sombre Portland stone, which are to be found in all but the smallest cemeteries.[1]

It is impossible to visit these cemeteries today without being moved by the scale of the sacrifice in 1916. The cemeteries are beautifully maintained by the gardeners and stonemasons of the Commonwealth War Graves Commission. A blend of traditional British flowers are mixed with plants common in that part of France. The cemeteries are immaculate and provide oases of peace and quiet in which to reflect on the scale of the losses. In addition, more than one hundred separate memorials commemorate the actions of individual divisions or battalions. By exploring the battlefields today it is possible to gain some understanding of the dreadful odds that faced the soldiers trying to advance across this landscape.

What follows is a very brief guide to the sites accessible to the visitor today at some of the locations referred to in this text. From north to south:

Gommecourt No. 2 Cemetery is located in the centre of what was No Man's Land on 1 July 1916. It began as a burial ground for men from the 56th (London) Division who went over the top here. One of these was Arthur Hubbard, who was badly traumatised by the experience (see Chapter 7). The cemetery provides a good view of Gommecourt Wood and contains 1,357 bodies (682 unidentified).[2]

The **Sheffield Memorial Park** commemorates many of the Pals battalions that went over the top in this sector just west of Serre, including the 12th Yorks and Lancs, known as the Sheffield City Pals (see Chapter 1). The 31st Division was a New Army division made up of twelve battalions, of which ten came from Yorkshire. The land was acquired by the city of Sheffield in 1928, and in the park it is possible to pick out the outlines of many shell craters and trenches. In the south-east corner, where as the 11th East Lancashires they went over the top, is a monument to the Accrington Pals.

Beaumont-Hamel is the site of the large **Newfoundland Memorial Park**, preserved by the Canadian government; it includes an orientation centre and walks across the section of the front where the Newfoundland Battalion was massacred (see Chapter 5). The park is still full of shell craters and some trench lines. At the far side is a statue of a giant Highlander standing on a cairn; a memorial to the 51st Highland Division, which finally took Beaumont-Hamel on 13 November (see Chapter 8), it is known as the 'Jock on the Rock'. A short distance to the west of the village is the sunken road in the middle of what was No Man's Land where Geoffrey Malins filmed the 1st Lancashire Fusiliers about to go over the top (see Chapter 5). The Beaumont-Hamel British Cemetery, a little to the east, contains many of these soldiers' graves.

The **Ulster Memorial Tower** was built near the site of the Schwaben Redoubt, stormed magnificently by the men of the 36th Ulster Division in their assault on the morning of 1 July (see Chapter 6). Its design was based upon a well-known Ulster landmark, Helen's Tower in County Down, where the 36th Division trained. It is easy to see the difficulty faced by the Ulstermen that morning as they charged up the steep slope in front of the tower. There is a café next to the memorial, staffed by friendly Ulstermen and women, and several cemeteries nearby where the Ulstermen who fell are buried. 1 July is still marked with solemn ceremonies across Northern Ireland.

Dominating the Somme skyline today is the **Thiepval Memorial**, commemorating more than 72,000 British and South African soldiers who died on the Somme and have no known grave. Designed by Sir Edwin Lutyens, clad in brick and faced in Portland stone, it has a central arch 140 feet (43 metres) high. Inaugurated in 1932 by the Prince of Wales and the President of France, it is an ugly monument but one that is still the centrepiece of many visits to the Somme today. It contains a visitor centre, an exhibition and a bookshop. It also serves as an Anglo-French memorial and a reminder that the battle was not an exclusively British operation. A ceremony of commemoration is held here annually on 1 July.

The **Lonsdale Cemetery**, Authuille is a remote and beautiful spot just in front of Authuille Wood where the 11th Borders, the Lonsdales, assembled on the night of 30 June. Their advance towards the Leipzig Salient at 8.30 a.m. on 1 July took place about 500 metres east of the cemetery in full view of the Nab Valley and the Nord Werk, the German machine gun position (see Chapter 6). The cemetery contains 1,542 burials, not only from the Lonsdales but also from the 1st Dorsets, who were alongside them, and from several other units who tried to advance in this section of the front. Lieutenant-Colonel Percy Machell is not buried here, as his body was taken down the line; he lies in the Warloy-Baillon Communal Cemetery, about five miles west of Albert.

Pozières, the village on the ridge successfully captured by the Australians at the end of July (see Chapter 8), attracts many visitors. The memorial to the 1st Australian Division is now linked to a walk that takes in seven other stations in a circuit around the village. A few hundred metres further east is the site of the windmill finally captured by the Australians on 4 August. Here a plaque commemorates the fact that the Australian dead lay 'more thickly on this ridge than on any other battlefield of the war'. On the other side of the road is the Tank Memorial, surrounded by four models and marking the advance at nearby Flers and the first use of tanks on 15 September.

The **Lochnagar Crater** just south of La Boiselle has been left intact as a reminder of the scale of the huge mining explosions under the German lines that ushered in the assault just before 7.30 on the morning of 1 July. It was the biggest of the explosions as the mine was packed with 60,000 lb of ammonal. Earth rose some 4,000 feet into the air. The huge crater, 300 feet (91 metres) in diameter and 70 feet (21 metres) deep, is privately owned but is open to the public as a Garden of Remembrance. Nearby is the area known as the Glory Hole; here a group of volunteers are carrying out archaeological work in the craters and dugouts that make up this section of the front, where the British and German lines were only 50 yards (45 metres) apart.

The **Devonshire Cemetery** is a small and very moving memorial just south of Mametz. Here the 8th and 9th Devonshires went over the top on 1 July in their suicide assault (see Chapter 5). The location of the German machine gun that cut them down can be seen in a civilian cemetery on the other side of the valley. Despite the massacre of the two Devonshire battalions, the attack here was one of the success stories of 1 July and Mametz was captured during the day. About 160 bodies were brought back and buried in the old front-line trench, inspiring the epitaph 'The Devonshires held this trench. The Devonshires hold it still.'

The **New Zealand Memorial** at Longueval marks the Switch Line near High Wood, successfully captured by the New Zealand Division on 15 September (see Chapter 8). A short distance away is the Caterpillar Valley Cemetery, where many New Zealand dead are buried.

Delville Wood, where Archibald Burgoyne (see Prologue and Chapter 7) fought and where the South African Brigade 'covered themselves with glory', is now the site of the huge **South African Memorial**. Built to commemorate all South Africans who fought and died in the Great War, the memorial was unveiled in 1926.

The last cemetery to be constructed along the Western Front was at Fromelles, just over thirty miles north of the Somme at the site of the disastrous diversionary attack on the night of 19–20 July (see Chapter 8). In May 2008 a mass grave of 250 bodies, mostly British and Australian, was uncovered. The Germans had buried the bodies immediately after the battle and details of its location had been lost. Using a variety of modern techniques of forensic archaeology, including DNA profiling, a little under half of the bodies were later positively identified. A new cemetery called **Pheasant Wood Cemetery** was inaugurated in 2010. The process of finding, identifying and burying the dead who had lain in mass graves for nearly one hundred years has been described as making 'a new cemetery for a new century'.[3]

Acknowledgements

The idea for this book came out of research carried out on my previous book, *Secret Warriors*, whose subject was the role of scientists in the First World War. Researching and writing this study has offered me an opportunity to dig deeper into one specific area that had broad implications for the conduct of the war.

Much has been written in recent years on the subject of shell shock and the psychiatric casualties of the First World War. One research institute alone published sixty-four papers on subjects relating to shell shock and war trauma in the years 2013 and 2014. As I explain in the Prologue, much of this recent interest and research has explored the psychological debate around shell shock as the first step on the long journey to an understanding of what is now called post-traumatic stress disorder. My approach to the subject is quite different, focusing on the military response to shell shock during the long Battle of the Somme from July to November 1916. But I am very aware of my debt to some of the outstanding histories of shell shock published in recent years. Ben Shephard was a pioneer with *A War of Nerves: Soldiers and Psychiatrists 1914–1994* (2000). Peter Barham's *Forgotten Lunatics of the Great War* (2004) and Fiona Reid's *Broken Men:*

Shell Shock, Treatment and Recovery 1914–1930 (2010) were both inspirational. And Edgar Jones and Simon Wessely's superb textbook *Shell Shock to PTSD* (2005) is a must-read for anyone interested in the subject. The many other works from which I have drawn inspiration and information are listed in the Bibliography. Wherever possible I have tried to use as source material documents or publications written at the time or very soon afterwards, when memories were fresh even if emotions were still raw. I have also found the many official histories written in the 1920s and 30s a superb source of detail as well as a guide to official thinking about the Great War in the inter-war years. Brigadier Sir James Edmonds' volume, telling the story of the build-up to and the events of 1 July 1916, is still a powerful and enthralling read today, just as it must have been eighty years ago. And Charles Bean's *Australian Official Histories* provide a gripping read, informed as they are by Bean's work as a war reporter, living alongside and suffering with the soldiers about whom he writes.

Several leading historians have in conversation helped to inspire and encourage me. I should like to thank Professor David Cannadine of Princeton, Professor Gary Sheffield of Wolverhampton, and Professor Jeremy Black of Exeter. Professor Edgar Jones of the King's Centre for Military Health provided help on the statistical record of shell shock during the Somme. Dr Walter Busuttil, the Medical Director of Combat Stress, the principal mental health charity dealing with military veterans in the UK today, was very generous with his time in showing me around a twenty-first-century version of Craiglockhart.

Historians are always reliant upon the vital work done by archivists in collecting, assembling, cataloguing and preserving the records that are the raw material for all historical writing. I am particularly grateful to Anthony Richards,

Head of Documents and Sound at the Imperial War Museum, who was also behind the republication ten years ago of the essential 1922 *Report of the War Office Committee of Enquiry into 'Shell Shock'*. Anthony gave me invaluable advice on exploring the private papers held in the museum's Documents Section. I am grateful to the Trustees of the Imperial War Museum for allowing me access to the papers in the Documents and Sound Section of the IWM and for granting me permission to quote from the papers for which the Crown holds the copyright. I am also grateful to Gillian Ankers for permission to quote from the Archibald McAllister Burgoyne papers. With many of the letters and diaries written one hundred years ago it has proved difficult to trace the copyright owners, although every reasonable effort has been made to contact them and seek their permission. Any omissions will be rectified at the first opportunity.

I am also very grateful to the archivists and librarians at the Basil Liddell Hart Military Archives at King's College, London; at the Wellcome Library in Euston; at the National Archives in Kew; at the London Library; and at the Institute of Historical Research at Senate House, part of the University of London's School of Advanced Study. I spent a fascinating few days at Cumbria's Museum of Military Life, located in the magnificent Carlisle Castle, researching the story of the 11th Battalion The Border Regiment. I am very grateful to the museum's curator, Stuart Eastwood, and assistant curator, Tony Goddard, for sharing so much information from their archive with me.

At Little, Brown it has been my pleasure and privilege to work with the same highly professional team as before. I should wholeheartedly like to thank Iain Hunt for his hard work as editor, Linda Silverman for tracking down the photographs and Steve Gove for his work on the manuscript. Tim Whiting has overseen the whole project from the first discussions to the final edits and as ever he has been tremendously positive in providing encouragement and direction.

Anne has lived through all the stages of writing this book and has cheered me up when researching some of the tragic stories related here got me down. As always, my final thanks are to her.

Taylor Downing
September 2015

Notes

Abbreviations used

BLHMA: Basil Liddell Hart Military Archives, King's College, London
Cumbria: Cumbria's Museum of Military Life, Carlisle
IWM Art: Imperial War Museum Art Department, London
IWM Documents: Imperial War Museum Documents Department, London
IWM Film: Imperial War Museum Film Archive, London
IWM Sound: Imperial War Museum Sound Department, London
RWOCESS: Report of the War Office Committee of Enquiry into 'Shell Shock'
TNA: The National Archives, Kew
Wellcome: Wellcome Archives and Manuscripts, The Wellcome Collection, London

Prologue

1 All extracts from Burgoyne's diary are taken from IWM Documents 20330: Papers of Archibald McAllister Burgoyne.
2 Burgoyne seems to have been more severely wounded later in the war, he returned to South Africa and died in Mafeking in 1920, aged forty-six; TNA: WO 154/36, 9th Division War Diary.
3 Letter extracts from IWM Documents 12825: Papers of Major F. St J. Steadman.
4 BLHMA: Montgomery-Massingberd Papers 7/41, *The Official War Diary of Fourth Army*. The breakdown is 18,057 officers and men killed (this is lower than the actual figure confirmed later); 81,104 wounded; 26,372 missing. Of those listed as missing the diary

notes that 'about 50% were subsequently found wounded in CCSs, 25% were probably killed and the remaining 25%, wounded and unwounded, [were] prisoners in the enemy's hands.'

5 Sir Archibald Montgomery assumed the additional name of Massingberd in 1926 when his wife, Diana Massingberd, inherited through her mother the Massingberd estates in Lincolnshire. During the war he was known as Montgomery, so for simplicity I shall refer to him by this surname throughout. He was no relation of the famous Second World War general, Sir Bernard Law Montgomery.

6 BLHMA Montgomery-Massingberd Papers MM10/11, Draft Autobiography, p. 22.

7 BLHMA Montgomery-Massingberd Papers MM7/3: submission by Brig. Reginald John Kentish.

8 Alan Clark, *The Donkeys*, p. 6. Although Clark adopted the phrase 'lions led by donkeys' as a quote from General Ludendorff's chief of staff, he later admitted that he had made up the phrase; see David Reynolds, *The Long Shadow*, p. 331. There was, however, a book published in 1927 by Capt. P.A. Thompson with the title *Lions Led by Donkeys*.

9 For the latest interpretations of the war see, for instance: Adrian Gregory, *The Last Great War: British Society and the First World War*; Gary Sheffield, *Forgotten Victory: The First World War: Myths and Realities*; Gary Sheffield, *The Chief: Douglas Haig and the British Army*; Dan Todman, *The Great War: Myth and Memory*; William Philpott, *Bloody Victory: Sacrifice on the Somme*; David Stevenson, *With Our Backs to the Wall: Victory and Defeat in 1918*. For the myths portrayed in the television programmes marking the centenary of the Great War see Stephen Badsey, 'A muddy vision of the Great War' in *History Today*, Vol. 65(5), May 2015, pp. 46–8.

10 Jay Winter, 'Shell shock and the cultural history of the Great War', in *Journal of Contemporary History*, Vol. 35 (1), January 2000, pp. 7–11.

11 See, for instance, over the last twenty years: Anthony Babington, *Shell Shock: A History of the Changing Attitudes to War Neuroses*; Ben Shephard, *A War of Nerves: Soldiers and Psychiatrists 1914–1994*; Peter Leese, *Shell Shock: Traumatic Neuroses and the British Soldiers of the First World War*; Edgar Jones and Simon Wessely, *Shell Shock to PTSD: Military Psychiatry from 1900 to the Gulf War*; Fiona Reid, *Broken Men: Shell Shock, Treatment and Recovery in Britain 1914–1930*. See also Edgar Jones and Simon Wessely, 'Battle for the mind: World War 1 and the birth of military psychiatry' in *The Lancet*, Vol. 384, 2014, pp. 1708–14.

12 *Report of the War Office Committee of Enquiry into 'Shell Shock'* (hereafter *RWOCESS*), p. 63.

13 Reid, *Broken Men*, p. 5.

1 The Pals Battalions

1   Harold Macmillan, *Winds of Change*, p. 59, and Gerald Brenan, 'A Survivor's Story', in George Panichas (ed.), *Promise of Greatness*, p. 39.

2   The latest study on these secret negotiations is by politician David Owen, *The Hidden Perspective: The Military Conversations 1906–1914*. The book contains much fascinating material and Owen compares these secret negotiations before the First World War with discussions between Tony Blair and President George Bush and secret arrangements that committed Britain to support the US in its invasion of Iraq in 2003.

3   Herbert Asquith to Venetia Stanley, 5 August 1914, in Michael and Eleanor Brock (eds), *H.H. Asquith: Letters to Venetia Stanley*, p. 157.

4   *The Times*, 3 August 1914.

5   Violet Bonham Carter, *Winston Churchill as I Knew Him*, p. 316.

6   Peter Simkins, *Kitchener's Army*, p. 35; the remark was made to Sir Percy Girouard.

7   This description of Kitchener's first Cabinet meeting comes from Winston Churchill, *The World Crisis, Vol. 1*, p. 191.

8   David Lloyd George, *War Memoirs Vol. 1*, p. 499.

9   A comment he made to Foreign Secretary Lord Grey, quoted in Simkins, *Kitchener's Army*, p. 41.

10 *The Times*, 30 August 1914 (in a special Sunday edition). For a review of press censorship in the early stages of the war and of Kitchener's role in it, see Taylor Downing, *Secret Warriors*, pp. 271–5.

11 Simkins, *Kitchener's Army*, p. 61.

12 Ibid., pp. 83–5.

13 Paul Oldfield and Ralph Gibson, *Sheffield City Battalion*, pp. 25–33.

14 For more details see Downing, *Secret Warriors*, pp. 273ff.

15 Simkins, *Kitchener's Army*, p. 86.

16 IWM Art: PST 2734. The latest analysis of the poster says that its impact has been vastly exaggerated and that the numbers coming forward declined after it became universal; see James Taylor, *'Your Country Needs You': The Secret History of the Propaganda Poster*, pp. 21–45.

17 David Cannadine has summed this up, saying that in the late nineteenth and early twentieth century 'there was a noticeable pro-

liferation of the "lower middle class"; that army of clerks and office workers who were neither factory labourers nor factory owners, but who merged into the working class beneath and the prosperous middle class above'; see David Cannadine, *Class in Britain*, p. 117.

18 Rupert Brooke, 'Peace', the first of five sonnets in his sequence called *1914*.

19 Hew Strachan, *The First World War: Vol. 1 To Arms*, p. 136.

20 David Parker, *The People of Devon in the First World War*, pp. 59–60.

21 A.T.Q. Stewart, *The Ulster Crisis*, p. 234; Simkins, *Kitchener's Army*, p. 95.

22 The traditional province of Ulster consisted of nine counties, all of which were represented in the UVF. After Partition in 1922, the region entitled Northern Ireland consisted of six counties.

23 Captain C. Falls, *The History of the 36th (Ulster) Division*, pp. 5–7.

24 Col H.C. Wylly, *The Border Regiment in the Great War*, pp. 28–9.

25 Cumbria: Roll of warrant officers, NCOs and other ranks, who served in the Lonsdales during the First World War.

26 Gary Sheffield, *Leadership in the Trenches*, p. 1.

27 Niall Ferguson, *The Pity of War*, p. 102.

28 Lloyd George, *War Memoirs Vol. 1*, p. 361.

29 Rudyard Kipling, *The New Army in Training*, pp. 61–3.

30 John Keegan, *The Face of Battle*, p. 221.

31 Vera Brittain, *Testament of Youth*, pp. 213–14.

2 Training a Citizen Army

1 R.H. Mottram, 'Stand To', in Panichas (ed.), *Promise of Greatness*, pp. 206–7.

2 Simkins, *Kitchener's Army*, pp. 194–5.

3 C.E. Montague, *Disenchantment*, p. 6.

4 Macmillan, *Winds of Change*, p. 59.

5 Oldfield and Gibson, *Sheffield City Battalion*, pp. 33–4.

6 Cumbria: 'V.M.', *Record of the XIth (Service) Battalion Border Regt (Lonsdale)*, pp. 6ff.

7 For a discussion of Haldane's reforms and the attempt to introduce a more scientific outlook, see Edward Spiers, *Haldane: An Army Reformer*, pp. 11ff.

8 Quoted in Tim Travers, *The Killing Ground*, p. 39.

9 *The Neglect of Science*, report of proceedings of a conference held in the rooms of the Linnean Society, Burlington House, Piccadilly, 3 May 1916, presided over by Lord Rayleigh and attended by H.G. Wells and other distinguished scientists.

10   There were technical schools in Britain and some of the universi-
     ties, especially the newer universities of Leeds, Manchester and
     Liverpool, were beginning to develop closer links to industry,
     while Cambridge was pioneering various new scientific studies.
     See Downing, *Secret Warriors*, pp. 33ff.

11   Quoted in Travers, *The Killing Ground*, p. 41.

12   H.G. Wells, *Anticipations*, p. 212.

13   Ibid., p. 189. Wells expanded on this concept in a famous short story
     in the *Strand Magazine* in 1903 called simply 'The Land Ironclads';
     this would later be cited as one of the sources of the idea of the
     development of the tank in 1915–16.

14   Ibid., p. 208.

15   Ibid., p. 213.

16   Graham Farmelo, *Churchill's Bomb*, p. 18.

17   H.G. Wells, 'Of a cross-channel passage', *Daily Mail*, 27 July 1909.

18   Quoted in Travers, *The Killing Ground*, p. 67.

19   Sir Philip Joubert de la Ferté, *The Fated Sky*, p. 32.

20   For more detailed coverage of the debates relating to the develop-
     ment of military aviation before the First World War, see David
     Edgerton, *England and the Aeroplane*, pp. 1–17, and Downing, *Secret
     Warriors*, pp. 51–74.

21   Gary Sheffield, *The Chief*, pp. 59–62.

22   John Blair, *In Arduis Fidelis*, p. 77.

23   Quoted in Mark Harrison, *The Medical War*, p. 125.

24   During the Great War inoculations against typhoid fever were
     credited with saving the lives of 130,000 men and preventing nearly
     900,000 men from being invalided out of the army; as his obituary
     for the Royal Society noted, 'For this achievement, Leishman must
     be accounted to have been one of our most successful generals
     in the Great War.' See Guy Hartcup, *The War of Invention*, p. 171;
     Downing, *Secret Warriors*, p. 216.

25   Blair, *In Arduis Fidelis*, p. 80.

26   Fiona Reid, *Broken Men*, p. 12.

27   Charles Myers, *Shell Shock in France 1914–1918*, pp. 16–17.

28   Oldfield and Gibson, *Sheffield City Battalion*, pp. 35–7.

29   Strachan, *The First World War: Vol. 1*, pp. 1065–60.

30   Basil Liddell Hart, 'Forced to Think', in Panichas (ed.), *Promise of
     Greatness*, p. 99.

31   Simkins, *Kitchener's Army*, p. 212.

32   Ibid., p. 221.

33   R.C. Sherriff, 'The English Public Schools in the War', in Panichas
     (ed.), *Promise of Greatness*, p. 137.

34 Sheffield, *Leadership in the Trenches*, p. 35; Sheffield says the number might have been as high as 27,000.
35 Cumbria: 'V.M', *Record of the XIth (Service) Battalion Border Regt (Lonsdale)*, pp. 6–8.
36 Cumbria: Letters of Percy Machell dated 2 November and 28 November 1914.
37 Keegan, *The Face of Battle*, p. 225.
38 A.J.P. Taylor points out that the four-letter word, 'fuck', came out of the trenches. Used by the men, it was copied by officers, and 'its universal use was first observed by the literate classes' during the war; see A.J.P. Taylor, *English History 1914–1945*, p. 62.
39 Siegfried Sassoon, *Sherston's Progress*, pp. 304–5 is one of many examples of this.
40 Macmillan, *Winds of Change*, p. 100, and Sheffield, *Leadership in the Trenches*, p. 136.
41 Quoted in Travers, *The Killing Ground*, p. 40.
42 Quoted in John Terraine, *Douglas Haig*, p. 160.
43 Simon Robbins, *British Generalship on the Western Front*, p. 16.
44 Robert Graves, *Goodbye to All That*, p. 152.
45 Robert Foley, *German Strategy and the Path to Verdun*, p. 103.
46 Quoted in Harrison, *The Medical War*, p. 23.
47 Aubrey Herbert, *Mons, Anzac and Kut*, p. 11.
48 Strachan, *The First World War: Vol. 1*, p. 278.
49 Brigadier-General John Charteris, *At G.H.Q.*, p. 59.
50 Brigadier-General Sir James E. Edmonds, *History of the Great War Based on Official Documents, Military Operations France and Belgium, 1915 Vol. 1*, p. 51.

3 The Shell Shock Enigma

1 Lord Moran, *The Anatomy of Courage*, p. 3.
2 Ben Shephard, *A War of Nerves*, pp. 1, 21; see also Downing, *Secret Warriors*, Chapter 11 'The Mind', pp. 241–66.
3 This description is from German medical officer and psychologist Walter Ludwig, published in 1920 and quoted in Alexander Watson, *Enduring the Great War*, p. 27. From the beginning shell shock was a problem that had to be confronted by all the armies on the Western Front; see Appendix 3.
4 Captain Wilfrid Harris, a physician attached to the Springfield Hospital, Wandsworth, quoted in Edgar Jones and Simon Wessely, *Shell Shock to PTSD*, p. 23.
5 The best recent account of the Torres Strait expedition and the

intellectual journeys taken by its members over the following decades is Ben Shephard, *Headhunters*, pp. 23ff.

6   Myers, *Shell Shock in France*, p. 14.
7   Ibid., pp. 13–14.
8   *The Lancet*, 13 February 1915, pp. 316–20.
9   Gerald Brenan, 'A Survivor's Story', in Panichas (ed.), *Promise of Greatness*, p. 47.
10 Grafton Elliot Smith and T.H. Pear, *Shell Shock and Its Lessons*, p. 2.
11 *RWOCESS*, p. 16.
12 Ibid., p. 34.
13 Shephard, *A War of Nerves*, pp. 10–11.
14 Peter Barham, *Forgotten Lunatics of the Great War*, p. 39.
15 Quoted in Elliot Smith and Pear, *Shell Shock and Its Lessons*, p. 109.
16 Elliot Smith and Pear, *Shell Shock and Its Lessons*, pp. 115, 121, 131.
17 Barham, *Forgotten Lunatics of the Great War*, p. 45.
18 Frederick W. Mott, *War Neuroses and Shell Shock*, pp. 1–5, 130ff.
19 Harold Wiltshire, 'A contribution to the etiology of shell shock' in *The Lancet*, Vol. 1, 1916, p. 1212.
20 Myers, *Shell Shock in France*, p. 26.
21 Elliot Smith and Pear, *Shell Shock and Its Lessons*, pp. 1–2.
22 Myers, *Shell Shock in France*, pp. 28, 40; Mark Harrison, *The Medical War*, pp. 111–12.
23 Myers, *Shell Shock in France*, pp. 95–6.
24 Ibid., pp. 42–8.
25 Edgar Jones, 'An atmosphere of cure: Frederick Mott, shell shock and the Maudsley' in *History of Psychiatry*, 25, 2014, p. 415; Emily Mayhew, *Wounded*, p. 207.
26 Myers, *Shell Shock in France*, pp. 36, 38.
27 W. Johnson and R.G. Rows, 'Neurasthenia and War Neuroses', in Macpherson et al. (eds), *History of the Great War Based on Official Documents: Diseases of the War Vol. II*, p. 2.
28 *RWOCESS*, p. 14.
29 *The Times*, 25 May 1915.
30 *The Manchester Guardian*, 26 April 1915.
31 Ian Whitehead, *Doctors in the Great War*, p. 182.
32 Johnson and Rows, 'Neurasthenia and War Neuroses', p. 9.
33 *RWOCESS*, p. 64.
34 For more details on the structure of medical care along the Western Front from 1915 to 1918, see Downing, *Secret Warriors*, pp. 221–6.
35 Myers, *Shell Shock in France*, p. 90.
36 *RWOCESS*, pp. 30–1.
37 Moran, *The Anatomy of Courage*, p. xxii.

38 Myers, *Shell Shock in France*, p. 53.

39 *RWOCESS*, p. 76.

40 IWM Documents 9188: Papers of H.E. Fayerbrother quoted in Malcolm Brown, *Tommy Goes to War*, p. 89.

41 *RWOCESS*, p. 30.

42 Edgar Jones, 'An atmosphere of cure: Frederick Mott, shell shock and the Maudsley', p. 416.

43 IWM Documents 1859 for Claire Tisdall's unpublished memoir; Leese, *Shell Shock,* p. 37.

44 *RWOCESS*, p. 16.

45 Ibid., pp. 14–15.

46 Ibid., p. 30.

47 Ibid., pp. 88–91.

48 Myers, *Shell Shock in France*, pp. 97–8.

4 The Big Push

1 Gary Sheffield, *The Chief*, p. 127.

2 Brigadier Sir James Edmonds, *History of the Great War Based on Official Documents, Military Operations, France and Belgium, 1916, Vol. I* (hereafter *Official History, 1916 Vol. I*), p. 16.

3 Robertson to Haig, 5 January 1916 in Robert Blake (ed.), *The Private Papers of Sir Douglas Haig 1914–1919*, p. 122.

4 There is considerable debate over this phrase. Falkenhayn later said he had used it in December 1915 and that he had never intended to break through at Verdun. However, no copy of any document using the words has ever been found and Crown Prince Wilhelm openly spoke of the 'capture of the fortress of Verdun' as an objective. Falkenhayn used the phrase in his memoirs, written after the war, possibly as a way of justifying the battle of attrition at Verdun and the huge German losses there.

5 Gary Sheffield and John Bourne (eds), *Douglas Haig: War Diaries and Letters, 1914–1918*, 26 May 1916, p. 188.

6 Quoted in William Philpott, *Bloody Victory*, pp. 98–9.

7 Quoted in Philpott, *Bloody Victory*, p. 113.

8 Quoted in Gen. Sir Frederick Maurice (ed.), *The Life of General Lord Rawlinson of Trent From His Journals and Letters*, p. 130.

9 It has to be said on the other hand that Rawlinson had told the King's aide-de-camp during a visit that this was 'Capital country in which to undertake an offensive' and had written in his diary, 'one gets an excellent view of the enemy's positions which could I think be captured without much trouble'. These comments are from

his private papers at the Churchill Archive Centre, Cambridge and suggest that, like all the commanders on the Somme, he expressed different views about his hopes and ambitions at different times; quoted in Philpott, *Bloody Victory*, p. 107.

10 Quoted in Maurice (ed.), *The Life of General Lord Rawlinson of Trent*, p. 157.

11 Philpott, *Bloody Victory*, p. 119.

12 Quoted in Maurice (ed.), *The Life of General Lord Rawlinson of Trent*, p. 158.

13 Downing, *Secret Warriors*, p. 93; by the end of the battle of the Somme the RFC had taken some 19,000 photos and from these 430,000 prints had been made.

14 Peter Simkins, 'Building Blocks: Aspects of Command and Control at Brigade Level in the BEF's Offensive Operations 1916–1918' in Gary Sheffield and Dan Todman (eds), *Command and Control on the Western Front*, pp. 158–9.

15 Gary Sheffield, *The Somme*, p. 19.

16 Keegan, *The Face of Battle*, p. 219.

17 Sheffield and Bourne (eds), *Douglas Haig: War Diaries and Letters, 1914–1918*, 29 March 1916, p. 183.

18 Quoted in Maurice (ed.), *The Life of General Lord Rawlinson of Trent*, pp. 155–6.

19 Edmonds, *Official History, 1916 Vol. I*, p. 491.

20 Letter from Haig to his wife, 14 October 1915, quoted in Sheffield, *The Chief*, p. 147.

21 Edmonds, *Official History, 1916 Vol. I*, p. 294.

22 Ibid., pp. 299–307.

23 Ibid., p. 288.

24 Quoted in Peter Hart, *The Somme*, p. 90.

25 Gerry Harrison (ed.), *To Fight Alongside Friends*, p. 212. I am grateful to Malcolm Brown for drawing my attention to Charlie May in *The Imperial War Museum Book of the Somme*, p. 54.

26 Quoted in Martin Middlebrook, *The First Day on the Somme*, p. 107.

27 The letter was published anonymously on 29 July 1916 and is quoted in Brown, *The Imperial War Museum Book of the Somme*, pp. 57–8.

28 Maurice (ed.), *The Life of General Lord Rawlinson of Trent*, p. 161.

29 Charteris, *At G.H.Q.*, p. 151.

30 Sheffield and Bourne (eds), *Douglas Haig: War Diaries and Letters, 1914–1918*, 30 June 1916, p. 195.

31 Edmonds, *Official History, 1916 Vol. I*, p. 315.

32 Harrison (ed.), *To Fight Alongside Friends*, p. 213.

33 Edmonds, *Official History, 1916 Vol. I*, p. 483.

5 Epidemic

1   Gerald Brenan, 'A Survivor's Story' in Panichas (ed.), *Promise of Greatness*, p. 44.

2   Travers, *The Killing Ground*, p. 140.

3   Edmonds, *Official History, 1916 Vol. I*, pp. 122–4, 356.

4   Middlebrook in *The First Day on the Somme*, p. 88 says it was 'as high as one third'.

5   Travers, *The Killing Ground*, pp. 133, 139.

6   There is a sequence in the film *All Quiet on the Western Front* (dir. Lewis Milestone, 1930, based on the book by Erich Maria Remarque, *Im Westen nichts Neues*, 1929) in which a group of German soldiers go slowly hysterical in a dugout under intense artillery fire that lasts for several days. One of them shakes uncontrollably; another suffers from nightmares; yet another screams out during the relentless hail of shells, 'Why don't we fight? Let's do something, let's go after them.' One of the soldiers breaks and runs up into the trench where he is badly injured by a shell. They are also attacked by a plague of rats which they try to kill with their spades. When the barrage ends the company races from its dugout to take up positions in the front trench. This sequence vividly enacts what it must have been like for the defenders on the Somme front during the seven-day artillery bombardment.

7   Stephan Westmann, *Surgeon with the Kaiser's Army*, pp. 74–5. Westmann served as a medical officer on the Western Front, was awarded the Iron Cross First Class, and became a surgeon in Berlin after the war. A vociferous anti-Nazi, he fled from Germany in 1933 and came to Britain, where he eventually opened a practice in Harley Street. In 1940 he changed his name to Stephen Westman and volunteered to run an emergency hospital for British forces in Glasgow taking the honorary rank of colonel, enabling him to say in later life that he had served 'under two flags'. In his heavily accented English, he gave a memorable interview for the BBC's *The Great War* series in 1964 in which he recited, almost word for word, this extract from his memoirs, which appears in episode 13 'The Devil is Coming'. His account might have been influenced by the scene in *All Quiet on the Western Front* described in n. 6 above.

8   Quoted in Brown, *The Imperial War Museum Book of the Somme*, pp. 4, 67.

9   Middlebrook, *The First Day on the Somme*, p. 280.

10 Quoted in Middlebrook, *The First Day on the Somme*, p. 157.

11 The images recorded by Geoffrey Malins and the other cameraman on the Somme front that day, J.B. McDowell, who was filming

further south with 7th Division, were edited into a feature documentary called *The Battle of the Somme*. Released in August 1916 while the battle was still raging, the film created a huge impact and it is estimated that 20 million people went to the cinemas to see it. It is today one of the crown jewels of the Imperial War Museum film archive, IWM Film ref: IWM 191. For the story of the making of the film, the use of fakes and an analysis of its impact, see Downing, *Secret Warriors*, pp. 298–310.

12 Middlebrook, *The First Day on the Somme*, p. 213. Gary Sheffield questions whether this telephone call ever actually took place; see Sheffield, *The Chief*, pp. 172, 432.

13 See Appendix 1 for a detailed analysis of the figures.

14 Johnson and Rows, 'Neurasthenia and War Neuroses', pp. 16–17.

15 Ibid., pp. 2–8.

16 Quoted in Harrison, *The Medical War*, p. 72.

17 Quoted in Brown, *The Imperial War Museum Book of the Somme*, pp. 246–7.

18 Major-General Sir W.G. Macpherson, *History of the Great War Based on Official Documents: Medical Services General History, Vol. III* (hereafter *Official History, Medical Services Vol. III*), p. 45.

19 T. Howard Somervell, *After Everest*, pp. 25–7.

20 Macpherson, *Official History, Medical Services Vol. III*, pp. 46–9.

21 Maurice (ed.), *The Life of General Lord Rawlinson of Trent*, p. 162.

22 Harrison, *The Medical War*, p. 110.

23 *The Times*, 18 July 1916, p. 8.

6 'No More'

1 Cumbria: 'V.M', *Record of the XIth (Service) Battalion Border Regt (Lonsdale)*, p. 14.

2 Ibid., pp. 15–19.

3 Quoted in Travers, *The Killing Ground*, p. 140.

4 That is, 15 shell shock cases out of 90 wounded.

5 TNA: WO 95/2403/1; a copy of the 11th Battalion Border Regiment War Diary is also held at Cumbria's Museum of Military Life. I am grateful to Stuart Eastwood of the museum for his analysis of some of the other regimental War Diaries.

6 Edmonds, *Official History, 1916 Vol. I*, p. 400.

7 Wylly, *The Border Regiment in the Great War*, p. 84.

8 Quoted in Middlebrook, *The First Day on the Somme*, p. 164.

9 Cumbria: 'V.M', *Record of the XIth (Service) Battalion Border Regt (Lonsdale)*, pp. 42, 44.

10 *Penrith Observer*, 11 July 1916, held at Cumbria's Museum of Military Life.

11 This was under the old style; the Battle of the Boyne is today remembered on 12 July.

12 Falls, *The History of the 36th (Ulster) Division*, p. 52.

13 Edmonds, *Official History, 1916 Vol. I*, p. 423.

14 Brigádier F.P. Crozier, *A Brass Hat in No Man's Land*, pp. 111–13.

15 Watson, *Enduring the Great War*, p. 30; Sheffield, *The Somme*, p. 68.

16 Interestingly, the 46th Division had the lowest casualty rate of any of the front-line divisions on 1 July, with losses of 2455; by comparison the 56th Division suffered losses of 4314. See Edmonds, *Official History, 1916 Vol. I*, p. 474.

17 Gerald Brenan, 'A Survivor's Story' in Panichas (ed.), *Promise of Greatness*, pp. 44–5.

18 The following account comes from a document entitled 'Proceedings of a Court of Enquiry dealing with the failure of part of an infantry battalion to carry out a raid ... ' Copies are held at Wellcome, ref: RAMC/446/18, and in the RAMC Archives with the same reference number.

19 Sheffield, *Leadership in the Trenches*, p. 152.

20 Gary Sheffield, 'An Army Commander on the Somme: Hubert Gough' in Sheffield and Todman (eds), *Command and Control on the Western Front*, pp. 84–5.

21 Although Kirkwood was reduced to the ranks he carried on administering medical aid during the war in the 91st Field Ambulance. According to the *London Gazette* he was reappointed a temporary lieutenant in the RAMC in June 1917, no doubt far away from General Gough's command. In December 1917 he was promoted to captain and he ended the war at this rank with the 8th Field Ambulance, never serving again as a battalion MO. He went back to South Africa after the war and died there, aged fifty-two, in 1931.

7 Attrition

1 This and all Hubbard's letters are from IWM Documents 22009: Papers of Arthur Hubbard.

2 *RWOCESS*, p. 31.

3 Moran, *Anatomy of Courage*, pp. 10–11.

4 Quoted in Watson, *Enduring the Great War*, p. 88.

5 Watson, *Enduring the Great War*, p. 91.

6 Denis Winter, *Death's Men*, p. 129.

7 J.G. Fuller, *Troop Morale and Popular Culture*, pp. 143–53.

8   Moran, *Anatomy of Courage*, pp. 75–6.

9   John Terraine, *White Heat: The New Warfare 1914–1918*, p. 95.

10 Major T.J. Mitchell and Miss G.M. Smith, *History of the Great War Based on Official Documents: Medical Services: Casualties and Medical Statistics of the Great War*, p. 41, and from German official statistics published in 1938, quoted in Watson, *Enduring the Great War*, p. 15.

11 *RWOCESS*, p. 34.

12 A.E. Wrench in his diary, quoted in Watson, *Enduring the Great War*, p. 28.

13 Moran, *Anatomy of Courage*, p. 42.

14 Quoted in Watson, *Enduring the Great War*, p. 31.

15 *RWOCESS*, pp. 77–9.

16 Ibid., p. 63.

17 From Norman Gladden, *The Somme 1916*, quoted in Winter, *Death's Men*, p. 133.

18 Maurice (ed.), *The Life of General Lord Rawlinson of Trent*, p. 163.

19 BLHMA: MM7/3: letter from Maj.-Gen. Furse to Maj.-Gen. Montgomery, 26 July 1916.

20 Captain Wilfrid Miles, *History of the Great War Based on Official Documents: Military Operations 1916, Vol. II* (hereafter *Official History, 1916 Vol. II*) , pp. 86–7. The conventional memory of this event is of horsemen charging 'with their lances and with pennants flying, up the slope to High Wood … They simply galloped on through all that [machine gun fire] and horses and men dropping on the ground, with no hope against the machine guns … It was an absolute rout', as in Lyn Macdonald, *The Somme*, pp. 137–8. Richard Holmes in *Tommy: The British Soldier on the Western Front*, pp. 440–1 showed this memory of the cavalry charge to be completely erroneous.

21 Sheffield, *The Somme*, pp. 83, 85.

22 Horne to his wife, 12 August 1916, in Robbins, *British Generalship during the Great War*, p. 123.

23 Gerald Brenan, 'A Survivor's Story' in Panichas (ed.), *Promise of Greatness*, p. 45.

24 See Prologue.

25 IWM Documents 20330: Papers of Archibald McAllister Burgoyne.

26 Miles, *Official History, 1916 Vol. II*, p. 108.

27 Major C.A. Bill, *The 15th Btn Royal Warwickshire Regt (2nd Birmingham Btn) in the Great War*, p. 44.

28 See Prologue.

29 IWM Documents 12825: Papers of Major F. St J. Steadman.

30 Sheffield, *Leadership in the Trenches*, p. 140.

31 IWM Sound 8764 (reel 3) interview, recorded 1985.

32 *RWOCESS*, p. 73.

33 Robertson to Lord Esher, 22 July 1916, quoted in Philpott, *Bloody Victory*, p. 318.

34 Miles, *Official History, 1916 Vol. II*, pp. 174–5.

35 Johnson and Rows, 'Neurasthenia and War Neuroses', p. 10.

36 TNA: WO 95/45/8, WO 95/447/6.

37 Johnson and Rows, 'Neurasthenia and War Neuroses', p. 10.

38 *RWOCESS*, pp. 123–5.

39 TNA: WO 95/45/9.

40 Myers, *Shell Shock in France*, p. 108.

41 *RWOCESS*, pp. 39–41.

42 IWM Documents 612: Papers of Captain L. Gameson. Gameson kept this typed notice in his papers and was generally hostile to the official attitude towards shell shock.

43 Gordon Holmes estimates between 4 per cent and 10 per cent, *RWOCESS*, p. 39; Johnson and Rows, 'Neurasthenia and War Neuroses', p. 18, has the lowest estimate at 2.5 per cent.

44 *RWOCESS*, p. 81.

45 Quoted in Johnson and Rows, 'Neurasthenia and War Neuroses', p. 15.

8 Yard by Yard – From Pozières to the Ancre

1 *RWOCESS*, p. 25.

2 Sheffield, *Leadership in the Trenches*, p. 167.

3 Charles Bean, *The Official History of Australia in the War, Vol. III, The Australian Imperial Force in France, 1916* (hereafter *Australian Official History Vol. III, 1916*), p. 70.

4 See Chapter 5. Newfoundland in 1916 was not part of Canada but was independent.

5 See Chapter 7. The quote is from Miles, *Official History, 1916 Vol. II*, p. 108.

6 Miles, *Official History, 1916 Vol. II*, p. 134.

7 http://www.awm.gov.au/wartime/36/article.asp (accessed February 2015).

8 For a full account of the discovery, identification and reburial of the bodies see Julie Summers (compiler), *Remembering Fromelles*.

9 Bean, *Australian Official History Vol. III, 1916*, p. 468.

10 From Cadmus, *Posiers*, in the State Library of New South Wales, Sydney, quoted in Philpott, *Bloody Victory*, p. 246.

11 Quoted in Terraine, *Douglas Haig*, p. 214.

12 Bean, *Australian Official History Vol. III, 1916*, p. 471.

13 Quoted in Bean, *Australian Official History Vol. III, 1916*, p. 494.

14 Ibid., p. 519.

15 Ibid., p. 534.

16 Quoted in Bean, *Australian Official History Vol. III, 1916*, pp. 553–4.

17 Ibid., pp. 579–81.

18 See Appendix 1.

19 Bean, *Australian Official History Vol. III, 1916*, p. 597.

20 Quoted in Bean, *Australian Official History Vol. III, 1916*, p. 591.

21 Sheffield and Bourne (eds), *Douglas Haig, War Diaries and Letters*, entry for 29 July 1916, p. 211.

22 Miles, *Official History, 1916 Vol. II*, p. 208.

23 Quoted in Bean, *Australian Official History Vol. III, 1916*, pp. 658–61.

24 Ibid., p. 720.

25 Ibid., p. 724.

26 BLHMA: Montgomery-Massingberd Papers MM7/3. It was to this questionnaire that Brigadier Reginald John Kentish, who had been in charge of the 76th Brigade during the long bitter fighting for Delville Wood, sent a reply headed 'The Limits of Endurance of the Infantry Soldier'; see Prologue.

27 From the Australian War Memorial, Canberra, quoted in Philpott, *Bloody Victory*, p. 248.

28 Quoted in Bean, *Australian Official History, Vol. III, 1916*, p. 876.

29 The *Australian Official History* was published in twelve volumes between 1920 and 1942; Bean wrote six of the volumes.

30 A.F. Wedd (ed.), *German Students' War Letters*, pp. 322–3.

31 See David Fletcher, *The British Tanks*; Downing, *Secret Warriors*, pp. 193ff.

32 Christy Campbell, *Band of Brigands*, pp. 184, 207, 220. The officer who had trained and prepared the tank crews for action later had a nervous breakdown and shot himself; see *Band of Brigands*, p. 402.

33 Lloyd George blamed him at the time; others have blamed him since, including Winston Churchill, *The Great Crisis*, and Basil Liddell Hart, *The First World War*, p. 262.

34 *The Times*, 18 September 1916.

35 Miles, *Official History, 1916 Vol. II*, p. 343.

36 Quoted in Col. H. Stewart, *The New Zealand Division, 1916–1919*, p. 107.

37 Miles, *Official History, 1916 Vol. II*, p. 524.

38 TNA: WO 95/2403/1; Cumbria: 11th Borders War Diary, 18 November 1916.

39 Miles, *Official History, 1916 Vol. II*, p. 535.

40 Churchill, *The World Crisis, Vol. III, 1916–1918 Part 1*, pp. 195–6.

Others who took a similar view include Liddell Hart, *History of the First World War*, Chapter 6.

41 See for instance Terraine, *Douglas Haig*, pp. 229–30; Sheffield, *The Somme*, pp. 157–60; Philpott, *Bloody Victory*, p. 8.

42 The British *Official History* claimed that total British losses, killed, wounded, missing and taken prisoner on the Somme between 1 July and 30 November were 419,654 and French losses were 194,451 (total Allied losses of 614,105); the British losses include a small percentage listed as missing at the time who later returned. See Edmonds, *Official History, 1916 Vol. I*, pp. 496–7. The Germans had a different system for adding up casualties, which did not include wounded who later returned to their units; they claimed their losses were about 500,000 (not including the seven-day offensive before 1 July). The British *Official History* controversially estimated German losses as high as 680,000; see Edmonds, Preface in Miles, *Official History, 1916 Vol. II*, p. xv. Recent calculations put German losses at somewhere between 500,000 and 600,000; see Sheffield, *The Somme*, p. 151.

43 Sheffield, *The Somme*, pp. 155–6.

44 Dudley McCarthy, *Gallipoli to the Somme*, p. 254.

45 Ibid., pp. 261, 268ff.

46 For a brief account of the establishment of the Imperial War Museum see Downing, *Secret Warriors*, pp. 331ff.

9 Rough Justice

1   Myers, *Shell Shock in France*, p. 83.

2   Robert Graves, *Goodbye to All That*, p. 112.

3   Gerard Oram, *Death Sentences*, p. 15.

4   *RWOCESS*, pp. 43–4.

5   TNA: WO 93/49; Julian Putkowski and Julian Sykes, *Shot at Dawn*, pp. 13ff.

6   Putkowski and Sykes, *Shot at Dawn*, pp. 23–6.

7   Sheffield, *The Chief*, p. 145.

8   Wellcome: RAMC/446/18. Also held in the RAMC Archives with the same ref no.

9   Sheffield and Bourne (eds), *Douglas Haig: War Diaries and Letters*, p. 259; entry for 6 December 1916.

10 There are several websites devoted to the cases of those 'shot at dawn', for instance www.ww1cemeteries.com/othercemeteries/ shotatdawnlist.htm.

11 *RWOCESS*, p. 66.

12   Ibid., p. 17.

13   Ibid., pp. 28–9.

14   Ibid., p. 48.

15   TNA: WO/95/2587/2: War Diary of 17th Sherwood Foresters.

16   TNA: WO 93/49; Putkowski and Sykes, *Shot at Dawn*, p. 106.

17   TNA: WO/95/2587/2: War Diary of 17th Sherwood Foresters.

18   TNA: WO 93/49; Putkowski and Sykes, *Shot at Dawn*, pp. 117–18; Babington, *Shell Shock*, p. 93.

19   TNA: WO 71/509.

20   Putkowski and Sykes, *Shot at Dawn*, pp. 41, 145 and passim.

21   Crozier, *A Brass Hat in No Man's Land*, p. 47.

22   *Hansard Parliamentary Debates*, House of Commons, 1917, Vol. 11, column 1499, 14 December 1917.

23   Babington, *Shell Shock*, p. 115; the statement was read out in the House of Commons on 14 March 1918.

24   See Chapter 11.

25   *RWOCESS*, p. 140.

26   *Paths of Glory*, A Bryna Production for United Artists, 1957. Directed by Stanley Kubrick, produced by James Harris; screenplay by Stanley Kubrick, Calder Willingham and Jim Thompson; starring Kirk Douglas, Adolphe Menjou, George Macready. The film differs significantly from Cobb's 1935 book, moving the character of Colonel Dax (played by Kirk Douglas) from the periphery to the centre of the story as the commander of the battalion that is accused by the divisional commander General Mireau (George Macready) of displaying cowardice. Dax is presented as having been a lawyer before the war and mounts a spirited defence of the three men, but the court refuses to listen to any evidence and is clearly determined to find the men guilty. The film ends with the brutal shooting of the three men as the camera faces them head on. There is nowhere else for the viewer to look. Earlier, the film also contains an interesting scene relevant to the present book when General Mireau walks through the front trench asking soldiers 'Are you ready to kill more Germans?' All the French soldiers mumble something appropriate, except for one poor man who can barely get any words out at all. 'He has shell shock,' says his sergeant. 'There is no such thing as shell shock,' shouts Mireau, who insists the man must be removed from the battalion and tells the sergeant, 'I won't have brave men contaminated by him.'

27   Oram, *Death Sentences*, p. 14; records from the Indian army have not survived.

28   Bean, *Australian Official History Vol. III, 1916*, p. 871.

10 Laboratory of the Mind

1 *The Times*, 4 November 1914.
2 *RWOCESS*, pp. 39–41.
3 Moran, *Anatomy of Courage*, p. 25.
4 Johnson and Rows, 'Neurasthenia and War Neuroses', pp. 27–8.
5 Babington, *Shell Shock*, p. 81.
6 Dr Arthur Hurst, quoted in *RWOCESS*, p. 26.
7 Dr Bernard Hart, quoted in *RWOCESS*, p. 79.
8 Myers, *Shell Shock in France*, p. 39.
9 Both case studies from Johnson and Rows, 'Neurasthenia and War Neuroses', pp. 32–3.
10 Myers, *Shell Shock in France*, p. 45.
11 C.S. Myers, 'Certain cases treated by hypnosis' in *The Lancet*, 1916, I, p. 69.
12 Shephard, *A War of Nerves*, p. 50.
13 W.H. Rivers, *Conflict and Dreams*, p. 6.
14 Quoted in Barham, *Forgotten Lunatics*, pp. 157–8.
15 Wendy Holden, *Shell Shock*, p. 55. The quote is based on an interview with Pear's daughter; see also Elliot Smith and Pear, *Shell Shock and Its Lessons*, p. 25.
16 Edgar Jones, 'An atmosphere of cure: Frederick Mott, shell shock and the Maudsley', p. 416.
17 Lewis Yealland, *Hysterical Disorders of Warfare*, pp. 3–4.
18 Ibid., pp. 7–15.
19 Stefanie Linden, Edgar Jones and Andrew Lees, 'Shell shock at Queen Square: Lewis Yealland 100 years on' in *Brain: A Journal of Neurology*, February 2013, p. 11.
20 For instance, Elaine Showalter finds Yealland's 'Orwellian scenes of mind control ... painfully embarrassing to contemporary readers', and writes that 'If Yealland was the worst of military psychiatrists, Sassoon's therapist, Rivers, was the best'; *The Female Malady*, pp. 178 and 181. Pat Barker creates a dramatic contrast between the techniques of Yealland and those of Rivers in her 1992 novel *Regeneration*.
21 Johnson and Rows, 'Neurasthenia and War Neuroses', p. 35.
22 The films are available to view on www.britishpathe.com/workspaces/BritishPathe/shell-shock

Sadly, being silent films, it is impossible to hear Hurst's voice as he persuades, cajoles and instructs his patients. Pathé cameramen also filmed Yealland carrying out his electrotherapy techniques on two patients on the roof of the Queen Square Hospital, but unfortunately no copies of this film have survived.

23 Elliot Smith and Pear, *Shell Shock and Its Lessons*, p. 21.

24 IWM Documents 7915: Papers of Lt. J. Butlin. The letters from Craiglockhart extend from 5 May to 9 July 1917.

25 The full text of Sassoon's declaration is to be found in *Memoirs of an Infantry Officer*, p. 218.

26 Siegfried Sassoon, *Sherston's Progress*, p. 17.

27 Ibid., pp. 11–51; Rivers, *Conflict and Dreams*, passim; Pat Barker's trilogy: *Regeneration* (1992), *The Eye in the Door* (1994) and *The Ghost Road* (1996). The 1997 film of *Regeneration*, directed by Gillies MacKinnon, starred Jonathan Pryce as William Rivers, James Wilby as Siegfried Sassoon and Stuart Bunce as Wilfred Owen.

28 Winter, *The First of the Few*, pp. 146, 191.

29 Edmund Blunden had edited an edition of Owen's poems in 1931, keeping his verse in print, but it was not until the explosion of interest in the First World War in the 1960s and the publication of an edition of his *Collected Poems* in 1963 that Owen's story and his poetry became iconic; see Reynolds, *The Long Shadow*, pp. 342ff.

30 Norman Fenton, *Shell Shock and Its Aftermath*, p. 37.

31 Reid, *Broken Men*, p. 75.

32 TNA: WO 95/45/9.

33 Johnson and Rows, 'Neurasthenia and War Neuroses', p. 11.

34 *RWOCESS*, p. 40.

35 Johnson and Rows, 'Neurasthenia and War Neuroses', p. 16.

36 Myers, *Shell Shock in France*, p. 101.

37 Winter, *Death's Men*, p. 136; Fenton, *Shell Shock and Its Aftermath*, p. 22.

38 Johnson and Rows, 'Neurasthenia and War Neuroses', p. 41.

39 Ibid., pp. 44–5.

40 Jones and Wessely, *Shell Shock to PTSD*, pp. 31–3.

41 Fenton, *Shell Shock and Its Aftermath*, p. 29.

42 Ibid., pp. 22–9; see Appendix 3 for further analysis of these figures.

11 The Ghosts of War

1 Moran, *Anatomy of Courage*, pp. 67–9.

2 *RWOCESS*, p. 58.

3 Barham, *Forgotten Lunatics*, pp. 231ff.

4 Ibid., pp. 170–1.

5 According to MeasuringWorth.com, using a mix of the retail price index and the GDP deflator.

6 Taylor, *English History 1914–1945*, p. 76.

7 Jones and Wessely, *Shell Shock to PTSD*, pp. 144ff.

8 IWM Documents 612: Papers of Lt J. Gameson.

9   Reid, *Broken Men*, p. 87.
10 *The Times*, 25 February 1919; this number does not include payments to widows or dependents.
11 Johnson and Rows, 'Neurasthenia and War Neuroses', pp. 57–60.
12 Barham, *Forgotten Lunatics*, pp. 168–9.
13 IWM Documents 7915: Papers of Lt. J. Butlin; these letters were dated 2 March and 29 March 1918.
14 Barham, *Forgotten Lunatics*, p. 196.
15 Montagu Lomax, *The Experiences of an Asylum Doctor*, pp. 197–9; see also Barham, *Forgotten Lunatics*, p. 117.
16 Reid, *Broken Men*, p. 111.
17 Approximately 400,000 men among the British and Dominion troops were diagnosed with venereal diseases in the period Aug 1914–Nov 1918; of these the vast majority, 66 per cent or 264,000, were diagnosed with gonorrhea and 24 per cent or 96,000 with syphilis. By the end of the war, twenty military hospitals in the UK and eight hospitals in France were given over exclusively to the treatment of venereal disease; see *Official Medical History: Diseases of War Vol. II*, pp. 118, 130.
18 Barham, *Forgotten Lunatics*, p. 173.
19 See Barham, *Forgotten Lunatics*, pp. 196ff for many tragic cases; also Reid, *Broken Men*, pp. 105ff.
20 The charity, now called Combat Stress, still exists today; see Epilogue.
21 Reid, *Broken Men*, p. 88.
22 *The Times*, 2 July 1919.
23 In July 1921 Haig was elected the first President of the British Legion, which soon acquired as its symbol the red Flanders poppy. The first 'Poppy Day' was held on Armistice Day in November 1921 and was a huge success; by November 1926, 25 million poppies a year were being sold in aid of the 'Haig Fund'. In other countries like France and even more so in Germany, veterans' associations became heavily politicised groups, but Haig ensured that the British Legion remained a largely conservative organisation mostly concerned with the welfare of ex-servicemen and to provide social facilities for veterans; see Sheffield, *The Chief*, pp. 348–59; Jones and Wessely, *Shell Shock to PTSD*, pp. 148ff.
24 Quoted in Reid, *Broken Men*, p. 93.
25 IWM Podcast 33 on Shell Shock.
26 *Daily Herald*, 28 October 1918, quoted in Reid, *Broken Men*, p. 94.
27 *Hansard Parliamentary Debates*, House of Lords, Vol. 39, No. 29, column 1094; 28 April 1920.

28   *RWOCESS*, p. 3.

29   Ibid., p. 92.

30   Ibid., pp. 125, 140.

31   Ibid., p. 92.

32   Ibid., pp. 190–3.

33   Barham, *Forgotten Lunatics*, p. 4.

34   Felipe Fernandez-Armesto, *Millennium*, p. 469.

35   *The Return of the Soldier* had a big impact in 1918 but was then largely forgotten until being revived in recent decades by Virago Press, when the emphasis was on West's treatment of feminist issues like the role of women in a patriarchal society, and masculinity and war. In 1982 *The Return of the Soldier* was made into a film starring Julie Christie, Glenda Jackson and Alan Bates, directed by Alan Bridges.

36   Dorothy Sayers, *Whose Body?*, Chapters 8 and 9. Sayers wrote eleven Lord Peter Wimsey novels between 1923 and 1937. Some were unsuccessfully turned into films but were later successfully adapted by the BBC for television starring Ian Carmichael in a series from 1972–5 and by Edward Petherbridge in 1987.

37   Robert Graves, *Goodbye to All That*, pp. 220–1.

38   See Reynolds, *The Long Shadow*, pp. 201ff, and Jay Winter, 'Shell Shock and the Cultural History of the Great War' in *Journal of Contemporary History*, January 2000, Vol. 35 (1), pp. 10–11.

39   Stevenson, *British Society 1914–45*, p. 306.

40   *The Times*, 2 July 1919.

Epilogue

1   Jones and Wessely, *Shell Shock to PTSD*, p. 128.

2   There was intense debate about PTSD in 1980. Most psychiatrists claimed that the disease was entirely legitimate and that at last a clear definition had been found for the delayed psychological damage caused to soldiers in combat or civilians in situations of extreme stress or danger. However, some American psychiatrists claimed that the politics of the anti-war movement had invaded the world of medicine. They argued there was no epidemiological evidence for the existence of PTSD and that it was a disease entirely invented by modern society, where, for instance, 'flashbacks' in films and literature have become a common device and so have entered the psychological experience. See Jones and Wessely, *Shell Shock to PTSD*, pp. 132–6; Shephard, *A War of Nerves*, pp. 355ff.

3   Jones and Wessely, *Shell Shock to PTSD*, p. 134.

4 Mart Tarn, Neil Greenberg and Simon Wessely, 'Gulf War syndrome – has it gone away?' in *Advances in Psychiatric Treatment*, Vol. 14, 2008, pp. 414–22.

5 The report was from No Offence! CIC, a research organisation focused on the criminal justice network. In 2014, there were approximately 2.8 million veterans in the UK, although this includes all Second World War veterans still living and 64 per cent of this total are over sixty-four. The vast majority of ex-servicemen in prison (about 77 per cent) are ex-army personnel over the age of forty-five.

6 The Veterans' Transition Review, p. 8: http://www.veteranstransition.co.uk/vtrreport.pdf (accessed May 2015).

7 BBC News, 21 December 2014, 'Ex-services personnel to get more help in prison': http://www.bbc.co.uk/news/uk-30558280 (accessed May 2015).

8 The Combat Stress website contains a great deal of information about the charity and many well-told stories of ex-servicemen and their families who have suffered from various forms of trauma: https://www.combatstress.org.uk/veterans/ (accessed May 2015).

9 Interview with the author, 15 May 2015.

10 Richard Holmes, *Firing Line*, pp. 36–56.

11 For a clear expression of this sense of survivor's guilt see Macmillan: 'We almost began to feel a sense of guilt for not having shared the fate of our friends and comrades [who had died in the war]. We certainly felt an obligation to make some decent use of the of the life that had been spared to us' in *Winds of Change*, p. 98.

12 See for instance, Arthur Marwick, *The Deluge: British Society and the First World War*.

Appendix 1: Numbers

1 *RWOCESS*, p. 7.

2 Johnson and Rows, 'Neurasthenia and War Neuroses', p. 11.

3 Shephard, *A War of Nerves*, p. 41.

4 The psychiatrist was Edward Mapother, the first Superintendent of the Maudsley Hospital; quoted in Watson, *Enduring the Great War*, pp. 238–9.

5 Maj-Gen. Sir W.G. Macpherson, *History of the Great War Based on Official Documents: Medical Services General History Vol. III*, p. 41.

6 Bean, *The Australian Imperial Force in France, 1916 Vol. I*, p. 597; see also Chapter 8.

7 See Chapter 6.

8   The total number of wounded on the Somme from 1 July to 30 November was 316,073; see Macpherson, *History of the Great War: Medical Services General History Vol. III*, p. 50.

9   Edgar Jones, Adam Thomas and Stephen Ironside, 'Shell Shock: an outcome study of a First World War "PIE" unit' in *Psychological Medicine*, Vol. 37, 2007, pp. 213–23.

10 Edgar Jones and Simon Wessely, 'Psychiatric battle casualties: an intra- and interwar comparison' in *British Journal of Psychiatry*, Vol. 178, 2001, pp. 242–7.

11 Fenton, *Shell Shock and Its Aftermath*, pp. 24–5.

12 Johnson and Rows, 'Neurasthenia and War Neuroses', p. 10.

13 See Chapter 10.

14 A total of 5,707,416 men served in the British army during the war; figures quoted in Watson, *Enduring the Great War*, p. 240. The German figure is given in Appendix 3.

Appendix 2: War Trauma before the First World War

1   *RWOCESS*, p. 8.

2   Babington, *Shell Shock*, pp. 7ff; Shakespeare, *Henry IV Part 1*, Act II, Scene 3.

3   Quoted in Jones and Wessely, *Shell Shock to PTSD*, p. 4.

4   This was Doctor George Burr, an army surgeon who counted 130 such cases in military hospitals; see Babington, *Shell Shock*, p. 19.

5   Jones and Wessely, *Shell Shock to PTSD*, p. 13.

6   Capt R.L. Richards, 'Mental and nervous diseases in the Russo-Japanese War' in *Military Surgeon*, Vol. 26, 1910; quoted in Babington, *Shell Shock*, p. 40.

Appendix 3: Shell Shock in other First World War armies

1   Quoted in Jones and Wessely, *Shell Shock to PTSD*, p. 25.

2   Quoted in Shephard, *A War of Nerves*, p. 102.

3   Shephard, *A War of Nerves*, p. 103; Downing, *Secret Warriors*, p. 262.

4   Quoted in Watson, *Enduring the Great War*, p. 239.

5   Shephard, *A War of Nerves*, pp. 98–100.

6   Fenton, *Shell Shock and Its Aftermath*, pp. 22–9.

Appendix 4: The Somme battlefield today

1   An excellent recent account of the debates that raged around the work of Fabian Ware and the establishment and early work of the

Imperial War Graves Commission can be found in David Crane, *Empires of the Dead*. See also Rose Coombs, *Before Endeavours Fade*, p. 156.

2 The website of the Commonwealth War Graves Commission has information on every official cemetery and is an easy place in which to search for the location of a grave: www.cwgc.org

3 For a full account of the discovery, identification and reburial of the bodies, see Julie Summers (compiler), *Remembering Fromelles*.

Bibliography

PRIMARY SOURCES

Government publications and official histories

C.E.W. Bean, *The Official History of Australia in the War of 1914–1918, Volume III: The Australian Imperial Force in France, 1916*. Sydney: Angus & Robertson, 1929

Brigadier-General Sir James E. Edmonds, *History of the Great War Based on Official Documents, Military Operations: France and Belgium, 1915, Vol. I*. London: Macmillan & Co, 1927

——, *History of the Great War Based on Official Documents, Military Operations: France and Belgium, 1916, Vol. I*. London: Macmillan & Co, 1932

Major-General Sir W.G. Macpherson, Major-General Sir W.P. Herringham, Colonel T.R. Elliott and Lieutenant-Colonel A. Balfour (eds), *History of the Great War Based on Official Documents, Medical Services, Diseases of the War, Vol. II*. London: HMSO, 1923

Major-General Sir W.G. Macpherson, *History of the Great War Based on Official Documents, Medical Services, Vol. III: Medical Services during the Operations on the Western Front in 1916, 1917 and 1918*. London: HMSO, 1924

Captain Wilfrid Miles, *History of the Great War Based on Official Documents, Military Operations: France and Belgium, 1916, Vol. II*. London: Macmillan & Co, 1938

Major T.J. Mitchell and Miss G.M. Smith, *History of the Great War Based on Official Documents, Medical Services: Casualties and Medical Statistics of the Great War*. London: HMSO, 1931; republished by The Imperial War Museum and The Battery Press, 1997

Report of the War Office Committee of Enquiry into Shell Shock. London:

HMSO Cmd 1734, 1922 (facsimile republished by the Naval and Military Press in Association with the Imperial War Museum, 2004)

Unit histories

Major C.A. Bill, *The 15th Btn Royal Warwickshire Regt (2nd Birmingham Btn) in the Great War.* Birmingham: Cornish Brothers, 1932

Captain C. Falls, *The History of the 36th (Ulster) Division.* Belfast: McCaw, Stevenson & Orr, 1922

Paul Oldfield and Ralph Gibson, *Sheffield City Battalion: A History of the Battalion Raised by Sheffield in World War One.* Barnsley: Pen & Sword, 2010 (first published 1994)

Colonel H. Stewart, *The New Zealand Division, 1916–1919.* Auckland: Whitcombe & Tombs, 1921

Colonel H.C. Wylly, *The Border Regiment in the Great War.* Aldershot: Gale & Polden, 1924

Wartime and post-war studies of shell shock

Grafton Elliot Smith and T.H. Pear, *Shell Shock and Its Lessons.* Manchester: Manchester University Press, 1917

Norman Fenton, *Shell Shock and Its Aftermath.* London: Henry Kimpton, 1926

Montagu Lomax, *The Experiences of an Asylum Doctor: With Suggestions for Asylum and Lunacy Law Reform.* London: George Allen & Unwin, 1921

Lord Charles Moran, *The Anatomy of Courage.* London: Constable, 1945; reprinted London: Robinson, 2007

Frederick W. Mott, *War Neuroses and Shell Shock.* London: Hodder & Stoughton, 1919

Charles Samuel Myers, *Shell Shock in France 1914–1918: Based on a War Diary.* Cambridge: Cambridge University Press, 1940

William Halse Rivers, *Conflict and Dream.* Cambridge: Cambridge University Press, 1922

Ernest Thurtle, *Military Discipline and Democracy.* London: C.W. Daniel, 1920

Lewis R. Yealland, *Hysterical Disorders of Warfare.* London: Macmillan & Co, 1918

Diaries, journals, letters and memoirs

Robert Blake (ed.), *The Private Papers of Douglas Haig, 1914–1919: being selections from the private diary and correspondence of Field Marshal the Earl Haig of Bemersyde.* London: Eyre & Spottiswoode, 1952

Edmund Blunden, *Undertones of War*. London: Cobden-Sanderson, 1928 (republished as a Penguin Modern Classic, 2000)

Michael and Eleanor Brock (eds), *H.H. Asquith: Letters to Venetia Stanley*. Oxford: Oxford University Press, 1982

Violet Bonham Carter, *Winston Churchill as I Knew Him*. London: Eyre & Spottiswoode and Collins, 1965

Brigadier-General John Charteris, *At G.H.Q.* London: Cassell & Co, 1931

Winston S. Churchill, *The World Crisis 1911–1918*. London: Thornton Butterworth, 5 volumes from 1923 to 1931

Brigadier-General F.P. Crozier, *A Brass Hat in No Man's Land*. London: Jonathan Cape, 1930

Norman Gladden, *The Somme 1916*. London: William Kimber, 1974

Robert Graves, *Goodbye to All That*. London: Jonathan Cape, 1929 (republished as a Penguin Modern Classic, 2000)

Gerry Harrison (ed.), *To Fight Alongside Friends: The First World War Diaries of Charlie May*. London: William Collins, 2014

Aubrey Herbert, *Mons, Anzac and Kut by an M.P.* London: E. Arnold, 1919; new edn ed. Edward Melotte, Barnsley: Pen and Sword, 2009

Sir Philip Joubert de la Ferté, *The Fated Sky: An Autobiography*. London: Hutchinson, 1952

Rudyard Kipling, *The New Army in Training*. London: Macmillan, 1914

David Lloyd George, *War Memoirs* (6 vols). London: Ivor Nicholson & Watson, 1933–6

Harold Macmillan, *Winds of Change, 1914–39*. London: Macmillan, 1966

Frederic Manning, *The Middle Parts of Fortune* (2 vols). London: Piazza Press, 1929. Republished in a censored form as *Her Privates We*. London: Peter Davies, 1930 (republished as a Penguin Modern Classic, 2014)

Major-General Sir Frederick Maurice (ed.), *The Life of General Lord Rawlinson of Trent: From his Journals and Letters*. London: Cassell & Co, 1928

Charles Edward Montague, *Disenchantment*. London: Chatto & Windus, 1922

Siegfried Sassoon, *Memoirs of an Infantry Officer*. London: Faber & Faber, 1930 (republished as a Faber Classic, 2000)

——, *Sherston's Progress*. London: Faber & Faber, 1936 (republished as a Penguin Classic, 2013)

Gary Sheffield and John Bourne (eds), *Douglas Haig: War Diaries and Letters 1914–1918*. London: Weidenfeld & Nicolson, 2005

T. Howard Somervell, *After Everest: The Experiences of a Mountaineer and Medical Missionary*. London: Hodder & Stoughton, 1936

A.F. Wedd, *German Students' War Letters: Translated and Arranged from the Original Edition of Dr Philipp Witkop*. London: Methuen, 1929 (republished by First Pine Street Books, Pennsylvania, 2002)

H.G. Wells, *Anticipations: Of the Reaction of Mechanical and Scientific Progress Upon Human Life and Thought*. London: Chapman & Hall, 1902

Stephan Kurt Westman, *Surgeon with the Kaiser's Army*. London: William Kimber, 1968 (republished by Pen and Sword, Barnsley, 2014)

Literary sources

Richard Aldington, *Death of a Hero*. London: Chatto & Windus, 1929 (republished as a Penguin Classic, 2013)

——, *Roads to Glory*. London: Chatto & Windus, 1930

Humphrey Cobb, *Paths of Glory*. London: Viking, 1935 (republished as a Penguin Classic, 2011)

A.P. Herbert, *The Secret Battle*. London: Methuen, 1919

Erich Maria Remarque, *All Quiet on the Western Front (Im Westen nichts Neues)*. New York: Little, Brown, 1929 (republished in English many times and now available as a Vintage paperback)

Dorothy Sayers, *Whose Body?* London: Fisher Unwin, 1923 (plus ten other Lord Peter Wimsey books, the last of which was *Busman's Honeymoon* in 1937 – all are available in paperback through a variety of publishers)

Rebecca West, *The Return of the Soldier*. London: Nisbet, 1918 (republished by Virago Press, 2010)

Virginia Woolf, *Mrs Dalloway*. London: Hogarth, 1925 (republished as a Penguin Classic, 2000)

SECONDARY SOURCES

Anthony Babington, *For the Sake of Example*. London: Leo Cooper, 1983

——, *Shell Shock: A History of the Changing Attitudes to War Neurosis*. Barnsley: Pen and Sword, 1997

Peter Barham, *Forgotten Lunatics of the Great War*. New Haven: Yale University Press, 2004

John S.G. Blair, *In Arduis Fidelis: Centenary History of the Royal Army Medical Corps*. Edinburgh: Scottish Academic Press, 1998

Malcolm Brown, *The Imperial War Museum Book of the Somme*. London: Macmillan-Pan Books in association with the IWM, 1997

——, Christy Campbell, *Band of Brigands: The First Men in Tanks*. London: Harper, 2007

David Cannadine, *Class in Britain*. New Haven: Yale University Press, 1998

Alan Clark, *The Donkeys*. London: Hutchinson, 1961

Rose Coombs, *Before Endeavours Fade*. London: After the Battle, 1976

David Crane, *Empires of the Dead: How One Man's Vision led to the Creation of WW1's War Graves*. London: William Collins, 2013

Taylor Downing, *Secret Warriors: Key Scientists, Code-breakers and Propagandists of the Great War*. London: Little, Brown, 2014

David Edgerton, *England and the Aeroplane: An Essay on a Militant and Technological Nation*. Basingstoke: Macmillan, 1991

Graham Farmelo, *Churchill's Bomb: A Hidden History of Science, War and Politics*. London: Faber & Faber, 2013

Niall Ferguson, *The Pity of War*. London: Allen Lane, 1998

Felipe Fernandez-Armesto, *Millennium*. London: Bantam, 1995

David Fletcher, *The British Tanks 1915–19*. Marlborough: Crowood Press, 2001

Robert Foley, *German Strategy and the Path to Verdun: Erich von Falkenhayn and the Development of Attrition, 1870–1916*. Cambridge: Cambridge University Press, 2005

J.G. Fuller, *Troop Morale and Popular Culture in the British and Dominion Armies, 1914–1918*. Oxford: Oxford University Press, 1990

Adrian Gregory, *The Last Great War: British Society and the First World War*. Cambridge: Cambridge University Press, 2008

Mark Harrison, *The Medical War: British Military Medicine in the First World War*. Oxford: Oxford University Press, 2010

Peter Hart, *The Somme*. London: Cassell, 2006

Guy Hartcup, *The War of Invention: Scientific Developments 1914–18*. London: Brassey's Defence Publishers, 1988

Wendy Holden, *Shell Shock: The Psychological Impact of War*. London: Channel 4 Books, 1998

Richard Holmes, *Firing Line*. London: Jonathan Cape, 1985

——, *Tommy: The British Soldier on the Western Front*. London: HarperCollins, 2004

Edgar Jones and Simon Wessely, *Shell Shock to PTSD: Military Psychiatry from 1900 to the Gulf War*. Hove: Psychology Press, 2005

John Keegan, *The Face of Battle: A Study of Agincourt, Waterloo and the Somme*. London: Jonathan Cape, 1976

Peter Leese, *Shell Shock: Traumatic Neurosis and the British Soldiers of the First World War*. Basingstoke: Palgrave Macmillan, 2002

Basil Liddell Hart, *The Real War, 1914–1918*. London: Faber & Faber, 1930 (republished as *History of the First World War*. London: Cassell & Co, 1970)

Lyn Macdonald, *Somme*. London: Macmillan, 1983

Arthur Marwick, *The Deluge: British Society and the First World War*. London: Macmillan, 1965

Emily Mayhew, *Wounded: From Battlefield to Blighty, 1914–1918*. London: The Bodley Head, 2013

Dudley McCarthy, *Gallipoli to the Somme: The Story of C.E.W. Bean*. London: Secker & Warburg, 1983

Martin Middlebrook, *The First Day on the Somme: 1 July 1916*. London: Allen Lane, 1971

Gerard Oram, *Death Sentences Passed by Military Courts of the British Army 1914–1924*. London: Francis Boutle, 1998

David Owen, *The Hidden Perspective: The Military Conversations 1906–1914*. London: Haus, 2014

George A. Panichas (ed.), *Promise of Greatness: The War of 1914–1918*. London: Cassell, 1968

David Parker, *The People of Devon in the First World War*. Stroud: The History Press, 2013

William Philpott, *Bloody Victory: The Sacrifice on the Somme*. London: Little, Brown, 2009

Julian Putkowski and Julian Sykes, *Shot at Dawn*. Barnsley: Wharncliffe, 1989

Fiona Reid, *Broken Men: Shell Shock, Treatment and Recovery in Britain 1914–1930*. London: Continuum, 2010

David Reynolds, *The Long Shadow: The Great War and the Twentieth Century*. London: Simon & Schuster, 2013

Simon Robbins, *British Generalship on the Western Front*. Abingdon: Routledge, 2005

——, *British Generalship during the Great War: The Military Career of Sir Henry Horne (1861–1929)*. Farnham: Ashgate, 2010

Michael Roper, *The Secret Battle: Emotional Survival in the Great War*. Manchester: Manchester University Press, 2009

Gary Sheffield, *Leadership in the Trenches: Officer-Man Relations, Morale and Discipline in the British Army in the Era of the First World War*. London: Macmillan, 2000

——, *Forgotten Victory: The First World War: Myths and Realities*. London: Hodder, 2002

——, *The Somme*. London: Cassell, 2003

——, *The Chief: Douglas Haig and the British Army*. London; Aurum, 2011

Gary Sheffield and Dan Todman (eds), *Command and Control on the Western Front: The British Army's Experience 1914–1918*. Staplehurst: Spellmount, 2004

Ben Shephard, *A War of Nerves: Soldiers and Psychiatrists 1914–1994*. London: Pimlico, 2002

——, *Headhunters: The Search for a Science of the Mind*. London: The Bodley Head, 2014

Elaine Showalter, *The Female Malady: Women, Madness and English Culture 1830–1980.* London, Virago, 1987

Peter Simkins, *Kitchener's Army: The Raising of the New Armies 1914–1916.* Barnsley: Pen and Sword, 2007 (reprint of original 1988 edition)

Edward Spiers, *Haldane: An Army Reformer.* Edinburgh: Edinburgh University Press, 1980

David Stevenson, *With Our Backs to the Wall: Victory and Defeat in 1918.* London: Penguin, 2011

John Stevenson, *British Society 1914–45.* London: Penguin, 1984

A.T.Q. Stewart, *The Ulster Crisis: Resistance to Home Rule, 1912–14.* London: Faber & Faber, 1967

Hew Strachan, *The First World War: Vol. 1 To Arms.* Oxford: Oxford University Press, 2001

Julie Summers (compiler), *Remembering Fromelles: A New Cemetery for a New Century.* Maidenhead: CWGC Publishing, 2010

A.J.P. Taylor, *English History 1914–1945,* The Oxford History of England Vol. 15. Oxford: Oxford University Press, 1965

James Taylor, *'Your Country Needs You': The Secret History of the Propaganda Poster.* Glasgow: Saraband, 2013

John Terraine, *Douglas Haig: The Educated Soldier.* London: Hutchinson, 1963

——, *White Heat: The New Warfare 1914–18.* London, Leo Cooper, 1992

Dan Todman, *The Great War: Myth and Memory.* London: Hambledon Continuum, 2005

Tim Travers, *The Killing Ground: The British Army, the Western Front and the Emergence of Modern War 1900–1918.* Barnsley: Pen and Sword, 2009 (reprint of original 1987 edition)

Alexander Watson, *Enduring the Great War: Combat, Morale and Collapse in the German and British Armies, 1914–1918.* Cambridge: Cambridge University Press, 2008

Ian R. Whitehead, *Doctors in the Great War.* Barnsley: Leo Cooper, 1999

Denis Winter, *Death's Men: Soldiers of the Great War.* London: Penguin, 1979

——, *The First of the Few: Fighter Pilots of the First World War.* London: Allen Lane, 1982

Index